NO JUSTICE IN THE SHADOWS

NO JUSTICE IN THE SHADOWS

How America Criminalizes Immigrants

ALINA DAS

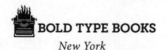
BOLD TYPE BOOKS
New York

Bold Type Books
116 East 16th Street, 8th Floor, New York, NY 10003
www.boldtypebooks.org
@BoldTypeBooks

Printed in the United States of America

First Edition: April 2020

Published by Bold Type Books, an imprint of Perseus Books, LLC, a subsidiary of Hachette Book Group, Inc. Bold Type Books is a copublishing venture of the Type Media Center and Perseus Books.

The Hachette Speakers Bureau provides a wide range of authors for speaking events. To find out more, go to www.hachettespeakersbureau.com or call (866) 376-6591.

The publisher is not responsible for websites (or their content) that are not owned by the publisher.

Print book interior design by Jeff Williams.

Library of Congress Control Number: 2019950511

ISBNs: 978-1-56858-946-6 (hardcover), 978-1-56858-945-9 (e-book)

LSC-C

10 9 8 7 6 5 4 3 2 1

CONTENTS

PROLOGUE

I SPENT THE LAST EVENING OF BARACK OBAMA'S PRES-
idency at the home of the Rev. Donna Schaper in New York City.
Donna invited together a small group to support our friend, and
my client, Ravi Ragbir. An immigrant rights leader who organized
faith communities across the country, Ravi fought for the rights
of other immigrants for a decade while his own deportation case
hung in the balance. He lived and breathed the immigrant rights
movement alongside his wife and fellow advocate, Amy Gottlieb.

The last several years had been tumultuous. But on this night,
the stakes never felt higher. As the minutes slipped away, so too did
our hope of protecting Ravi and Amy from what was to come.

For months, we had clung to the hope that President Obama
would grant Ravi a pardon. Ravi's deportation hinged on a single conviction that he had received fifteen years earlier, when his
employer accused him of fraud. Ravi fought for his innocence
at trial but was convicted. Like one in three adults in America,
he now lived with a criminal record.[1] But long after he had paid
his debt to society, Ravi faced a second, much more devastating punishment of deportation. Although he had a green card,

Ravi was not an American citizen. For that reason, his single conviction threatened to strip him from his home, family, and community—permanently.

Ravi's battle against deportation was bruising. A federal immigration judge ordered his deportation without considering the hardship it would cause him or his family. Ravi spent two years in an immigration jail fighting his deportation order before he was released pending appeal. By that time, life as he knew it had been destroyed.

Ravi did not give up hope. After his release, he became an organizer. He answered desperate calls from people in immigration jails and came to other advocates like me to brainstorm ways to help people stay with their families. He eventually joined the New Sanctuary Coalition, mobilizing faith communities across the country to stand in solidarity with immigrants facing deportation. He later became the coalition's executive director.

Ravi and I became friends, and when I learned that he had a case of his own, I became his lawyer. We fought like hell for the day in court he never had—a chance to tell his story and prove he shouldn't be deported. The law was not kind to us. But with every setback in his case, Ravi worked twice as hard to save someone else.

When the time came to pursue a pardon for Ravi from President Obama, the community stood with Ravi. Immigrant and civil rights leaders wrote endless letters, and thousands of community members signed petitions. Donna, Ravi's longtime pastor and senior minister at Judson Memorial Church, was one of many prominent faith leaders who urged President Obama to grant Ravi this reprieve.

We knew, of course, that it would be an uphill battle. President Obama made a concerted effort late in his presidency to consider sentencing commutations, but he granted few pardons—a full and unconditional erasure of the consequences of a conviction—compared to prior administrations.[2] The list of pending pardon applications was long, and time was running out. No matter, we thought. We could always shift our focus to the next president.

Then came the election of Donald Trump, a man who vowed to build a "beautiful wall" between the United States and Mexico, ban Muslims, and deport the "bad hombres."[3] How would Ravi survive this next presidency? Suddenly the hope of being among President Obama's last remaining pardons was all we had left.

Hope. It was President Obama's promise, yet so fleeting for immigrants. President Obama's policies had helped to build a vast machinery for deportation. Three million people had been forcibly deported from the United States during the Obama administration—more than during any other prior presidency.[4]

It wasn't that President Obama shared his successor's anti-immigrant views. To the contrary, he cared deeply about immigrants. He urged Congress to take on immigration reform and, in the vacuum, stepped in. Pushed by young activists, he created Deferred Action for Childhood Arrivals (DACA), a temporary, two-year reprieve from deportation for people who came to the United States as children. While he ramped up deportations—focusing primarily on people who had criminal records—he also urged immigration officials to exercise discretion in light of people's individual circumstances.

To President Obama, and the long line of political leaders before him who straddled similar lines, these approaches went hand in hand. On one side were the worthy few who deserved to stay. DACA's youthful recipients, for example, came here "through no fault of their own." In the words of President Obama, these young people and their families deserved to "come out of the shadows and get right with the law."[5]

On the other side were those who, by comparison, were not so deserving. "We're going to keep focusing enforcement resources on actual threats to our security," President Obama explained. "Felons, not families. Criminals, not children."[6]

With these words, President Obama gave voice to the views held by millions of Americans who believe that we can achieve a more just immigration system by bringing the "good immigrants" out of the shadows. But where did that leave a person like Ravi—a hardworking man with a family *and* a felony conviction?

On which side of the line between good and bad immigrants did he belong?

And so the shadows spread, as our political leaders debated who among us deserved to come into the light, just in time for a new administration to target more immigrants than ever before. As we feared, Ravi would be on that list.

⸻

FOR MANY YEARS, the dividing lines in our immigration policies were largely invisible to me. Immigrant communities were always being asked to "get right with the law." We were rarely encouraged to ask whether the law is right.

My parents came to the United States from India decades ago. They were green card holders when my brother and I were born here, and they decided to stay. My parents still have a faded copy of the US Constitution that they were given when they became citizens.

America is our home, and it is the only home I have ever known. But in time it became clear that how we viewed America, and how America viewed us, were two different things. We loved our country. But not everyone here believed that we belonged. My parents' accents, our brown skin, what we ate, how we prayed— these were the telltale signs that collectively marked us as foreigners despite our citizenship status.

It began to bother me as a child that people like me were not automatically accepted as American. It was that otherness that drove me, years later, to attend law school. The law, I thought, would be the tool to fight for inclusion and justice for all, regardless of where you were born or the color of your skin.

But when I began representing immigrants who faced deportation, I learned that the law itself is part of the problem. The law is rarely on the side of those who seek to come to the United States and thrive here. Rather than welcome people, the law excludes, exploits, and punishes. For many years, it did so explicitly on the basis of race. Had my parents sought to come to the United States much earlier than they did, they would have been barred from entry because they were Indian.

The fall of most racial barriers to immigration by the 1960s brought demographic change to the United States. But, as I would come to learn, it did not fundamentally alter the character of the law. Immigration law still excludes, exploits, and punishes. It still targets people of color. And while many immigrants do succeed and thrive in the United States, they do so despite the law, not because of it.

America criminalizes immigrants. People become suspects before they even set foot on this soil. And the moment they falter, the law sweeps in to do its worst.

⁕

AS WE HAD feared, Ravi was plunged back into the darkness after President Trump came into power. At a routine immigration appointment with Immigration and Customs Enforcement (ICE) on January 11, 2018, immigration officers handcuffed Ravi and led him away for deportation. Men surrounded him, ignoring the questions and tears from his wife, Amy, and brushing aside our arguments for why their actions were wrong. Ravi handed me the rosary beads that his friend, a Catholic priest, had given him before the appointment. Ravi knew that he could not take them where he was going. One set of officers led him down the hallway as another officer escorted me out of the room. I did not know if I would ever see my friend again.

ICE claimed that it was taking action because Ravi had a criminal conviction. It didn't matter that nearly two decades had passed, that he had become a community leader, that he had been reporting to immigration officials without incident for years, or that he had been given permission to stay. ICE claimed, after all this time, that Ravi was a threat.

Ravi was a threat. Not to the public, but to the deportation system itself. He spoke out tirelessly against US immigration policy and the cruelty of deportations. He brought elected officials into federal immigration buildings and led prayer vigils outside. He spoke openly and honestly about what he saw. And it galvanized the community to fight back.

The public outcry was instantaneous, with hundreds rallying outside the federal building where Ravi was detained. Eighteen people, including two members of the New York City Council, were arrested as they attempted to block the vehicle taking Ravi away from the building.[7] We filed a lawsuit challenging Ravi's detention, arguing the case as crowds of people packed the courtroom. Nearly three weeks after Ravi's detention, in a stunning rebuke to the Trump administration, a federal judge denounced ICE's actions as "unnecessarily cruel"—actions associated with "regimes we revile."[8] The judge ordered Ravi's immediate release. By that evening, Ravi was back with us, safe at home. He still lived under the threat of deportation, but he did so surrounded by the community that loves him.

Some in the media questioned why the community chose to rally around Ravi—a man with a felony conviction.[9] Federal immigration officials dismissed the public support. They defended their decision to take action against him as an "aggravated felon." They counted on the willingness of the public to sacrifice Ravi to this label. But, as one headline aptly read, Ravi was "freed by the movement he helped build"—a more inclusive movement that does not allow our community to be divided into good and bad, deserving and undeserving.[10] And so we lived to fight another day.

Few can say the same. Ravi is one of millions of people who have faced banishment from America because of a vast, crime-based deportation machine. Most who are plunged into the shadows by this machine disappear, forced to leave their heartbroken families and communities behind.

It doesn't have to be this way.

IIIIIII

THIS BOOK TELLS the story of America's crime-based deportation machine. It is a machine that relies on the tools of criminalization and mass incarceration—policing, prosecution, and prison—to punish immigrants with deportation. It can deprive people of everything they have—family, job, home, liberty, and even life—with limited or no access to a lawyer, a neutral judge, and many of the other procedural protections we associate with justice.

The machine is cruel by design. As one coalition of immigration and civil rights groups recently explained, the laws that expanded the criminal grounds for deportation were written to "treat people of color as disposable and criminal until proven otherwise."[11] The Antiterrorism and Effective Death Penalty Act (AEDPA) and the Illegal Immigration Reform and Immigrant Responsibility Act (IIRIRA), both signed by President Bill Clinton in 1996, were part of a package of punitive legislation that targeted welfare, immigration, and prisons for draconian reforms. These laws transformed the immigration system by dramatically merging it with the criminal legal system.[12]

While these laws remain the blueprint for today's crime-based deportation machine, the Clinton administration and the 104th Congress were hardly writing on a blank slate. From the beginning, when the United States enacted its first federal laws restricting migration in the late 1800s, political leaders have relied on criminality to justify racial exclusions in immigration law. By the 1920s, Congress established formal racial quotas for immigration, created the US Border Patrol, and criminalized border crossing. President Herbert Hoover addressed the threat of "criminal aliens" in his 1930 State of the Union address, and a growing immigration enforcement bureaucracy capitalized on the concept at key moments over the next few decades. When the racial quotas on immigration finally ended in 1965, the rise of crime control policies in the post–civil rights era allowed the targeting of "criminal aliens" to take on heightened significance, continuing the work that formal racial exclusion had done before.[13]

The 1996 laws were built on this long-standing foundation of racialized criminalization in immigration law, but few people saw it that way at the time. Even as the harsh impact of AEDPA and IIRIRA became clear—as longtime residents became subject to mandatory deportation overnight—proponents of ameliorating these harms were no match for those who demonized the "criminal alien."

Rather than reverse course on criminalization, political leaders gave immigrant communities more of the same. Congress poured millions, and then billions, of dollars into immigration enforcement. After President George W. Bush and Congress created the Department of Homeland Security (DHS) in 2002, the footprint of immigration enforcement expanded even more. Soon enough, DHS—which oversees Border Patrol and ICE—began receiving more federal funding than all other federal law enforcement agencies combined.[14]

ICE in particular became a stealth force for what it calls the "interior enforcement" of immigration law in neighborhoods across America. Toting guns and vests that say "POLICE" in capital letters while conducting warrantless raids, ICE officers have arrested hundreds of thousands of people who have been living in the United States for years—lawful permanent residents, refugees, and undocumented immigrants alike.

When President Obama was elected, things went from bad to worse. The Obama administration expanded interior enforcement, using crime-based deportation grounds to drive up deportations in the hope of brokering reform that never came. In an attempt to reduce the harm, the Obama administration encouraged federal immigration officers to exercise restraint, but the net widened dramatically nonetheless.

By the time President Trump rose to power, a potent mix of law and policy had already created a well-oiled crime-based deportation machine. From there, President Trump simply "took the shackles off" federal immigration officers.[15] It did not take long for those shackles to end up on our community members instead—people like Ravi.

This book takes us through the history and the harms of America's crime-based deportation machine. It addresses the purposeful conflation of crime and immigration policy, and how prejudice and fear have led to harsh deportation laws that make us less safe. It lays the groundwork for a different path forward—one that centers the dignity of all people in our vision for justice rather than dividing ourselves into good and bad.

Ultimately, this is a book of stories—of the laws that fuel the crime-based deportation machine and of the people whose lives the machine seeks to tear apart. Although the machine targets anyone who comes in contact with the criminal legal system, including many who have committed no crimes, I focus primarily on the stories of people who do have criminal records—the so-called "criminal aliens." It is their humanity that is too often overlooked even by those who seek to build a more humane immigration system.

I wrote this book because of people like Ravi: people who have experienced the devastation of the crime-based deportation machine firsthand and seek to dismantle it. I wrote this book for people who are open to learning about—and standing with—those who have been criminalized in the shadows.

IN MANY WAYS, President Trump made it easy to criticize US immigration policy. Within days of his inauguration, he had initiated his long-promised "Muslim ban." In time, he announced the end of DACA. He expanded "zero tolerance" family separation at the border, literally tearing children from their parents. He stripped asylum seekers of their rights as people died in the desert. And all the while, he continued to target those who have always been targeted, his so-called "bad hombres."[16]

Each new horror splashed across the papers and drummed up fresh outrage. People took to the streets. "This time he crossed the line," many would say, pointing to the Muslim PhD student, the DACA recipient, the child sobbing for her parents, all threatened with deportation.

But the problem, as people like Ravi have long known and as I have learned, is not Trump. We made it easy for him to cross the line because we drew the line through our own communities. Our laws divide America into citizen and noncitizen, deserving and undeserving, good and bad. We then apportion justice and human dignity accordingly—and become outraged when those in power disagree with how we divided up our people.

The criminalization of immigrants began long before Trump was elected president, and if we are not careful, it will last long after he is gone. The fight to restore immigrant rights cannot simply be about regaining the ground we've lost. It requires us to question the fault lines that left us so vulnerable in the first place.

As this book will show, those who seek to expand deportation power have long used the racialized rhetoric of the "criminal alien" as a weapon against communities of color. But we can disarm them. The humanity of those who battle the injustices of both the immigration and criminal legal systems can help us transcend the good-versus-bad immigrant narrative in political debate and break the cycle of criminalization hurting communities of color in this country.

We do better by Ravi, and the millions of people like him who are at risk of being banished from this country, by rejecting the divisive politics of punishment that drive America's crime-based deportation machine. We do better by standing up for due process and human dignity for all.

Chapter One

THE "CRIMINAL ALIENS" AMONG US

"294."

When the court clerk called out the last three digits of Ely's "Alien number," we stood up and made our way to the front of the courtroom. A Black man with graying hair and stooped shoulders, Ely was one of my older clients. We moved our way slowly through the crowded aisle.

We were far more relaxed than many of the people in the room. The presiding immigration judge had already ruled in Ely's favor once before, a decision that we had defended successfully on appeal. Today's proceedings were simply a formality, a chance for the judge to rubber-stamp her prior decision that Ely should not be deported.

Such optimism is a rarity in an otherwise foreboding deportation system. In many ways, immigration courts look and feel like many other courtrooms in America: cold and bureaucratic. The fates of the "respondents"—immigrants facing deportation, who are mostly people of color—are decided by immigration judges and government lawyers who are mostly White. Unlike in criminal courts, there is no right to government-appointed counsel for immigrants who cannot afford an attorney. So the majority of them fight their deportation cases alone.

At 26 Federal Plaza in New York City, where Ely and I were that morning, people milled about in the hallways, peering into crowded, windowless courtrooms. Our courtroom, like those beside it, was marked with a seal of the Executive Office for Immigration Review, a division of the US Department of Justice. Our immigration judge, a Justice Department employee, sat at the front of the courtroom, draped in a black robe, presiding over a massive caseload. To the left, a lawyer for ICE, the bureau within the Department of Homeland Security that enforces deportation laws, sat at a table absorbed in a pile of case files. Nervous men, women, and children fidgeted in the back of the courtroom on hard wooden benches, waiting their turn. The ones who were represented by counsel craned their necks to look for their lawyers. Eye contact was seldom made as people's fates were being decided, sometimes in a matter of minutes.

It was a bleak picture. People were at very real risk of separation from their families and even persecution or death if deported. These were "death penalty cases in a traffic court setting," as one prominent immigration judge described it.[1]

Nonetheless, Ely and I knew that we were lucky to be in this courtroom, especially given the alternative. Federal immigration officials had initially arrested Ely in New York City when they began their deportation case against him. They took him to an immigration jail across the river in New Jersey. The law at the time made him eligible to be released on bail, which allowed him to attend court as a free man. But under today's law, his criminal record for drug possession would bar his release. He would have remained imprisoned, his case transferred to a "detained court." He probably would have been forced to appear in court by video conference from the jail. His likelihood of finding a lawyer would have plummeted—only 14 percent of people in immigration jail do—as would his likelihood of winning his case.[2] Ely's freedom was a precious thing.

Ely and I also knew that we were fortunate to be in court at all. In some cases immigration officers can deport people with the stroke of a pen—no lawyer, no judge, no oversight. The use of these kinds of one-sided summary proceedings has grown rapidly over the past decade, leading to hundreds of thousands of deportations annually.[3]

Ely easily could have been one of those shackled in immigration jail or swept away with no judge's intervention. But he was one of the "lucky" ones. He was released from immigration jail. He received a day in court. He had a lawyer. We knew that we had a good judge who would stand by her initial decision. And she did.

After skimming through the paperwork in the case, the judge spoke. She would reinstate her prior decision to cancel his deportation case. Ely slowly exhaled as she announced the news and handed me her written order.

Then she looked up at Ely. "Welcome to America," she said.

We took her written order, handed a copy to the government attorney, and got out of the courtroom as quickly as possible. We were relieved and grateful, but I could not get the judge's final, congratulatory words out of my head. Ely was a sixty-year-old grandfather who had lived in the United States longer than I had been alive. He had worked here, married, and raised his family here. He was as American as they come. The reason for his deportation case—minor drug possession convictions he had received and had been punished for long ago—were part of his American story. Yet US immigration officials had pursued his permanent exile from this country for a decade, and they very nearly got what they wanted.

Ely is not alone in this experience. He is one of millions of immigrants in America who have faced deportation on criminal grounds over the past two decades. Using the tools of the criminal legal system, federal immigration officials and politicians have deemed people like Ely to be "criminal aliens"—public safety threats who deserve nothing but banishment.

Ely's story is the story of the "criminal alien"—the target of every administration, vilified in public discourse through a lens that leaves little room for empathy, until you look behind the label.

Welcome to America.

||||||

THERE IS NO one legal definition of the term "criminal alien." An "alien" is defined in federal immigration law as someone who is neither a citizen (by birth or naturalization) nor a national (those born in a US territory) of the United States.[4] But the term "criminal alien" is not defined with the same precision. Over the years, political leaders and federal immigration officials have used the term broadly to refer to those who lack US citizenship and have some kind of criminal arrest or conviction on their record.

The targeting of so-called "criminal aliens" accounts for the vast majority of immigration enforcement today. More than 87 percent of the over 150,000 immigration arrests inside the United States in fiscal year 2018 targeted people who have a criminal record—the majority of which consist of immigration, drug, and traffic offenses.[5] When President Trump was elected, criminal prosecutions for so-called "immigration crimes" like illegal entry and reentry made up a majority of federal prosecutions, outpacing all other federal crimes combined and transforming the criminal legal system at our borders.[6]

Federal agencies like ICE and Border Patrol celebrate these statistics as proof of a job well done. But what has this targeting accomplished? Behind each statistic is a person—most likely a person of color, and often a person with deep ties to the United States. A person like Ely.

Ely's experience of becoming both an "alien" and a "criminal," like so many who live with that label, is an American experience—born of historical decisions that our political leaders have made to criminalize people rather than solve societal problems. Federal immigration officials' dogged pursuit of Ely's deportation did not address harm. It perpetuated it.

||||||

ELY CAME TO the United States from Jamaica in the wake of the Hart-Celler Act of 1965, which marked the end of decades of overtly racial exclusions in US immigration law. Ely and his family settled in New York City while the country was still reeling from momentous changes in race relations.

It was a time of both progress and backlash for Black people in the United States. Civil rights leaders had fought tirelessly to end legalized racial discrimination in housing, employment, and voting. Elected officials responded by turning to a law-and-order rhetoric to justify a new wave of punitive legislation. A brewing "war on crime" funneled millions of federal dollars into local policing, even as funding for education and employment opportunities in heavily segregated urban centers dried up. The crime war was soon followed by the "war on drugs," leading to the proliferation of laws, policies, and programs that heavily criminalized drug use and sale, particularly in impoverished Black communities.[7]

Ely was an immigrant with a green card. He was also a Black man living in America. During this period of social upheaval, he experienced firsthand the growing crises of poverty and violence that rocked many communities as new forms of racial segregation took shape and urban communities lost their economic base. Ely did well for himself for a time—he married, had children, and worked a steady blue-collar job at a paper factory. But by the mid-1990s, his fortunes had reversed. His marriage fell apart, and his wife divorced him. His father was hit by a stray bullet and killed near his parents' doorstep, a victim of the growing violence in their neighborhood. And the job that provided Ely with economic stability eventually filled his lungs with so much paper dust that after fifteen years he was too ill to work.

Around this time, crack cocaine had spread into his neighborhood. Ely succumbed to drug addiction, which had at first been his escape but was ultimately his downfall. He lost what remaining stability he had, becoming homeless. It was an experience so indelible that years later, as his immigration judge would observe at his first hearing, Ely "could recall vividly what it is like to sleep on a bench with a cardboard box as a cover" even as other memories began to fade with age. Rather than receiving care, housing, or treatment during that period of homelessness, Ely got misdemeanor drug possession convictions.

It took a few years, but Ely was able to overcome his demons. He got sober and moved in with his daughter, an adult with children of her own, who wanted to pursue her education. Ely helped take care of his grandchildren while his daughter went to school. As it turned out, living in service to his family proved to be the secret to his continued sobriety, just as surely as the loss of his wife and father all those years ago had been his undoing.

But the stability Ely had struggled to re-create—the solutions he had found for his problems—was jeopardized again, this time by the looming threat of deportation. Federal immigration officials decided to charge him with deportability based on his drug offenses.

Ely's family hired lawyers who initially secured him a court hearing seeking cancellation of removal—a form of relief from deportation that permitted an immigration judge to weigh the positive aspects of his life and his rehabilitation against his drug possession misdemeanors. Ultimately, in 2004, his immigration judge canceled his removal, concluding that Ely had, in fact, turned his life around, and that deporting him would create a terrible hardship for him and his family.

The many years of living in limbo during these proceedings, facing a second punishment for his convictions, were hard enough. But then Ely learned that his fight against deportation was just beginning. ICE appealed the immigration judge's decision. The federal officials weren't arguing that the judge had weighed the facts about his life incorrectly. They were arguing that, because of his criminal record, the judge should have deported Ely without giving him a hearing about hardship at all.

‖‖‖‖‖

SINCE THE TURN of the twentieth century, federal immigration officials have obsessed over the connection between immigration and crime—despite facts that stubbornly refuse to support their obsession. In 1911, a special congressional committee called the Dillingham Commission produced an immigration report that characterized US crime trends in terms of both race and nationality, comparing the crime rates of immigrants from various countries to those of native-born White and Black people. It ultimately concluded that immigration as a whole had no disproportionate impact on crime rates.[8]

Then came the Wickersham Commission in 1929, charged by President Herbert Hoover with reviewing the effectiveness of law enforcement in the United States. The commission devoted an entire volume of its report to the enforcement of deportation laws. While it too acknowledged that immigration as a whole was not connected to increasing crime, the Wickersham Commission report nonetheless asserted that "the most important function of deportation laws would seem to be to rid our country of the alien criminals."[9]

President Hoover, eager to name an enemy in the throes of the Great Depression, issued his own rallying cry to target "criminal aliens." In his 1930 State of the Union address, President Hoover urged "the strengthening of our deportation laws so as to more fully rid ourselves of criminal aliens" and those "who have entered the country in violation of the immigration laws." He emphasized that the "very method of their entry indicates their objectionable character, and our law-abiding foreign-born residents suffer in consequence."[10] Hoover was among many politicians who used criminality to divide immigrants into "good" and "bad."

The precise definition of "criminal alien" didn't really matter for political purposes. Politicians and law enforcement agencies labeled immigrants as criminals as part of broader campaigns, often racially and economically motivated, to get rid of undesirable groups of immigrants regardless of whether individuals actually had criminal records. Hoover launched a "Mexican repatriation" program that continued through the subsequent administration, thanks to local enthusiasm for deportations. Federal authorities joined with local police and vigilantes to deport as many as two million people of Mexican heritage, an estimated majority of whom were US citizens, to Mexico in the 1930s—scapegoats of America's economic woes and racist anxiety.[11]

Criminalization wasn't limited to immigrants whose only alleged crime was to cross a border, or to resemble someone who did. The definition of "criminal alien" included immigrants who came to the United States lawfully and later committed crimes. As law enforcement officials realized that they had another tool at their disposal, deportation became a second punishment, used to rid the community of undesirable immigrants. The same year as President Hoover's speech urging "the strengthening of our deportation laws," the New York Police Department established the Bureau of Criminal Alien Investigation, the first of its kind nationwide. New York City Police Commissioner Edward Pierce Mulrooney announced the formation of the bureau, whose purpose was to "round up and investigate all aliens with criminal records to establish possible grounds for deportation."[12]

Today, we often distinguish between how we treat immigrants who are "criminalized" for being here without status and those who are deemed "criminals" because of the unlawful acts they commit while building their lives here. It's the difference, in current parlance, between being labeled an "illegal alien" for being undocumented and a "criminal alien" for committing a crime. People have pushed back on the first label with a powerful response: "No human being is illegal." Many elected officials, community organizations, and media outlets have "dropped the I-word" in recognition of the dehumanizing frame of illegality.[13] But the second label lingers on—conveying the same message that people who break the law don't deserve its protections. With the term "criminal alien," few push back.

This is by design. Immigrants didn't suddenly decide to start breaking the law, leading America to adopt deportation policies to deal with the threat. Rather, America chose to criminalize immigrants—and their acts—to justify more deportation. It's a cycle that repeats itself through history. First comes rhetoric associating immigrants with criminality. Next, political leaders transform that rhetoric into laws that criminalize acts associated with immigrants. And finally, government officials use those laws to punish immigrants who commit these acts with incarceration, deportation, or both. It then becomes easy to point to all those who are punished for breaking the law—law that is too often created with immigrants, and people of color more broadly, in mind—as proof that immigrants were criminals all along. And so the cycle continues.

People may hear terms like "criminal alien" today and believe that deportation is justified. But when they actually look at the individuals behind such labels—individuals like Ely—it becomes clear how misleading the labels really are.

ICE OFFICIALS ARGUED that Ely's record made him the worst kind of "criminal alien," one ineligible for any opportunity to plead for mercy from an immigration judge. He had, in their words, been convicted of a "drug trafficking aggravated felony."

Ely was bewildered by ICE's argument. He had been convicted of drug possession misdemeanors. There was, in fact, no trafficking, no aggravating factor, no felony.

In 1988, Congress invented the term "aggravated felony" to target what it viewed as the most dangerous "criminal aliens." Under the law, federal immigration officials would detain and deport people with aggravated felonies when their criminal sentences were completed. They would receive no bail from immigration jail, and—after more legislative amendments—no hearing on hardship to family or rehabilitation, regardless of how compelling their personal circumstances might be. If they attempted to return to the United States after deportation, they would face lengthy prison time.[14]

The invention of the aggravated felony breathed new life into the long-standing frenzy over "criminal aliens." At first, the term applied to people convicted of murder, drug trafficking, or firearms trafficking. By 1996, Congress had dramatically expanded the list several times to include nearly two dozen subcategories of offenses and added additional criminal grounds for deportation. Congress also increased the potential criminal penalty for reentry into the United States after an aggravated felony conviction to twenty years in prison.[15]

Federal immigration officials were particularly aggressive in interpreting the new deportation grounds. As the subcategories expanded, so too did the government's imagination. Aggravated felonies did not need to be aggravated or felonies. And in the drug trafficking context, they did not need to involve trafficking. Using a series of statutory cross-references in the law, federal immigration officials took the position that even a simple drug possession offense could be a drug trafficking aggravated felony. Immigration judges—most of them—went along.

Not Ely's judge. She couldn't see how misdemeanor drug possession offenses equated to drug trafficking. She ruled against the government and held a cancellation hearing for Ely. It was the first ruling he received that made sense to him.

But federal immigration officials doubled down and appealed. The Board of Immigration Appeals, an administrative division of the Justice Department charged with reviewing immigration judge decisions, sided with ICE. If no one intervened, Ely would be deported, as if his hearing—and the life he had built after his convictions—never happened.

||||||||

I FIRST LEARNED of Ely's case when I was a young attorney at the Immigrant Defense Project. Founded in 1997 by Manny Vargas, the Immigrant Defense Project was one of the first immigrant rights organizations to specialize in the intersection of immigration and criminal law. As an immigration lawyer, Manny had seen the writing on the wall when Congress vastly expanded the criminal grounds for deportation. He founded the Immigrant Defense Project to ensure that criminal defense attorneys could defend immigrant clients from deportation consequences as early in the arrest-to-deportation pipeline as possible. Over the years, the Immigrant Defense Project took its battles to federal court, becoming a national hub for litigating against immigration officials' increasingly expansive interpretation of the criminal grounds for deportation.

I joined the Immigrant Defense Project in 2006 and became part of a team of lawyers trying to challenge the government's harsh application of the "drug trafficking aggravated felony" label. Advocates had just won a victory at the Supreme Court that year in *Lopez v. Gonzales*, which concluded that a single, simple drug possession conviction could not be deemed a drug trafficking aggravated felony.[16] But the government quickly pivoted to pushing its argument that a second drug possession offense could be a drug trafficking aggravated felony because federal law sometimes punished recidivist drug offenses harshly. With no right to counsel in deportation proceedings, immigrants had to fight these nonsensical arguments on their own, and many immigration courts were quick to side with the government. We often found ourselves trying to chase down cases and intervene before it was too late.

By the time we learned of Ely's case, he was no longer able to afford his private counsel. We helped him navigate his case, and when I transitioned to begin my teaching position at the New York University School of Law's Immigrant Rights Clinic, I took over Ely's appeal. With the support of the Immigrant Defense Project and others, I argued his case to a three-judge panel at the US Court of Appeals for the Second Circuit, a federal appeals court in New York.

It was clear at the federal appeals hearing that the judges were disturbed by the government's position. "How is it that you can urge that, as a matter of law," one judge pointedly asked the government attorney, "that we are obliged to treat these aliens as having been punished as the equivalent as federal felons?" I internally flinched at the judge's casual use of the terms "aliens" and "felons," but the intent of her question was clear. The government's argument defied common sense.

When the federal appeals hearing concluded, Ely asked me what I thought his chances were. After all he had been through, hope in the legal system felt like a luxury. "Whatever happens," I replied, "we'll keep fighting."

And so we waited, one of many agonizing waits for justice. After a few months, we received the judges' ruling. The Board of Immigration Appeals decision would be reversed. The immigration judge had correctly found Ely eligible for a hearing to cancel his deportation.

My heart went to my throat as I called Ely with the news. "You won," I said simply. In his stunned silence, I could hear the sound of his grandchildren in the background. Ely finally spoke, his voice thick with emotion: "This is a blessing." We were finally able to return to immigration court, vindicated, to receive the immigration judge's order ending his deportation case once and for all.

The victory was bittersweet. It would take another two years for the Supreme Court to reject the government's harsh position on multiple drug possession offenses nationwide in a 2010 case, *Carachuri-Rosendo v. Holder*.[17] By then, countless people had been deported without hearings. Those who, like Ely, had managed to stay and fight for their rights under the law had endured years of painful uncertainty. Ely still gets overwhelmed when he thinks about what he went through. Living each day in fear that he would be forced to restart his life alone as an elderly disabled man in Jamaica—a country he had not seen, as he told the immigration judge, "since Nixon was president."

It was not the first time federal immigration officials would use the criminal legal system to expand their power to deport those deeply rooted in the United States, nor was it the last. In the decade after the Supreme Court's first drug deportability decision in 2006, three other cases about drug deportability, including *Carachuri-Rosendo,* made their way to the Supreme Court. Each time, the justices struck down the government's overreaching interpretation of the law. Each time, federal immigration officials adapted, developing different arguments to uproot those with criminal records. For every person who staved off deportation, thousands more were banished in the shadows—exactly as the system was designed.

SO MUCH HAS changed in the two decades since Ely was first placed in deportation proceedings—for Ely and for the immigrant rights movement in this country. More people than ever recognize the harms of deportation, the cruelty of our immigration policies. And yet they stop short of acknowledging, let alone embracing, people like Ely.

How did we get to this point? Where we can call drug possession "drug trafficking" with a straight face, just to deprive a person of the right to a hearing before he gets deported? Where a man who did everything he was asked to do following a drug offense— pay his debt to society and get drug treatment—can face a second punishment even harsher than the one he got in the criminal legal system? Where so few question the deportation of millions based on such rationales?

You could explain what happened to Ely as a consequence of our failed war on drugs. As a Black man, Ely experienced a legal system that criminalized his addiction and punished him with jail time. You could tell that story, and it would be true. But it would not be complete. The war on drugs and the racialized underpinnings of the criminal legal system have had a clear impact on Ely's life. But so too have the war on immigrants and the racialized underpinnings of the immigration system. In fact, it is the intertwining of these two systems that most clearly explains what happened to Ely from a historical standpoint.

The long history of racialized exclusion in US immigration law is often overlooked in the popular American historical narrative. But buried even further in our history is the symbiotic and destructive relationship between racial exclusion and criminalization. Racism against immigrants has fueled and capitalized upon a public safety narrative to criminalize communities of color and justify harsh immigration policies against people with and without criminal records.

This story may sound familiar to those who know the history of racial justice in America. It echoes the larger story of mass incarceration in this country. As civil rights lawyer and scholar Michelle Alexander has written, American history has witnessed many forms of racialized social control of Black people. The mass incarceration of Black people today is a reincarnation of slavery and Jim Crow—prior legal and social systems that permitted White people to target Black people overtly based on race. After major social, legal, and legislative victories rejected these institutions and ushered in a supposedly colorblind society, racism found a new champion in the criminal legal system. "Although this new system of racialized social control purports to be colorblind, it creates and maintains racial hierarchy much as earlier systems of control did," Alexander explains. Through thinly veiled, anti-Black rhetoric in the wake of the civil rights victories of the 1950s and '60s, elected officials sought "law and order," eventually declaring a war on drugs that spurred massive growth in the criminal legal system. Black people have borne the brunt of the "new Jim Crow": racially disparate rates of arrests, charges, and convictions; mandatory minimum sentences; and postincarceration impediments to voting, housing, and employment.[18]

Few turn this lens on the immigration system, but the same pattern exists. Criminalization has ensured the deportation of millions of people of color from the United States. Government officials have used public safety grounds to help justify every anti-immigrant measure since the beginning of restrictive federal immigration law. Where such a narrative was permitted to mingle with overtly racist language, it did so. And when overtly racist language was no longer legally or socially acceptable, the immigrant-as-criminal narrative emerged to help justify what the overtly racist narrative once did—the large-scale exclusion and expulsion of communities of color from the United States.

Ely came close to losing everything as a result of these forces. But he survived. A decade after we last stood together in immigration court, Ely is still living with his daughter, helping to raise his grandkids. He is welcome in his America: the home he has built around his family, Sunday dinners, walks to the park, enjoying the twilight years of his life. But the scars are still there. He can never shake off the vague sense of uncertainty that comes with being a Black immigrant with a criminal record.

Facing deportation as a "criminal alien" nearly destroyed Ely's life. But the hardship he faced is not an example of a broken system. To the contrary, Ely's experience fighting deportation is the result of a vast crime-based deportation machine that is working exactly as intended. It is part of a larger story of racism and criminalization that is two centuries in the making. Understanding this history—and the critical role that racism has played in the construction of the "criminal alien"—is the first step in breaking the cycle of criminalization that has targeted immigrants like Ely all along.

Chapter Two

ORIGINS OF CONTROL

IN THE SUMMER OF 2017, A TROPICAL STORM FORMED IN the Atlantic. Picking up strength as it entered the Gulf of Mexico, it became the first Category 4 hurricane to make landfall in the continental United States in a decade. In late August Hurricane Harvey drenched Houston, Texas, and the surrounding areas with torrential rain. The rapidly rising floodwaters displaced tens of thousands of families. Reports of destroyed homes and lost lives flashed across the news as Governor Greg Abbott declared a state of emergency.

A hundred miles north, in Lufkin, Texas, Alonso Guillén saw the painful images. He and two friends drove down to the disaster zone, boat in tow, to join a group of volunteer rescuers searching for survivors. As they attempted to navigate the swollen waters, a rush of flooding swept their boat into a bridge, capsizing it. Alonso drowned in Cypress Creek. His family recovered his body a few days later.

Alonso's death made national headlines—not only because of his heroic spirit, but also because Alonso was a recipient of Deferred Action for Childhood Arrivals. DACA was an Obama-era program that gave roughly 800,000 undocumented people who came to the United States as children a temporary opportunity to live and work in the country without fear of deportation. Although a majority of Americans supported the program, it was politically controversial. A coalition of conservative states—led by Texas Attorney General Ken Paxton—condemned the program as "illegal amnesty." As Alonso was rushing down to Houston to help flood victims, Paxton and his allies were threatening to sue the Trump administration if it did not end the DACA program.

Alonso did not live to learn DACA's fate. The day after his body was recovered, Attorney General Jeff Sessions, a longtime immigration restrictionist, declared the end of DACA.

This was a coup for Sessions, who had honed his anti-immigrant views during his years as a US senator from Alabama. A "living monument to the Confederacy," as one grassroots group deemed him, Jefferson Beauregard Sessions III carried the name of Confederate States of America President Jefferson Davis, a legacy that was not lost on him.[1]

Sessions's abysmal record on civil rights issues dated back to his stint as a prosecutor in Alabama. His 1986 nomination to the federal judiciary was withdrawn after the Senate Judiciary Committee heard testimony regarding his racist comments and criticism of the National Association for the Advancement of Colored People and the American Civil Liberties Union. A decade later he was elected to the Senate, where he was primed for anti-immigrant sentiments by Washington lobbyists like Roy Beck, cofounder of NumbersUSA, an organization whose sole mission is to reduce immigration to the United States. Soon enough, Sessions began "finishing Mr. Beck's sentences" and became "the most reliable congressional ally of anti-immigration groups," according to a report in the *New York Times*.[2]

Trump's 2017 nomination of Sessions for attorney general immediately sent up red flags in immigrant rights circles. It came as no surprise when Sessions announced the death of DACA on September 5, 2018. With a tight-lipped smile and a hat tip to the "legal heritage" of "our founders," Sessions declared that the failure to enforce immigration laws "has put our nation at risk of crime, violence, and even terrorism." Ending this lawlessness, he claimed, would ensure public safety and "more effectively teach new immigrants our system of government and assimilate them to the cultural understandings that support it."[3] With those words, Sessions thrust the lives of 800,000 people in the United States, along with their families, into limbo.

Alonso's family was no stranger to the harshness of immigration policy. Like many of the eleven million or so undocumented individuals living in the United States, Alonso was part of a mixed-status family. He lived in Texas with his father, a lawful permanent resident who had no immediate means under immigration law to confer his status to his adult son. Alonso's mother, Rita, lived on the other side of the border in Mexico, without immigration status to join them in the United States.

The end of DACA was only one of many immigration policy choices that affected Alonso's family, and not necessarily the worst. Like many families who live close to our borders, Alonso's family had been kept apart by the immigration system during his life and, as it would turn out, even in death. When Rita learned of her son's death, she immediately attempted to come see him. But she was turned away at the border. Crossing the border without authorization—no matter what the reason—is a crime under US law. Only after the Mexican government advocated for her was she granted humanitarian parole so she could attend her son's funeral.

Sessions is among many who believe that immigration enforcement is a moral, not just legal, imperative. In defending the Trump administration's 2018 policy to separate parents from their children when they arrive at the border, Sessions cited not a federal statute or court case, but the Bible itself. "I would cite you to the Apostle Paul and his clear and wise command in Romans 13, to obey the laws of the government because God has ordained the government for his purposes," he said.[4] It was no coincidence that he drew upon the same biblical passage that lawmakers in the 1800s cited in defense of slavery. The purpose was the same—to convert a political choice into a God-given right.

This perspective is countered by another one held by the many people whose daily lives are affected by immigration enforcement. It was perhaps summarized best by Rita when she was turned away from the border as she tried to bury her son. "When we are with God, there are no borders," she said. "Man made borders on this earth."[5]

Over the years, I have thought often about Rita's words—a mother who, through her grief, stated so plainly a truth that political rhetoric tends to mask. There is nothing inherently moral or even natural about criminalizing movement across borders. Migration is a natural phenomenon. Throughout history, the human race has survived and flourished because of migration. Restrictions on migration—forcing or barring movement—are merely human inventions, subject to human failings.

One of those human failings is America's deep and entrenched embrace of racism. Accepted, legalized, and open racial discrimination has been a driving force behind the laws that kept Alonso's family separated by a criminalized border, even in a land that once belonged to their people. From the country's very first federal law of naturalization, reserving such rights to "free White persons" in 1790, immigration law has had a racist design.[6] That racism continues today as part of our crime-based deportation machine: a machine that punishes immigrants by criminalizing their acts and deporting them for their crimes.

Some may deny the role that racism has played in perpetuating this system of control. They may argue that criminality is a perfectly legitimate basis for deciding who may enter, and remain, in a country. But that view is precisely why uncovering the basis for the label of criminality is so important. If racist ideas lead to criminal labels, then those racist ideas justify the system, not criminality itself.

Racism is not, of course, the only divisive force at work in the formation of immigration law. America has always strived to protect itself from those deemed undesirable, while exploiting them at the same time. The people who initially colonized this land and displaced its indigenous inhabitants were, for the most part,

White, Protestant propertied men. They sought to protect their interests against all those whom they deemed threats. Their condemnation was sweeping. It included, during various points in our early history, British Loyalists, the French, the Irish, southern and eastern Europeans, Catholics, Jews, communists, and anarchists, to name a few disfavored groups. Over time, some of these groups have moved into the mainstream, while others have not. Nativism, sexism, classism, homophobia, transphobia, anti-Semitism, Islamophobia—there is a long list of intersectional prejudices that continue to render some groups undesirable. The targets have changed over time, but America has long been prone to these prejudicial agendas.[7]

I emphasize racism not to detract from these other prejudices but to underscore how significantly and consistently race has shaped the criminalization of immigrants. The founders wrote citizenship, naturalization, and immigration laws to preserve Whiteness, eradicate Blackness, and racialize immigrants through this hierarchy. Where migration was associated with the free movement of people of color, lawmakers quickly acted to regulate and, eventually, criminalize that movement.

In this way, racism has been a driving force behind punitive immigration laws from the beginning. It feeds the cycle of criminalization: first associating immigrants with criminality, then criminalizing acts associated with immigrants, and finally punishing immigrants with incarceration and deportation. Racism helps to explain why people of color—with or without criminal records, with or without immigration status—share a fate of criminalization in a system where deportation is the ultimate punishment.

America's earliest experiments with criminalizing immigrants— from the first restrictive citizenship and immigration laws through the end of racial immigration quotas in 1965—demonstrate that criminality has never been a neutral way of deciding who belongs in America. Much like the foundational laws governing US citizenship and immigration generally, the laws that gave rise to the crime-based deportation machine have been steeped in racism from the start.

Man made borders on this earth for political reasons, and in the United States, those reasons include the preservation of the nation's racial hierarchy.

IIIIIII

THE FERVENT ATTACK on safe havens from deportation like DACA—the program that tenuously preserved Alonso's place in this country during the last years of his life—is part of a much larger project in this country. The story of immigration regulation in America begins with the story of colonialism and slavery. Even before the concept of the "immigrant"—from the time of "colonists," "settlers," "slaves," "indentured servants," and "Indians"—laws concerning membership and belonging enforced a racial hierarchy to exploit people of color while preserving Whiteness in America.

The birth of colonial America began with the violent displacement of its indigenous residents. Colonists quickly reneged on their initial promises of protection and trade, touching off "Indian wars" aimed at pushing indigenous tribes off their ancestral land. With the expansion of its territorial conquests, colonial America had an interest in encouraging migration in various forms. To build and expand their colonies, colonists sought the voluntary migration of propertied White men from western Europe to provide the capital and fill the new settlements. Simultaneously, colonists relied on the involuntary migration of enslaved and indentured people to provide the necessary labor.

With these interests in mind, colonists eventually enacted laws to regulate migration and membership. As the colonists themselves hailed from another land, they were less concerned with foreign birth and more concerned with racial, ethnic, and economic desirability. As historian Kunal Parker has written, laws routinely rendered groups that colonists deemed undesirable as "foreign" within the colonies—including enslaved and free Black people, indigenous people, women, and the poor.[8] Colonies regularly prohibited the settlement of these undesirable individuals within their boundaries and precluded them from owning property and voting at the local level.

These colonial understandings of membership continued through the Revolutionary War. In the late eighteenth century, the newly formed United States of America defined citizenship at a national level, while individual states continued the colonies' tradition of regulating migration at a local level. These varied laws shared a common purpose: to preserve a hierarchy in which White people—initially Protestant, propertied, western European men—were afforded the greatest freedom of movement and security of membership in society. Black people—free and enslaved—and indigenous people were at the lowest rung of this hierarchy and subject to the most restrictions.

In no place is this hierarchy more evident than in the struggle around citizenship itself. Any assessment of modern immigrant struggles for societal inclusion—whether through liminal protections like DACA or paths to citizenship in immigration reform—must begin with an examination of the historical fight for birthright citizenship.

The framers drafted the US Constitution against a backdrop of *jus soli*, the English common law tradition of conferring citizenship to all those born within a country's jurisdiction.[9] Nonetheless, as legal scholar Ian Haney López has explained, birthright citizenship was restricted to White people for a century—a restriction influenced as much by racist ideas about Black and indigenous people as it was by broader concepts of foreignness.

The burden of challenging these racist concepts fell on people of color. Dred Scott was born into slavery in Virginia at the end of the eighteenth century. Although the United States banned the transatlantic slave trade a little over a decade after his birth, slavery flourished through internal "breeding" and domestic trade of enslaved people. Scott was sold and leased in various states before seeking to purchase freedom for himself and his family. When he was refused, he turned to the courts.

A series of lawsuits ultimately culminated in the infamous 1857 *Dred Scott* decision. The Supreme Court ruled that a Black man born in the United States could not be a citizen, and therefore could not seek intervention from the Court, because he was part of "a subordinate and inferior class of beings."[10] Such an "open, glaring, and scandalous tissue of lies," as abolitionist Frederick Douglass described the decision, fueled tensions between the states over slavery.[11]

After the Civil War, Reconstruction-era lawmakers hastened to invalidate the *Dred Scott* decision. Overcoming a presidential veto, Congress enacted the Civil Rights Act of 1866, which recognized the citizenship of all persons born in the United States. The provisions gained constitutional force through the Fourteenth Amendment, ratified two years later, which states, "All persons born or naturalized in the United States, and subject to the jurisdiction thereof, are citizens of the United States and of the state wherein they reside."[12]

Despite the seemingly plain words of the law, White nativists continued to guard citizenship jealously, arguing that the children of parents loyal to another government could not be said to be "subject to the jurisdiction" of the United States. The children of Asian immigrants were routinely denied citizenship based on this theory. When California-born Wong Kim Ark returned to the United States after a brief visit with his parents in China, immigration officials detained him, claiming that he could not be a US citizen. Wong Kim Ark, like Dred Scott, fought his case up to the Supreme Court. In 1898, three decades after the ratification of the Fourteenth Amendment, the Court finally declared that the native-born children of immigrants were birthright citizens of the United States.[13]

Yet citizenship hierarchies and exceptions remained. Indigenous people, some of whom sought the recognition of American citizenship, fared poorly. The Supreme Court rejected birthright citizenship for indigenous people in the 1884 *Elk v. Wilkins* decision. Legislation did not confer birthright citizenship to indigenous people until 1924.[14] And even that legislation left questions about the citizenship of indigenous people born after the law was passed.[15] It was not until the Nationality Act of 1940—more than a century and a half after the formation of the

United States—that federal law clarified that all persons born in the United States are citizens.[16]

Somehow, the debate over birthright citizenship lingers on even today. A small but vocal minority of people argue that birthright citizenship—as understood in the Supreme Court's *Wong Kim Ark* decision—cannot reach the American-born children of undocumented immigrants. According to the proponents of this fringe view, such undocumented parents are not "subject to the jurisdiction" of the United States as the framers understood it.

Although this reading of the law has been widely debunked by constitutional law scholars, its salience continues. Proponents of the narrow interpretation of birthright citizenship dislike the more popular, inclusive reading because, in their eyes, it acts as a "powerful magnet for people to violate our immigration laws."[17] In other words, birthright citizenship is hated precisely because it allows children born in the United States to escape the punishments heaped on their parents. No matter that a generation of racist laws prevented those parents from obtaining legal status in the first place.

GIVEN THE HISTORY of birthright citizenship, it should come as no surprise that naturalization—the process by which foreign-born individuals become citizens—was similarly fraught with racist ideas. In 1790, Congress passed the first federal naturalization law, limited to "any alien, being a free white person who shall have resided within the limits and under the jurisdiction of the United States for a term of two years."[18] For nearly a century, only White foreigners could naturalize.

During the Reconstruction era, Congress finally amended the law to extend the right to naturalize to "aliens of African nativity and to persons of African descent," but retained bars on indigenous and Asian naturalization.[19] Although the 1870 amendment did not distinguish between new African immigrants and those who had been brought to the United States enslaved, few viewed the amendment as an invitation for Black immigration. In the words of one federal judge, the law may ostensibly offer naturalization to the "savage and strange inhabitants of the 'dark continent,'" but "the Negroes of Africa were not likely to emigrate to this country, and therefore the provision concerning them was merely a harmless piece of legislative buncombe."[20]

Asian immigrants challenged the remaining restrictions in naturalization law. Attempting to marshal what they could from the burgeoning "science" of race that became popular during the early 1900s, many Asian immigrants attempted—and failed—to gain recognition as "free white persons" under the law. Rejecting those claims for immigrants from China, Japan, and India alike, the Supreme Court relied on the "understanding of the common man" in defining Whiteness.[21]

Only after World War II did a series of legislative acts slowly open up naturalization to people from Asian countries. In 1952, all explicit racial requirements for naturalization were eliminated in the Immigration and Nationality Act.[22]

The path to naturalization, however, remains complex. To enter the country in a lawful status, and then to remain as a lawful permanent resident—the status one must have before becoming naturalized—is often impossible. And even if one person in a family is able to get on that path—someone like Alonso's father, for example—sharing that status with family members is often impossible or made possible only through a process that takes decades.

More than 16.7 million people in America are just like Alonso—members of families with at least one member who lacks formal immigration status.[23] These include mixed-status families in which parents cannot convey their status to their adult children, at least not for years. The law is also written so that children born in the United States cannot convey their status to their parents until they turn twenty-one, and even then other bars may apply. In the interim, these family members are labeled as "illegal" or "criminal." And even when painfully modest programs like DACA enter into the political debate—not even to convey status but merely to prevent deportation—there are forces that will fight like hell to close those doors.

Those forces have always been with us. They persisted throughout the history of racially restricted birthright citizenship and naturalization, and as those battles were lost, they increasingly fixed their eyes on migration itself. Who is allowed to enter the United States? Who must leave? Cloaked today in sanitized discussions about the need to "protect American interests," the laws of exclusion and deportation are simply branches of a single tree, rooted in White supremacy.

⁙

A SIX-HOUR DRIVE south from where Alonso Guillén lost his life is Rio Grande City, Texas, home to the Starr County Jail. There, on May 13, 2018, guards found Marco Antonio Muñoz dead in a padded cell. The death was unreported to the public for days, until the *Washington Post* broke the story. Marco, father of two, had committed suicide after Border Patrol separated him from his wife and toddler.[24]

Two days earlier, Marco, his wife, Orlanda, and their three-year-old son had crossed the Rio Grande near the tiny border town of Granjeno, Texas. They had lived in the United States a few years ago and had their first son there, but eventually the family returned to their native Honduras. They grew coffee in rural Copán and had their second little boy. For a while, it seemed like they could build their lives there. But after Orlanda's brother was murdered, the family no longer felt safe. They put their older son, a US citizen by birth, on a plane to meet relatives in the United States, and then set off for the US-Mexico border to seek asylum.

The journey was treacherous, and Marco was exhausted by the time they made it to America. Border Patrol officers brought them to a station in nearby McAllen, Texas.

That's when the Border Patrol officers told Marco that he would not be able to stay with his wife and son. Instead, he would be criminally prosecuted for illegal entry under the Trump administration's zero tolerance policy.

Marco did not understand. He looked at his wife and his little boy, and then back at the officers. The men were taking his wife and son away. Marco hugged his three-year-old son and refused to let go. The officers physically pried him away from his child and locked him in a chain-link cage as Marco had what officers described as a panic attack. Long after his wife and child were no longer there, Marco was still rattling the cage, screaming for his family.

So Border Patrol drove him forty miles away to Starr County Jail, where corrections officers locked him in a padded cell. Within those four walls, Marco took off his sweater. According to jail officials, he tied one edge of the sweater to the grate in the middle of the floor and the other edge around his neck. Video footage showed him twisting his body around until he suffocated and died.[25]

The criminalization of the border has taken countless lives and separated families. Hundreds of people, including children, die on the journey north, some in the desert, and some in Border Patrol cells. Walls are built and ports of entry turn asylum seekers away, forcing many to make desperate trips across treacherous terrain.[26]

To make matters worse, since 2005 the federal government has engaged in a program of mass prosecution called Operation Streamline. Under the program, which now stretches across all federal courts covering the border with Mexico, federal prosecutors file charges against every adult who comes across the border without authorization, including asylum seekers like Marco. As a result of the large numbers, the program forces groups of people, as many as eighty at a time, to plead guilty in front of a single federal judge in a mass criminal proceeding that lasts minutes. Thousands of people seeking a better life in the United States have been imprisoned here instead. It is a reason why Latinx people are disproportionately incarcerated in federal prisons nationwide.[27]

People today increasingly recognize that these policies are violent and cruel. We weep at stories like Marco's and wonder how the crisis has grown so severe. But these types of policies aren't recent inventions. From the beginning, America's border criminalization policies were designed with this end in mind: to punish people like Marco for attempting to do what generations of western European immigrants once did without repercussion. The laws were written to redefine the American polity not only by whom we want to keep in, but by whom we want to keep out, even if the violence of incarceration is required to get there.

IIIIIII

PEOPLE LIKE MARCO were not the first to experience these kinds of criminalizing policies in America. The dehumanization of indigenous people and enslaved Africans thrived on violence— from the reservation to the plantation, the whipping post to the lynching tree. The separation of families—on the auction block or through conquest—was commonplace. The story about migration must begin with those whose movement was originally, and continues to be, the focus of much criminalization in America.

As with the racist rules that originally governed citizenship and naturalization, migration control in America was initially less about foreign birth (a trait of the early settlers themselves) than it was about race. Thus the power to regulate migration— at least for the first century of this nation's history—fell to those with the greatest interest in maintaining control over people of color: the states. And it was the states' desire to control Black people, free and enslaved, that legitimated the concept of borders and the regulation of undesirable presence in the United States in the first place.

Throughout the nineteenth century, states vigorously regulated the behavior and movement of Black people in ways that foreshadowed the regulation of immigrants today. Many states required free Black people to register and carry documents proving their free status and residency. Some states attempted to bar the entry of Black people, free or enslaved, entirely. States further criminalized those who facilitated unlawful entry, which the Supreme Court initially upheld as an appropriate exercise of states' police powers.[28] It was proper, the Court wrote in 1852, for states "to protect themselves against the influx either of liberated or fugitive slaves, and to repel from their soil a population likely to become burdensome and injurious, either as paupers or criminals."[29]

These racist laws were not confined to Southern slaveholding states. Northern states like Oregon, Indiana, and Illinois banned the settlement or immigration of Black people in their state constitutions.[30] Illinois, for example, amended its constitution to direct the legislature to "pass such laws as will effectually prohibit free persons of color from immigrating to and settling in this State; and to effectually prevent the owners of slaves from bringing them into this State, for the purpose of setting them free."[31]

Lawmakers in Northern and Southern states alike viewed the free movement of Black people as a threat to the institution of slavery and to the Whiteness of the country. While much of these fears focused on internal migration of freed Black slaves, changes abroad began to transform the concern to one of transnational migration. After a massive revolt of enslaved people in Saint-Domingue birthed the nation of Haiti in 1804, several states passed legislation to prohibit the entry of free Black people for fear that they would radicalize enslaved Black people or lead similar revolts.[32] Fears of foreign-born free Black people further heightened in 1833 when the British abolished slavery throughout its empire, including the British West Indies.[33]

The federal government was initially reluctant to weigh in on the governance of migration. Congress's early foray into immigration regulation, the Alien and Sedition Acts of 1798, fanned by fears of French influence, was widely criticized, and its deportation provisions were never enforced. Republicans questioned whether the federal government had the power to deport undesirable immigrants. A two-year sunset provision came and went without action, and nearly a century passed before the federal government attempted to engage in deportation.[34]

This did not mean, however, that the federal government rejected other forms of migration regulation in the interim. The Act Prohibiting Importation of Slaves, enacted in 1807, came on the heels of a similar British act curbing the transatlantic slave trade. But domestic trading continued, with a million native-born Black people subjected to slavery and internal forced migration within and across state lines.

As societal views on slavery splintered the country and enslaved people escaped to seek refuge in free Northern states, Congress enacted a series of fugitive slave laws to ensure the return of runaway slaves to the South.[35] As the United States expanded its territory, Congress also passed laws like the 1830 Indian Removal Act, resulting in the death of thousands of indigenous residents and the confinement of survivors in "reservations" as foreigners to the state.[36]

These acts set the stage for the ugly history of migration regulation yet to come. As legal scholar Dan Kanstroom has written, the fugitive slave laws and Trail of Tears are the "antecedents" of American deportation policy.[37] When the gaze of White nationalists expanded to include other people of color in their midst—Chinese people settling along the West Coast, Mexican people living on both sides of a changing southwestern border—they knew what to do.

Long before the US government stopped Alonso Guillén's grieving mother from entering America to bury her son, long before it decided to incarcerate and separate families who dared to cross the border, racism found a powerful tool in the criminalization of migration itself.

IIIIIII

THE NINETEENTH-CENTURY BORDERS of the United States were rapidly changing, as were the ethnicity of those who began to settle within the country. In 1845, the United States annexed the Republic of Texas. Relations between the United States and Mexico quickly took a turn toward war. The Mexican-American War ended in 1848 with the Treaty of Guadalupe Hidalgo, through which the United States acquired Alta California and Santa Fe de Nuevo México. A new border was created, running through Mexican communities in the south and southwest along the Rio Grande.[38]

Mexicans within the US territory were granted US citizenship and the right to naturalize, thereby legally recognized as White. But racism against Mexicans was prevalent, growing into more formal systems of segregation and discrimination as the population grew.[39]

The opening of the West also attracted Chinese merchants from across the Pacific, with an increased focus on the mutual benefits of Chinese-American trade. Initially welcomed for their goods and labor, Chinese immigrants began to settle in California in small numbers. Then came the gold rush of 1849—spurring thousands of people to migrate to California from various parts of the country and the world, including China.[40]

These new settlements sparked new racialized anxieties, drawing from old prejudices. But White settlers did not yet have a language to talk about the unwanted Chinese and Mexicans in their midst. So they borrowed one.

In 1853, a White man named George Hall attacked a Chinese miner at Bear River in California. When Ling Sing, another miner at the camp, attempted to intervene, Hall shot and killed him. A jury convicted Hall of murder on the testimony of Chinese witnesses. Hall appealed, citing a California law that "No Black or Mulatto person, or Indian, shall be permitted to give evidence in favor of, or against, any White person." Chinese people had no right, Hall argued, to testify against a White man.

The California Supreme Court agreed with Hall, reversing the conviction based on the trial court's consideration of Chinese witnesses. Deploying a profoundly racist legal logic, Chief Justice Hugh Murray wrote that the term "White" necessarily included the "Caucasian race" and excluded all others, while the term "Black" was defined as "the opposite of White." Chinese persons, although not named in the law, were prohibited from testimony as Black people—described as "the more degraded tribes of the same species, who have nothing in common with us, in language, country or laws."[41]

Motivating this ruling was not only a concern over the protection of White citizens from non-White testimony, but a preservation of the privileges of American Whiteness itself. In the words of Chief Justice Murray, "The same rule which would admit [the Chinese] to testify, would admit them to all the equal rights of citizenship, and we might soon see them at the polls, in the jury box, upon the bench, and in our legislative halls. This is not a speculation which exists in the excited and over-heated imagination of the patriot and statesman, but it is an actual and present danger."[42] Chief Justice Murray went on to label Chinese persons as not only inferior but as an immoral and dangerous force—capturing the prevailing view of many White Californians at the time.

Soon enough, groups like Chinese and Mexican people were labeled the West's "Negro problem." It didn't take long before White nationalists turned to the same toolkit to deal with this problem that they had long used against Black and indigenous people. And as the political and legal landscape evolved through the Civil War and its aftermath, so too did the tools. Criminalization became the key.

The backlash against immigrants in the West reached a fever pitch after the Civil War.[43] White voters demanded action. In addition to racist criminal procedure laws, the California legislature passed laws to tax foreign minors, restrict Chinese immigrants from land ownership, require ship captains to post bond when bringing Chinese women passengers from overseas, and promote segregation in schools.[44]

Many of these laws were initially upheld by state and federal courts. For years, the Supreme Court had recognized the authority of states to regulate immigration as a valid exercise of state "police power." As the Court explained in one 1837 case, state action was necessary and appropriate to guard "against the moral pestilence of paupers, vagabonds, and possibly convicts" within the state.[45] But in the 1849 Passenger Cases, the Supreme Court struck down state regulations imposing taxes on arriving foreign passengers as an invalid exercise of federal "commerce power."[46] Although states may protect their residents from threats, only the federal government can regulate commerce with foreign nations.

The idea that states' authority rested on the type of power exerted—police power versus commerce power—began to shift the way that states regulated immigrants. As legal scholar Kerry

Abrams has written, the uncertainty over whether a state immigration law would be upheld in court encouraged state lawmakers to frame their laws as exercises of police power—thus inviting states to label unwanted immigrants as paupers, vagabonds, and convicts.[47]

The legislative maneuvering came at an important time. Anger over Chinese immigrants exploded into lynchings and mob violence across the West, including mass murders in California, Wyoming, and Washington.[48] Rather than condemn the violence, local political leaders routinely described Chinese people as dangerous to the White population and inherently immoral. Chinese men, they argued, were kidnappers and human traffickers, and Chinese women were depicted as prostitutes.

In 1870, the California legislature targeted Chinese men and women through the Anti-Kidnapping Act and the Anti-Coolie Act. The Anti-Kidnapping Act criminalized the "kidnapping and importation of Mongolian, Chinese and Japanese females" and treated Asian immigrant women as presumptive prostitutes.[49] It required each Asian woman to obtain a license to enter the United States upon a showing that she was a "person of correct habits and good character."[50] The Anti-Coolie Act made a similar requirement of Chinese laborers.[51] Characterizing Chinese laborers as criminals, the law declared that "criminals and malefactors are being constantly imported from Chinese seaports," creating a "burdensome expense upon the administration of criminal justice."[52]

California legislators amended these laws several times, making it increasingly hard for Chinese men and women to immigrate to California. By 1874 ship captains were required to post a $500 bond for any immigrant passenger who fell within a broad set of undesired categories, including "convicted criminal" or "lewd or debauched woman."[53]

But the winds were changing. The United States was engaged in complex trade negotiations with China and was pursuing treaty obligations aimed at encouraging immigration and goods from China. At the same time, federal courts began to consolidate immigration authority within the federal government. Soon the

Supreme Court shifted even further away from its prior case law and held that only the federal government, not the states, had plenary power over immigration regulation.[54]

White Californians had to look beyond their state legislators to deal with unwanted Chinese immigrants. They sent elected officials to take the fight to Congress. Aaron Sargent, born in Massachusetts, moved to California in 1849 and was eventually elected to Congress. A lawyer and a Republican who became known as a champion of women's suffrage, Sargent embraced his fellow White Californians' disdain for the Chinese. In an 1862 debate over federalizing California's taxation of foreign minors, Representative Sargent declared, "In morals and in every other respect they are obnoxious to our people. The women are prostitutes, and the men petty thieves. But how can we get them out? . . . We are overrun with these pagans, and we are doing what we can to relieve ourselves in the mild form of taxation."[55]

Taxation, as Sargent and like-minded lawmakers soon learned, was not sufficient. Exclusion was the new goal. Fellow congressman Horace Page, also of California, took up the cause. Like Sargent, Page was born out east, in New York, and moved to California as a young man, where he was eventually elected to serve in Congress as a Republican. Pushing for a ban on Chinese immigration, Page echoed Sargent's theme of criminality. Page proclaimed in his speeches that Chinese people were doomed to criminality because "thieving, trickery, cheating, and fraud are taught and encouraged as the essential elements of success" in Chinese institutions.[56]

Page eventually succeeded where others had failed in securing more dramatic action against the Chinese. Taking some of the worst elements of the anti-kidnapping and anti-Coolie laws, Page drafted the first restrictive federal immigration law ever to be enforced against those seeking to migrate here.

The Page Act of 1875 criminalized the transportation of Chinese, Japanese, and other "Oriental" passengers without their consent, as well as the "importation" of women "for the purposes of prostitution."[57] The Page Act also excluded "persons who are undergoing a sentence for conviction in their own country of felonious crimes other than political . . . or whose sentence has been remitted on condition of their emigration" and "women 'imported for the purposes of prostitution.'"[58] The reference to remitted sentences lumped the issue of Chinese immigration with widespread hatred of policies from the 1700s that permitted the transportation of people convicted of crimes in Europe to America in lieu of receiving the death penalty. A new sweeping category of dangerous criminal immigrants was born, justifying the first federal exclusion law.

Emboldened by their success, anti-Chinese lawmakers quickly followed the Page Act with the Chinese Exclusion Act of 1882, which explicitly excluded Chinese laborers from entering the United States for ten years and criminalized anyone who helped a Chinese person enter with a sentence of up to one year in prison.[59] The lawmakers who had sought to criminalize Chinese immigrants to prevent their entry now achieved their greater goal—an outright ban on Chinese labor migration.

The Supreme Court upheld Chinese exclusion in its 1889 decision *Chae Chan Ping v. United States*, adopting much of the racist rhetoric of the West. Chinese laborers were a threat to the "material interests" and "public morals" of Americans, the Court concluded; "their immigration was in numbers approaching the character of an Oriental invasion, and was a menace to our civilization." The Court would not, therefore, scrutinize Congress's decision to exclude "the presence of foreigners of a different race in this country, who will not assimilate with us" and thus are "dangerous to its peace and security."[60]

Chinese exclusion was the law of the land. But it soon became clear that Chinese exclusion was not enough to appease White people in the West. As historian Kelly Lytle Hernández writes, "The Chinese Exclusion Act stemmed the rise of Chinese immigration into the United States, but it did not purge Chinese immigrants from the U.S. West."[61] Legislators claimed that Chinese laborers were evading the law and living in the United States unlawfully.[62]

Yet another congressman from California, Thomas Geary, attempted to close the gap. The Geary Act of 1892 not only indefinitely extended the bar on Chinese migration; it required Chinese laborers living in the United States to register and prove legal status through the testimony of White witnesses that they had entered the country before 1882.[63] The Geary Act specified that Chinese immigrants who could not prove legal residency could be convicted, sentenced to up to one year of imprisonment and hard labor, and deported.[64] The adjudication of these penalties—criminal and civil—involved a summary proceeding without a jury.[65] It was the first law to criminalize undocumented status within the United States.[66]

Chinese activists led a concerted battle to strike down the Geary Act, taking aim at both its incarceration and deportation provisions.[67] In *Wong Wing v. United States*, the Supreme Court held that Fifth and Sixth Amendment protections, including the right to a jury trial, must accompany the imposition of a criminal sentence of imprisonment and hard labor.[68] It was a significant victory for a group that had been relentlessly attacked.

But the question of deportation without trial remained open. Although states had expelled people for a variety of reasons in the past, never before had the federal government exerted this kind of deportation power over immigrants. New York resident Fong Yue Ting, a laundryman who refused to register under the Geary Act and was arrested under the law, took up the challenge.[69]

Only a few years had passed since the Supreme Court upheld Chinese exclusion in *Chae Chan Ping*, giving the political branches unchecked power to exclude people from the United States based on race.[70] But Fong Yue Ting hoped that the justices would view deportation power differently. Forcibly expelling someone from his home, Fong Yue Ting's lawyers argued, was different from preventing someone from entering at the border. At a minimum, deportation surely required a trial and similar procedural protections available in criminal cases.

In response, the US solicitor general defended deportation power before the Supreme Court, making a blatantly racist appeal. He normalized the deportation of Chinese people by pointing to long-standing federal policies permitting the "forcible removal" of indigenous peoples in the United States, along with the deportation of "Egyptians" and "Turks" by England. Deportation power was a sovereign right, he argued, required to safeguard the public from the dangerous "alien races." As he wrote in his legal brief on behalf of the federal government, "It is now generally conceded that the most insidious and dangerous enemies to the State are not the armed foes who invade our territory, but those alien races who are incapable of assimilation, and come among us to debase our labor and poison the health and morals of the communities in which they locate."[71]

The solicitor general's arguments landed well. Writing for the majority, Supreme Court Justice Horace Gray concluded that, having already recognized the right of the nation to exclude Chinese immigrants at the border, the right to deport was equally "absolute and unqualified."[72] Then came one of many legal fictions in immigration law. Deportation, Justice Gray wrote, "is not a punishment" and thus falls outside the protections provided to criminal defendants by the Constitution.[73]

In a dissent, Chief Justice Melville Fuller explained that deportation is "punishment without a judicial trial," "a legislative sentence of banishment, and, as such, absolutely void."[74] Another dissenter, Justice David Brewer, further derided the majority's view as divorced from reality. "Every one knows," he wrote, "that to be forcibly taken away from home and family and friends and business and property, and sent across the ocean to a distant land, is punishment, and that oftentimes most severe and cruel."[75] Justice Stephen Field similarly dissented: "It is cruel and unusual. As to its cruelty, nothing can exceed a forcible deportation from a country of one's residence, and the breaking up of all the relations of friendship, family, and business there contracted."[76]

Justice Field's dissent was of particular importance because he was the author of the *Chae Chan Ping* decision upholding Chinese exclusion. The power to deport was different, he believed, from the power to exclude. Quoting James Madison's 1798 statement condemning executive deportation power, he wrote: "If a banishment of this sort described be not a punishment, and among the severest of punishments, it will be difficult to imagine a doom to which the name can be applied." In Justice Field's view, deportation is unquestionably punishment, one "beyond all reason in its severity" and "out of all proportion to the alleged offense."[77] Treated as such, deportation power was far from "absolute and unqualified," as the majority concluded. It should have been subject to the constitutional protections that applied to all such criminal punishments.

Despite these vigorous dissenting views, the majority prevailed, and executive deportation power—as a civil rather than a criminal function—received the stamp of approval from the only court that could curb its excess.

It was an important lesson for federal lawmakers. Laws of exclusion were a way to prevent people of color from entering America, and now laws of deportation were a way to kick out the few who made it through.

SOON ENOUGH, THE list of grounds for deportation grew. Criminal grounds were popular, as lawmakers adapted a tool they had honed during the backlash to Reconstruction.

When citizenship and naturalization rights were extended to Black people in the Reconstruction era, many states passed and expanded legislation to control and criminalize Black people. Vagrancy laws were a key aspect of this legislation, known as the Black Codes. The Black Codes ensured that localities could selectively arrest and incarcerate Black people and subject them to involuntary labor through a convict-leasing system. It allowed Southern states to reap the economic benefits they lost because of emancipation and gave businesses a cheap source of exploitable labor.[78]

To maximize the political benefits of criminalization, several Southern states also passed laws that prohibited individuals with certain types of criminal records from voting. After Reconstruction, the goal was to disenfranchise Black men without running afoul of new constitutional protections. As a result, legislators chose to apply the bars to crimes involving "moral turpitude." Such crimes, in the minds of legislators, were at the heart of the Black Codes and could be easily associated with Black men.[79]

As legal scholar Julia Simon-Kerr has written, it was against this backdrop that the term "crime . . . involving moral turpitude" made its 1891 debut in immigration law as a ground of exclusion. The term was not defined in the immigration law, nor was there much debate during its inclusion. It was an easy way to ensure that a certain type of person could be excluded and deported.[80]

Targeting immigrants for deportation based on their crimes of "moral turpitude" was just the beginning. Anti-immigrant sentiment helped to fuel a growing movement to criminalize drug use. Like migration, the use and sale of drugs was widely unregulated in early American history. Most substances initially were heralded for their medicinal purposes.[81] Medical and pharmaceutical industries promoted opium, for example, in the 1800s.[82] But when opium became associated with Chinese immigrants, legislators began to use the tools of the criminal legal system to respond.[83] Anti-Chinese sentiment in the West prompted one of the nation's first criminal laws directed at drug use: an 1875 San Francisco ordinance penalizing any person who keeps or visits an opium den.[84]

As general anti-Chinese hysteria grew, so too did local and state ordinances criminalizing drugs. Political scientist Doris Marie Provine has documented how "advocates of vigorous enforcement . . . routinely exploited white fears of racial mixing" by framing opium as a substance by which Chinese immigrants would tempt white women and youth into addiction.[85] The initial opium laws were heavily enforced against Chinese immigrants. As one court observed in upholding such prosecutions, the laws may proceed "more from a desire to vex and annoy the 'Heathen Chinee' . . . than to protect the people from the evil habit."[86]

Similar steps were taken to associate other narcotics with people of color, particularly Black people, who were demonized by politicians and the media as illicit drug users. The racialized characterization of drug use played a significant role in the federal criminalization of drugs.[87] It led to several acts in the 1900s to regulate, tax, and eventually criminalize drug use and sale.[88]

It did not take long for these federal criminal drug laws to include a deportation provision—the first significant category of crime-based immigration penalties since prostitution and "crimes involving moral turpitude." The Narcotic Drugs Import and Export Act of 1922 both criminalized the importation of narcotics offenses and provided that "any alien who at any time after his entry is convicted [of such an importation offense] shall upon termination of imprisonment be taken into custody and deported."[89]

History repeated itself as cannabis—a substance that, like opium, was initially valued for its medicinal purposes—became associated with Mexicans as "marijuana." The fledgling Federal Bureau of Narcotics capitalized on the anti-immigrant sentiments of the time to drum up opposition to marijuana at the local and state levels. Claiming that marijuana was associated with violent crime from Mexican laborers, Black people, and others, the bureau led a campaign against the "marijuana menace." Eventually, marijuana trade became criminalized federally, and deportation grounds followed.[90]

The grounds for exclusion and deportation based on drug offenses would vastly expand over the next seventy-five years—at all times, taking a disproportionate aim at people of color. Anti-Black, anti-Chinese, and anti-Mexican sentiment were combined not only to justify deportation, but to criminalize acts that were simply not crimes before.

||||||

A BREWING "RACIAL science" pushed by eugenicists in the early twentieth century helped justify the characterization of immigrants as criminals. People of color were biologically more inferior, prone to immorality and criminality, eugenicists argued. As these ideas picked up steam, eugenicists took it upon themselves to use immigration law to protect the purity of the White race.

Eugenicists worked with Congress to craft a quota system of racial and ethnic preferences for immigration to the United States.[91] The National Origins Act of 1924 restricted immigration outside the Western Hemisphere to 155,000 people annually, and divided those numbers by country of origin, permitting migration from each country at a level no greater than 2 percent of their foreign-born population in the United States as of 1890, and barring immigration by those ineligible to naturalize.[92]

As a result of the new quotas, immigration from southern and eastern Europe, Africa, and the rest of the world beyond the Western Hemisphere was vastly limited; Asians, ineligible for citizenship under prior exclusionary laws, were barred.[93] This was intentional; as one congressional report stated, the purpose of the quotas was "to preserve, as nearly as possible, the racial status quo in the United States."[94] As historian Mae Ngai has written, "the law constructed a white American race" and "transform[ed] immigration law into an instrument of mass racial engineering."[95]

Over the next few decades, the National Origins Quota System effectively stemmed immigration from countries beyond western Europe.[96] To appease western and southern agribusiness interests, however, lawmakers agreed to exempt countries within the Western Hemisphere from the quotas. After all, the farms needed access to cheap labor. Black inhabitants of the colonized islands of the Caribbean remained restricted, subject to subquotas within the quotas given to the British Empire.[97] Laborers from Mexico, however, were not subject to quota restriction—and thus could provide the source of labor that American agribusiness required.

To ensure an exploitable workforce of Mexican immigrants, lawmakers developed and relied on other forms of regulation. Although Mexican immigrants were not subject to the new quota system, they were required to apply for and obtain expensive visas and pay head taxes upon entry.[98] Those who entered the United States without making the necessary payments could be quickly deported. Fear of deportation made it easy for agribusiness to hire Mexican immigrants cheaply and with few protections.

Enforcement of these new immigration laws fell to a fledging agency. Congress created the first federal agency to enforce immigration law in 1891. The Bureau of Immigration and Naturalization realized quickly that its budget depended on the priorities of Congress. In reports to Congress, the first commissioner of the bureau initially capitalized on anti-Chinese sentiment, celebrating the agency's growing tools for rooting out "illegal" Chinese— port inspectors, detention centers and jails, legal challenges. But he also bemoaned the lack of resources at the southern border to keep the unwanted from coming.[99]

Congress responded in 1924 by forming the US Border Patrol.[100] The imposition of quotas, visas, and head taxes made border policing a priority. The effect of these laws, and the new boots on the ground to enforce them, had an immediate impact. A growing segment of immigrants from Mexico found themselves subject to deportation for evading increasingly prohibitive requirements.[101] By 1929, more than fifteen thousand Mexicans were deported annually, seven times the number deported just four years earlier.[102]

Nativists wanted more. As historian Kelly Lytle Hernández has written, they found their champion in the White supremacist South Carolina Senator Coleman Blease. Senator Blease finally broke the stalemate between those who wanted an outright ban on Mexican migration and those who wanted to permit, but keep control over, Mexican labor. He proposed criminalizing, not just deporting, those who came without authorization.[103]

In 1929, Congress enacted the first law formally criminalizing entry and reentry to the United States.[104] Learning from the outcome in *Wong Wing,* Congress ensured this newly criminal offense carried the trial and due process rights that normally attended criminal prosecutions at the time. In the end, those rights didn't matter much. The crime itself was so broadly defined—aiming to cover anyone entering the United States in violation of the law—that the right to a trial and a lawyer did little to prevent successful prosecutions for illegal entry and reentry.

In the years that followed, no other law sent more Mexicans to federal prison than illegal entry and reentry.[105] By 1930, at the height of Prohibition, immigration convictions were second only to liquor charges in the federal system.[106] Prosecution of immigration crimes fueled the growth of the federal criminal system throughout the 1930s, spurring the federal government to build more prisons and laying the groundwork for the federal prison system we have today.[107] In the process, "Mexican immigrant" became synonymous with "criminal."

〜〜〜〜〜

SOME OF THE most racist elements of US immigration policy began to liberalize during the World War II era. The interests of the White majority finally converged with the interests of those subject to Chinese exclusion. Congress nominally repealed Chinese exclusion in 1943, largely in response to Japanese war propaganda that pointedly labeled the policy as racist. It was the first step in a series of enactments that slowly repealed other Asian exclusion laws to address what became viewed as a counterproductive policy in the war on communism.

At first the practical result of these actions was minimal. The National Origins Quota System remained in place and continued to do its intended work: vastly restricting migration from southern and eastern Europe, Africa, and Asia even under the somewhat liberalized postwar policies.[108]

Mexican immigrants, exempt from the quotas, continued to face discriminatory immigration policies in other ways. Criminal prosecutions for illegal entry and reentry were only the tip of the iceberg. During the Great Depression, the Hoover administration launched a massive deportation campaign that sent approximately 1.6 million Mexicans, including US citizens, to Mexico. As the American economy recovered, the United States created a temporary labor program to encourage Mexican migration once again. But as soon as the need for such labor was over, President Dwight Eisenhower authorized Operation Wetback—a reference to the racial epithet characterizing people who crossed the Rio Grande. Through Operation Wetback, government officials forcibly deported as many as four million people to Mexico, including, once again, US citizens.[109]

Congress continued to make immigration law more restrictive during this period. Under the leadership of anticommunist conservative Senator Pat McCarran, Congress passed the 1952 Immigration and Nationality Act. Over the veto of President Harry Truman, the law retained the national origins quotas. The overall cap of 155,000 immigrants per year remained unchanged despite the increase in the nation's population since 1924. The law even imposed new quotas on the former British colonies in the Caribbean, "a move that was designed to limit the migration of black people into the United States," as explained by Mae Ngai.[110] It removed all explicit racial bars to citizenship, seen as a barrier to foreign relations in Asia. But it imposed a global race quota in its place to restrict Asian immigration in the absence of Asian exclusion.[111]

The 1952 law also vastly expanded exclusion and deportation. It added grounds of deportability, narrowed the availability of discretionary relief, and eliminated the statute of limitations for most deportable offenses. It recognized certain procedural protections for deportation cases but expanded the power of immigration officials to deport people whose activities were suspect.[112]

But change was on the horizon. President Truman was vocal in his condemnation of the national origins quotas, and he was not alone. Lawmakers like Representative Emanuel Celler had been fighting against the quotas since their inception and blamed them rightly for America's failure to protect Jews fleeing Nazi Germany. As the civil rights movement began to take hold, the racism inherent in the quotas became more vulnerable to criticism.[113]

In his campaign for the presidency, John F. Kennedy made the abolition of the quotas a focus of his immigration platform. As president, he made good on his promise, working with lawmakers like Representative Celler to craft legislation that would end formal discrimination in immigration law. Although President Kennedy did not live to see the culmination of his efforts, President

Lyndon B. Johnson continued to push the legislation through. Forty years of national origins quotas came to an end when President Johnson signed the Hart-Celler Act in 1965.[114]

Some feared that the changes would dramatically affect immigration to the United States. Representative Celler tried to dismiss such claims, observing that the law retained caps on immigration overall. The elimination of the quotas would simply foster "equal opportunity." Visa preferences would now be based on family relationships and occupations instead of the desirability of one's race. As Celler explained, "Since the people of Africa and Asia have very few relatives here, comparatively few could immigrate from those countries because they have no family ties in the United States."[115] President Johnson echoed these claims when he signed the legislation. The bill "corrects a cruel and enduring wrong in the conduct of the American nation," he explained during the signing ceremony, but it "will not reshape the structure of our daily lives."[116]

The predictions of minimal demographic change were wrong. In 1960, 75 percent of foreign-born people in the United States were from Europe. By 1980, Europeans made up only 37 percent of the foreign-born population. Asian, African, and Latin American migration had become the new majority.[117]

The legislation's promise of equal opportunity was also misleading. In eliminating the racial quotas, the Hart-Celler Act extended the overall immigration cap worldwide. Western Hemisphere countries would now come under a 120,000 cap overall, which eventually translated into 20,000 visas per country—including Mexico. Hundreds of thousands of Mexicans who had been crossing in and out of the United States for decades were now forced to compete for 20,000 visas.[118] The law had rendered the vast majority of migration from Mexico illegal, laying the groundwork for a new era of punitive immigration law.

⁙

MAN MADE BORDERS on this earth, as Rita said. From the beginning, men crafted federal immigration laws to restrict the membership and movement of people of color in the United

States. Criminalization was one of many tools freely used to achieve these racist goals.

The end of national origins quotas in 1965 ushered in significant demographic change. This change, coupled with the growing number of people whose migration was now outside the law, were a potent mix. The new color of immigration—both newly legal and newly illegal—stoked the fears of many White Americans who had supported the national origins quotas for decades. Millions of people like Alonso Guillén and Marco Antonio Muñoz and their families sought to come to the United States only to find that the new rule of law had no place for them.

Civil rights reforms may have ended national origins quotas, but they did not stop the racism that drove the quotas in the first place. Tools of deportation and incarceration—given the stamp of approval during the era of Chinese exclusion and Mexican repatriation and left untouched by the civil rights reforms of 1965—took on heightened importance. And as the next decades of the post–civil rights era would prove, criminality would provide the justification for a vast crime-based deportation machine.

Chapter Three

RISE OF THE DEPORTATION MACHINE

OAKDALE FEDERAL DETENTION CENTER WAS ON LOCK-down. Prison guards forced men back into their cells, counting them rapidly as they went. The men were used to the occasional impromptu count. But they began to worry when they noticed that the television screens in the common areas had gone blank. Something was wrong.

It was not the first time that tensions had run high at Oakdale. Opened in 1986 to incarcerate Cuban asylum seekers who fled Fidel Castro's regime, the prison had filled quickly. Within a year, the Immigration and Naturalization Service (INS) had incarcerated one thousand men in Oakdale, 80 percent more than its capacity. With no relief in sight, the INS made promises to some of the men that they would soon receive parole hearings. But in 1987, word broke that the United States had negotiated an agreement with Cuba to deport an undisclosed list of 2,500 detained Cubans. The brewing tensions at Oakdale bubbled over into a full-fledged prison uprising. After years of incarceration, the asylum seekers refused to be deported without a hearing. It took several days and the intervention of a prominent bishop for the protest to come to an end.[1]

Many years have passed since those tumultuous days. What might have been scrapped as a failed experiment in human caging has instead expanded. Within two decades, the population of Oakdale resembled the United Nations. People hailed from across the world—including America.

These events were set in motion by America's punitive backlash to civil rights–era reforms. By the time Oakdale began imprisoning immigrants in the late 1980s, America was firmly entrenched in a war on drugs targeting Black communities. The drug war soon set its sights on immigrants, unleashing a massive expansion of deportation policies that only deepened with the emergence of the war on terror. From 1986 through 1996, Congress passed a series of laws that targeted immigrants with criminal records for deportation. By 1996, it did not matter if the immigrants were undocumented or green card holders, if they had lived in the United States for a single day or for sixty years. If they had almost any kind of criminal record—even for an old, minor, nonviolent offense—deportation was on the horizon.

As a result of these changes, hundreds of jails and prisons like Oakdale have been filled with both newly arrived asylum seekers and immigrants who have lived in the United States for many years, some for most of their lives. America has fully embraced a crime-based deportation machine: one that uses the tools of the criminal legal system and mass incarceration to deport millions of people without a meaningful day in court. For a person trapped by this machine, there is no telling when banishment will come.

So when, on a warm fall day in 2001, the Oakdale prison guards brought all the detained people inside their cells and switched off the televisions, the men inside feared the worst. But even they could not imagine the truth.

"A plane flew into the World Trade Center," one guard finally said. "Pentagon too." The guards were on high alert. Most lived just outside Oakdale, Louisiana, a tiny town of 800 people. Some had served in the military before becoming prison guards. The horrific terrorist attacks of September 11 felt both far away and close to home at the same time.

From one of the cells, a man tried to flag down a guard. "What's happening?" he asked. He had a wife, children, and a grandchild back in New York. "I need to call my family," he explained.

"No calls." The guard shrugged off his request. With no room to pace in his cell, the man lay down on his bunk, staring at the notches he had scratched on the rails. He had been in Oakdale for a year. But New York was his home.

His name was Yuen Shing, but everyone called him Lefty. He had gotten his nickname from using his left hand to play handball in the Bronx neighborhood where he grew up. The concrete walls of the handball courts were his refuge when he arrived in New York City with a green card in 1973, the day before his twelfth birthday.

By the time his family moved to Queens a few years later, Lefty easily blended into the New York City landscape. He had nearly finished school when he dropped out to work, but within a few years he had gotten his GED. He married young and divorced. After a bumpy road, things began to click into place. By the mid-1990s, Lefty was remarried and living in Brooklyn, with a good job as a delivery man and a steady paycheck to support his family. He was a New Yorker, through and through.

Back then, Lefty and his family never could have imagined that he could one day face permanent exile from the only country he considered home. But it was no coincidence that Lefty came to America when he did, or that he was swept into the deportation system when he was. The timing of these events coincided with monumental shifts in US immigration policy—changes shaped by both progress and regression for racial justice in America.

Lefty is one of millions of people who have faced deportation from America because of a massive crime-based deportation machine that arose in the wake of civil rights reforms. The door to immigration may have opened for many people of color in 1965, but over the next forty years, prison walls were built firmly in its place.

LEFTY'S TROUBLES BEGAN on an otherwise ordinary day, as he drove home from a visit with his parents in Queens. Pulling into a parking lot in his parents' neighborhood, he heard someone call his name. "Lefty, you mind giving me a ride?" It was the uncle of his first wife, the best man at their wedding. "Sure," Lefty said. He didn't give it much thought.

One drive became many more. It turned out his former uncle-in-law worked for the local water department and was involved in a scheme to fix people's water bills for a cut of the difference. Lefty drove him around, eventually introducing him to people who owned businesses in the neighborhood. Lefty knew he was getting in over his head, but he pushed those thoughts out of his mind.

Then came the inevitable. The water department caught on to the scheme. Federal prosecutors entered the picture, and everyone was arrested: Lefty's uncle-in-law, others at the water department, and Lefty.

It was the first time in Lefty's life that he was on the wrong side of the law. His family hired a private criminal defense lawyer, who quickly broke the bad news: prosecutors were going to charge Lefty with a federal felony, and he would be treated just like everybody else involved as part of the conspiracy. Then the lawyer presented him with a deal—six months in prison, six months home confinement. "It's a good deal," the lawyer said. "Plead guilty and you can get this over with." Lefty asked about his status—he had applied for citizenship a few months earlier, but the application was still pending. "You don't have to worry about deportation," the lawyer said. "You're a green card holder."

Lefty pleaded guilty and steeled himself to take responsibility for his actions. The thought of going to prison terrified him. He was sentenced to serve his time at Fort Dix, New Jersey. It was far enough to make it hard for his wife, Arlene, to visit, but she made the trips anyway. His entire family was counting down the days until his release.

A chicken pox outbreak at the prison pushed back the release date by a week. When the outbreak cleared and the new release date finally came, Lefty breathed a sigh of relief. So did Arlene, as she began the long drive from Brooklyn to Fort Dix to pick him up.

Lefty couldn't have been happier than when prison guards came as scheduled that morning, bagging up his possessions and leading him to the processing area to take off his handcuffs. It was only when he got there that Lefty noticed another set of officers.

"You're getting deported," one officer said. Lefty thought he was kidding. Lefty remembered his lawyer's assurances that deportation was off the table. "Is this for real?" was all he could think to say.

But Lefty knew it was real when the new officers brought out a different set of handcuffs: five-point shackles that they used to chain his wrists and ankles to his waist. As Lefty shuffled alongside the officers, he thought about Arlene waiting for him in the prison parking lot.

The officers led him and two other men onto a bus, which took them to a neighboring jail. After a few hours of paperwork, Lefty was finally able to call his wife to explain what had happened. Arlene was as shocked as Lefty was. She had come to Fort Dix expecting to take him home, only to be told by the prison guards that her husband was in immigration custody. Arlene hired an immigration lawyer to fight Lefty's case in immigration court.

Within a few weeks, a different set of officers took Lefty out of the New Jersey jail and onto a plane filled with other immigrants, all in chains. "Where are you taking us?" Lefty asked. "You're headed to Oakdale, Louisiana," an officer finally told him as the plane landed. Lefty caught a glimpse of the rural Louisiana landscape as they boarded a bus for the drive to the prison.

Lefty's time in immigration court in Oakdale came and went. The private lawyer his wife hired couldn't travel to Louisiana, and after he missed a telephonic hearing, the immigration judge took him off the case. So Lefty fought his deportation without a lawyer.

The fight didn't last long. To the immigration judge, the case was open and shut. "You've been convicted of an aggravated felony," the judge said. "That means mandatory deportation to China."

Lefty couldn't believe it. It was 2000. He hadn't stepped foot in Hong Kong in twenty-seven years. It was still a British territory when he lived there as a boy. The world had changed around him, and now he was facing banishment to a place he did not know. All he knew was that he needed to keep fighting.

Lefty was still fighting his deportation case when Oakdale went on lockdown on September 11, 2001. He hadn't been in New York since he reported to Fort Dix to serve his prison sentence in 1999. But his whole life was there—his parents, his wife, his children, and his grandchild.

After what felt like a lifetime, the lockdown was finally over. Oakdale guards let the men out of their cells in shifts and turned the televisions back on. Lefty stared up at the screen, horrified by what he saw. He waited in line for the phones to call Arlene.

It took a while, but eventually Lefty got through. "I'm OK," Arlene said, breathless on the other end of the line. "We're OK."

But they were not OK. They had survived the worst terrorist attack in US history, but they were still stuck in their own personal nightmare. The heart of their family—the man who loved and supported all of them—had been torn from them and stashed a thousand miles away in an immigration prison, facing permanent deportation to China.

Things were bad. Lefty and Arlene knew that. Years of anti-immigrant sentiment had been building in the country. With the dawn of the homeland security era, things could only get worse.

||||||

THE HART-CELLER ACT of 1965 ended decades of racialized national origins quotas and opened the possibility of increased immigration from countries outside western Europe. While the sponsors of the legislation believed that few immigrants in Asia or Africa would take up the invitation, the Hart-Celler Act ushered in significant demographic change. Lefty's family was one of thousands, and then millions, who came to the United States from Asia, Africa, and the Caribbean in the late 1960s, '70s, and '80s. America's growing footprint in places like Southeast Asia and

Central America contributed to greater flows of migration from those regions. The Vietnam War led to refugee resettlement the likes of which America had not previously experienced. US military interventions in El Salvador, Honduras, and Guatemala, the countries that compose the "Northern Triangle" in Central America, seeded violence and unrest that drove millions to flee north.[2]

America did not exactly welcome the new immigrants in its midst. Tensions bubbled over in fits and starts. When Vietnamese refugees settled in Galveston Bay, Texas, in the late 1970s, White residents rebelled. White and Vietnamese fishermen clashed over the burning of the refugees' fishing boats in the bay and, in one case, the death of a White fisherman. By 1981, the Ku Klux Klan had descended on the town, patrolling the bay in white hoods, brandishing guns and an effigy of a Vietnamese fisherman. Klan leader Louis Beam held rallies and "trained" White attendees on how to burn the Vietnamese fishermen's boats. Only intervention by the Southern Poverty Law Center and a ruling by a federal judge in Texas stopped the escalation of the violence.[3]

The agency in charge of deportations and border security at the time was the INS—the same group that had been cultivating the idea that immigrants were threats to Americans for decades. In the 1950s, in the heyday of Operation Wetback, when the INS forcibly removed nearly four million Mexicans from the United States, its Border Patrol unit began a rebranding campaign. As historian Kelly Lytle Hernández has described, Border Patrol officials in the Southwest encouraged their officers to drop the openly racist term "wetback" after observing that the term had elicited sympathy from the public. Instead, they suggested that officers describe immigrants as "illegal" and "criminal"—emphasizing the threat they posed.[4]

The Hart-Celler Act gave the Border Patrol's strategy some teeth. It extended the overall US visa caps to the Western Hemisphere. In 1976, most migration from Mexico became illegal as a 20,000-per-country visa cap went into effect. That same year, INS Commissioner Leonard Chapman took the rebranding campaign to the national stage, publishing an article in *Reader's Digest* titled

"Illegal Aliens: Time to Call a Halt!" In it, he claimed that Border Patrol was overwhelmed by the increasing threat of "illegal aliens" from Mexico and pitched a massive influx of funds to prevent this invading force.[5]

It did not take long before new lobbying groups formed, espousing a thinly veiled White nationalist ideology. In 1979, eugenicist John Tanton founded the Federation for American Immigration Reform (FAIR), an organization that the Southern Poverty Law Center has labeled as a hate group.[6] Tanton viewed immigration as a threat to White America: "As Whites see their power and control over their lives declining, will they simply go quietly into the night? Or will there be an explosion?" he wrote.[7] Tanton and FAIR gave rise to a number of like-minded organizations including the Immigration Law Reform Institute, the Center for Immigration Studies, and NumbersUSA, all seeking the restriction of immigration to the United States.

Their "invasion" trope soon found a new target as refugees began to leave the Caribbean en masse. It began with Haitians fleeing the Duvalier regime. First under President François "Papa Doc" Duvalier and then under his son, President Jean-Claude "Baby Doc" Duvalier, Haitian political dissent was brutally repressed through imprisonment, torture, and murder. The first boat of Haitians seeking to escape the Duvalier regime arrived in the United States in 1963, and were promptly denied asylum and deported. As the oppression deepened over the next several years, more than fifty thousand Haitians sought asylum in the United States, many by boat.[8]

At first, Haitians were permitted to at least apply for asylum upon reaching American shores. But Florida residents became upset with the growing number of Haitian refugees, Black people whom they perceived as "not only disease-ridden, but also uneducated, unskilled peasants," as anthropologist Alex Stepick has explained.[9] By the 1980s, Floridians had persuaded their local elected officials to pressure the INS to take harsher action.[10]

Similar tensions flared in 1980 during the Mariel Boatlift, a six-month period when Fidel Castro temporarily lifted restrictions preventing people from leaving Cuba. More than 125,000 people boarded boats departing from Mariel Bay, including some who had been released from prisons or mental institutions. Nearly all were stigmatized as dangerous. When then–Arkansas Governor Bill Clinton agreed to process several thousand Cuban refugees at Fort Chaffee, angry White mobs patrolled the streets outside the complex. Conditions quickly deteriorated, rioting broke out, and some refugees fled, prompting the Ku Klux Klan to converge on the town, rallying in support of White power.[11]

The INS responded to these racially charged protests by embracing mass imprisonment. Even before new federal immigration prisons could be built, the INS directed the immediate detention of Haitian asylum seekers in local jails and prisons, the denial of work permits for those released on bond, and the summary processing of their asylum claims. Eventually the INS adopted a policy of interdiction at sea—preventing Haitians from ever setting foot on US soil and detaining some in military facilities in Guantánamo Bay.[12]

Cuban refugees fleeing the Castro regime were treated differently. Over several decades, many Cubans fleeing communism were permitted to apply for political asylum and stay in the United States. But during the Mariel Boatlift, which included Cubans from Castro's prisons and many poor Cubans of African descent, the INS relied heavily on mass detention. Many of the "Marielitos" remained imprisoned for several years.[13]

By the late 1980s, immigration imprisonment had become the norm. It was the beginning of a new punitive chapter in the history of US immigration law. As recently as 1958, the Supreme Court had observed that the "physical detention of aliens is now the exception, not the rule, and is generally employed only as to security risks or those likely to abscond."[14] The Court proclaimed such limited use of imprisonment to "reflect the humane equalities of an enlightened civilization."[15] Yet by the late 1980s, imprisonment was openly used to deter asylum seekers.

Even as the immediate humanitarian crises from Haiti and Cuba subsided, Congress embraced this new tool. Legislators authorized the INS to hire more officers, build new facilities, and enter partnerships with county jails and with a burgeoning private prison industry that was literally invested in the future of anti-immigrant policies. The only question was how to justify the growth of the deportation machine.

The emerging war on drugs provided the legislative foundation for a new system of mass imprisonment for immigrants, asylum seekers, and "criminal aliens" alike. Explicit racism in immigration law was a thing of the past. Criminality now served as the dominant threat narrative.

||||||

THE PUNITIVE TURN of immigration law during this period was, perhaps, inevitable. For years, America had been cultivating criminalization as its chosen response to racial progress. This was how the nation ended up with mass incarceration more broadly—a phenomenon that too was tied to migration, but of a different sort.

From World War I through 1970, six million Black people left the South as part of an internal Great Migration. Fleeing widespread racial violence and segregation, Black people settled in urban centers across the North and made new homes. There, they found economic opportunities and some measure of safety, but not equality. Racial discrimination in education, voting, public accommodations, and most aspects of civic life relegated Black people to second-class citizenship.[16]

Black communities led massive social and legal campaigns to undo the structures of legalized oppression. Interests began to converge. Racial discrimination lowered America's standing across the world, a fact that worried US policymakers in the post–World War II fight against communism. At the same time, the civil rights movement was gaining ground through nonviolent and effective protest of segregated buses, schools, and lunch counters.[17]

By the 1960s, Black communities had achieved dramatic success in their campaigns against legalized racial discrimination, both in the courts and in Congress. The Supreme Court's 1954 decision in *Brown v. Board of Education* prohibited racial segregation in public schools, and several other landmark cases followed. Segregationists fought back, and the national spectacle that unfolded spurred calls for federal intervention. During the same period, outrage at highly publicized acts of police brutality against Black people erupted into protest in various cities, at times violent. President Johnson, following through on the promises of the late President Kennedy, pushed forward landmark civil rights legislation. In 1964, he signed the Civil Rights Act into law, followed by the Voting Rights Act of 1965. It was a new day for racial justice in America.[18]

Southern segregationists and other racist ideologues were forced to react to this changing landscape. As historian Khalil Gibran Muhammad has described, junk science had long permitted racists to associate Black people with inferiority and criminality.[19] Racists also quickly associated the tactics of civil rights activists and social unrest in Black communities as criminal. A new, purposeful law-and-order rhetoric emerged. With every so-called "race riot"—as many of the protests against police brutality were called, regardless of context—crime was increasingly associated with Black people.[20]

The undoing of legalized racial discrimination came at a time of other socioeconomic changes in America, and—not coincidentally—those changes prompted an intensified desire to clamp down on crime. The Federal Bureau of Investigation began reporting a dramatic increase in the crime rate during the post–civil rights era. The same politicians who had supported legalized racial segregation began to support crime control legislation instead. Although it remains unclear how much of the FBI's reported crime wave was attributable to changes in crime versus expansion in law enforcement and reporting, the statistics gave weight to segregationists' dire warnings connecting crime to the end of state-sanctioned discrimination against Black people.[21]

One of the major outcomes of the emerging emphasis on law and order was a dramatic increase in the resources given to law enforcement as a response to social problems as a whole, particularly in communities of color. The seeds of change had been planted during the civil rights era. As historian Elizabeth Hinton has chronicled, in addition to landmark civil rights legislation, President Johnson also signed the Law Enforcement Assistance Act and the Omnibus Crime Control and Safe Streets Act, laws that ensured massive federal funding for local policing.[22] Although President Johnson saw this as one feature of his Great Society, the influx of federal dollars opened the door for a new way to control Black people in the wake of civil rights reform.

Over the 1970s and '80s, as politicians competed to show who was tougher on crime, billions of federal dollars flowed into criminal law enforcement, strengthening police and prosecutors even as other public institutions began to falter. This coincided with major economic downturns, particularly as the manufacturing sector began to disappear in the 1970s. The absence of jobs, along with White flight, left many urban centers without a sufficient tax base to fund schools and other public institutions. Overwhelmed police departments were among the only institutions reliably receiving public funding.[23]

The changing dynamics made a potent political mix. Politicians quickly saw that fear of crime translated into conservative votes. Drug use in the 1970s and '80s became an opportunity, not for greater public health resources but for expanded criminalization. President Nixon infamously capitalized on the law-and-order rhetoric to call for a war on drugs, which President Reagan revived and implemented.[24]

The arrival of crack cocaine in inner-city neighborhoods in the mid-1980s all but cemented the success of the war-on-drugs strategy. Federal agencies like the Drug Enforcement Administration implemented highly successful media strategies to heighten concerns about a "crack epidemic" in Black communities. As civil rights lawyer and legal scholar Michelle Alexander explains, politicians also became adept at using carefully coded language to tap into racist characterizations of Black people as "welfare queens" and "predators"—thus undeserving of social welfare while deserving of criminalization.[25]

The drug scourge made front-page headlines day after day. A fearful public applauded expanded policing, mandatory minimum sentences, and other get-tough policies as an answer to this dangerous threat. Mass incarceration was born—just in time for a deportation machine to rise from its foundations.

||||||||

AS POLITICIANS AND the media whipped up public safety fears in the 1980s, America quickly embraced the solution of "governing through crime."[26] Immigration was not immune to these forces.

Republican leaders began to express alarm about the presence of "criminal aliens" within jails and prisons—an increasingly common concern as crime legislation sent jail and prison populations skyrocketing. In 1985, influential New York Republican Senator Alfonse D'Amato called for an investigation into the effectiveness of the INS in deporting immigrants with criminal records in the New York region. The resulting report, published by the Government Accountability Office in 1986, identified a "deportable criminal alien problem." Although available data was limited, the report concluded that the INS did not have the resources to deport all "criminal aliens" despite the likelihood of recidivism by those not deported.[27] The report marked the first of many reports and hearings that named the "criminal alien" as a core problem of immigration reform in the 1980s and '90s.

In 1986, Congress enacted the Immigration Reform and Control Act. The law provided amnesty to many undocumented immigrants so long as they passed background checks. At the same time, the law criminalized the employment of undocumented immigrants, bringing immigration enforcement to the workplace. These provisions involved significant debate before and after their enactment. But one aspect of the law that was relatively uncontroversial was a provision that directed the INS to focus on identifying and detaining immigrants in jails and prisons. It marked the first major piece of legislation in the modern era that targeted "criminal aliens" for deportation.[28]

Between Senator D'Amato's investigation and Congress's new directive, the pressure was on the INS to identify "criminal aliens" for deportation. The INS responded by creating the Alien Criminal Apprehension Program—later known as the Criminal Alien Program—to identify immigrants in prisons and jails that same year.[29] Initiatives to identify "criminal aliens" began springing up in jails and prisons across the country.

The war on drugs provided more targets. In 1986, the same year that Congress enacted the Immigration Reform and Control Act, it also passed the Anti-Drug Abuse Act. The law set lengthy mandatory minimum sentences for drug offenses and higher penalties for the possession of crack cocaine than for powder cocaine, driving up jail and prison populations. The law also included broad drug deportation provisions, turning a violation of any law relating to a controlled substance on the federal schedule into a deportable offense.[30] Drug offenses became a major driver of deportations.

In 1988, Congress enacted another Anti-Drug Abuse Act. This marked a new low in the drug war. The act expanded mandatory minimums for drug offenses and authorized the use of the death penalty in certain cases. It also expanded civil penalties for drug offenses, including possible eviction from public housing and bars to student loans.[31]

Perhaps the most severe civil penalties were reserved for immigrants. The Anti-Drug Abuse Act of 1988 gave birth to the term "aggravated felony," a new ground for deportation that began to dissolve judges' discretion.[32] A pet project of Senator D'Amato's, the aggravated felony provision was intended to target immigrants with serious criminal records—murder, drug trafficking, and firearms trafficking.[33] People with aggravated felony convictions would not only face deportation; they would face mandatory detention. Immigration judges would no longer have the power to grant bail in such cases.[34]

This concept—categorical, mandatory imprisonment—found no parallel in other types of civil proceedings. Bail was a staple of pretrial detention in criminal cases. But Congress set forth a different standard for immigrants facing deportation for aggravated felony convictions. Congress wanted them to be locked up until they could be deported. And Congress added a sentencing enhancement to the crime of illegal reentry for individuals who had been deported based on an aggravated felony.[35]

Expanding the grounds for deportation and mandating imprisonment without bail during deportation proceedings on aggravated felony grounds was not punitive enough. So long as judges could exercise their discretion in such proceedings, some immigrants who had contact with the criminal legal system could avoid deportation. Members of Congress soon shut off these safety valves through legislation that eliminated several forms of discretionary relief.

It was a dramatic change. Since 1917, judges had held the power to issue recommendations against deportation in many criminal cases, and immigration judges could waive criminal grounds for deportation for certain lawful residents. This discretionary authority was routinely used to prevent the deportation of longtime residents—generally European immigrants, as immigrants of color were largely barred from entry because of Asian exclusion and national origins quotas. During this period, prominent lawmakers like New York Governor and Senator Herbert Lehman would decry the deportation of European immigrants for old, petty crimes and in the same breath condemn the "wetback" from Mexico who arrived at America's so-called back door.[36] When national origins quotas ended and it became clear that the immigrants facing deportation for old criminal convictions were primarily people of color, they did not generate the sympathy as their European brethren.

In 1990, under President George H. W. Bush, Congress eliminated criminal judges' power to issue recommendations against deportation.[37] Congress also expanded the definition of an "aggravated felony" conviction and amended the law so that such a conviction eliminated an immigrant's eligibility for asylum, naturalization, and—if the offense involved five years in prison—waivers of deportation for lawful residents.[38]

The anti-immigrant groups that formed in the wake of the 1965 immigration reforms lobbied in support of these types of changes. In 1993, FAIR founder John Tanton and fellow White nationalist Wayne Lutton published an essay titled "Immigration and Crime" in which they suggested that America was experiencing a crime wave attributable to the opening of immigration in 1965. "Criminal activities in the U.S. run by Third World natives can be traced back to the Immigration Act of 1965 and failure to control illegal immigration," they wrote. "The social effects of the 1965 Act were not felt immediately. Only after a 'critical mass' of foreign colonists arrived here, did law enforcement agencies begin to learn about the presence of criminal elements among the new immigrants."[39] Tying drug activity in particular to ethnic groups, Tanton and Lutton expressed nostalgia for the pre–civil rights era of closed migration. "In past years, our elected representatives passed laws to try to keep criminals out, and then enforced those statutes," they wrote. "But our current leaders lack the will to deal forthrightly with this issue."[40]

This narrative set the stage for increasingly punitive legislation in the mid-1990s. The Clinton administration, eager not to be seen as soft on crime or immigration, took a tough approach on both. Anti-immigrant provisions targeting "criminal aliens" were included in the infamous 1994 crime bill. That same year, the Clinton administration announced Operation Gatekeeper, which swelled forces and resources at the southern border, militarizing it in unprecedented ways.[41]

The 1993 World Trade Center bombing cemented public perceptions of immigrants as inherently dangerous. When White US citizen Timothy McVeigh bombed a federal building in Oklahoma City two years later, many Americans were initially convinced that it was an act of foreign terrorism. Learning the truth did not stop the momentum for more draconian immigration policies.[42]

Rushing to mark the one-year anniversary of the Oklahoma City bombing, Congress passed, and President Clinton signed, the 1996 Antiterrorism and Effective Death Penalty Act. AEDPA, followed closely by the Illegal Immigration Reform and Immigrant

Responsibility Act (IIRIRA), dramatically expanded the criminal grounds for deportation and detention.[43] Under these two laws, the list of subcategories of aggravated felonies swelled to twenty-one, many with their own sub-subcategories. The criminal grounds for mandatory detention expanded beyond aggravated felonies to include a long list of offenses, including "crimes involving moral turpitude" in some circumstances and nearly all drug offenses. The few remaining forms of discretionary relief from deportation were repealed, with extremely limited new forms of relief left in their place. Judges could no longer grant reprieves from deportation in many cases.[44]

The impact was swift, severe, and long-lasting. Because both the AEDPA and the IIRIRA legislation were rush jobs, some of their harshest consequences came as a surprise. As stories about the people who had become deportable overnight slowly hit the national press, members of Congress began pleading ignorance about the legislation they had signed. Even Texas Republican Representative Lamar Smith, one of the principal architects of IIRIRA, called upon the INS to exercise discretion in cases that "cry out for compassion."[45] He and twenty-seven other members of Congress, including several prominent Republicans, submitted a letter to Attorney General Janet Reno and INS Commissioner Doris Meissner in 1999, urging them to exercise discretion in cases involving lawful permanent residents facing deportation for convictions at the "lower end of the 'aggravated felony' spectrum."[46] A momentum began building to "fix '96."

But then came September 2001. Another horrific terror attack, this one worse than all that had come before. Immigration reform—at least the humane kind—was soon off the table.

‖‖‖‖‖

THE DAY OF the September 11 attacks, the day Oakdale and the entire country went on lockdown, I was standing on MacDougal Street in Greenwich Village, staring in horror at the World Trade Center. Smoke billowed in the distance, pluming upward as the second tower suddenly fell.

I had just arrived in New York City. I was twenty-one and a first-year student at New York University School of Law. My parents had just helped me move into the dorm before heading back to their home in Kansas City. They too had spent their twenties in cities like Chicago and Los Angeles and New York, when they first moved to the United States from India. New York had changed dramatically over the past several decades, but some of the sights and sounds were familiar to them.

They were fond of the city, but they didn't love the idea of me living there on my own. And now I knew they would be terrified. I dialed their number on my cellphone. No signal. Every cell tower in the area was overloaded. It felt like a lifetime before I reached them to let them know I was OK. My law school classes had been canceled. Many of my classmates and I grew restless, weighed down by despair and helplessness. By the afternoon, we had wandered over to the nearest hospital, lining up to give blood, unaware that there would be few survivors to receive our donations. I faintly remember New York Governor George Pataki shaking my hand as he walked up and down the line of blood donors to thank us for our donations, a cameraman trailing behind him. He too must have felt helpless in those moments, comforted in our numbers.

I thought about that line at the hospital when, months later, another long line of New Yorkers materialized around a different building in Manhattan. This time, however, the line was solely of Brown men circling a federal immigration building. They were reporting for "special registration," a program billed as a way to prevent the next terrorist attack. Like those of us who lined up at hospitals on September 11, they were trying to do the right thing. What the men did not know was that many of them were signing up for their own deportation.

After the terrorist attacks, President George W. Bush and Congress appointed the National Commission on Terrorist Attacks Upon the United States, known as the 9/11 Commission. Their task was clear: to study and propose fixes to the loopholes and lapses in our laws that had permitted the September 11 perpetrators to commit these attacks on US soil. Following the 9/11 Commission's report, Congress enacted the 2002 Homeland Security Act, reorganizing several components of the INS into the Department of Homeland Security.

The reorganization, under the umbrella of a national security organization, had the effect of weaponizing deportation. Enforcement was broken down into two components, ICE and Customs and Border Protection, the latter of which housed the Border Patrol. Funding poured into the agencies, and their mandate was clear. In addition to pursuing programs like "special registration," they quickly announced a new plan, dubbed Operation Endgame, to deport every deportable immigrant by 2012.[47]

I would soon learn exactly what that meant. In the weeks and months after September 11, I began to see the toll that this unforgivable act of terrorism would have, not only on those who lost their lives and loved ones that day but also on the broader community. The lives of the brown-skinned among us were suddenly punctuated by new, more sinister questions of loyalty and terrorism.

Those questions intensified an old, familiar feeling. I grew up as the daughter of South Asian immigrants, spending most of my childhood in Baton Rouge, Louisiana. Born in the United States, I am a citizen. But with my brown skin and South Asian features, I was often presumed to be a foreigner by neighbors, classmates, and strangers. As I met other South Asian Americans, I learned that I was not alone in this experience. We were, along with others outside the Black-White divide in this country, the perpetual other.

September 11 set that othering on fire. Tensions ran high. The attacks hit too close to home for a grieving people to remember who the real enemy was. Angry glares followed us on the streets of Manhattan. Anger begot policy. Federal agents rounded up and disappeared Muslim, South Asian, and Arab men. Entire immigrant neighborhoods in Brooklyn and Queens were gutted. And that was just in New York. The whole country was captured by anti-immigrant sentiment.

By 2002, I had channeled my feelings of hopelessness into action. I joined NYU's Immigrant Rights Clinic, where I learned that this ugliness was only the latest chapter in a long history of anti-immigrant policies. And it was through my work at that clinic that I first met Lefty.

||||||

EVER SINCE LEFTY arrived at Oakdale, the days had been long. Some men kept to themselves, silenced by fear, language barriers, or the dread of impending deportation. Others got to know their fellow detainees, motivated by some mixture of the need for human connection, curiosity, and boredom. Lefty, who was nothing if not friendly, got to know the people around him. When not in his cell, Lefty made the most of his time, trying to keep his mind off what life would be like for him in China. He got a good work detail—as a cook in the prison kitchen—and spent his free time in the law library.

The name of the game in the law library was figuring out who was the smartest person in the room. Some people in detention had perfected the art of pro se legal defense. They would pore over old law books and faded case supplements, type up legal arguments for immigrants who had no lawyers—the majority of the people in Oakdale. Each time Lefty went to the law library, he would scan the room for the people his friends in detention had recommended and chat about his case.

Before long, Lefty had figured out that Robert, from Trinidad, and Luis, from Colombia, were the guys to talk to. They had helped more than one person get out. Lefty gave them his paperwork and explained his situation. Robert was interested. He did great legal work, but jailhouse lawyering sometimes came with a price. For Lefty, it was one of his two pairs of glasses. In exchange, Robert wrote Lefty a petition for a writ of habeas corpus.

Habeas corpus was fancy legal terminology for getting a federal court to assess the legality of the government's actions. Robert typed up a petition, which Lefty mailed to a federal court in his hometown of Brooklyn.

By then, Lefty had lost his immigration appeal before the Board of Immigration Appeals. He needed a federal court to review his case. The 1996 laws had stripped courts of judicial review of orders involving immigrants with aggravated felonies—until a 2005 law restored review for legal and constitutional questions—so a habeas petition was Lefty's last best hope for securing his freedom.

In the end, the pair of glasses was worth it.

〰〰〰〰

LEFTY'S PETITION LANDED on the desk of the Honorable Judge Sterling Johnson Jr. A former prosecutor nominated to the bench by Senator D'Amato, Judge Johnson was one of only a few Black judges on the federal bench. Serving in Brooklyn, with its active litigation docket, he presided over numerous criminal and civil trials.

Judge Johnson was no stranger to immigration controversies. As a special narcotics prosecutor, he had worked with Senator D'Amato when the senator drafted the aggravated felony provision of the Anti-Drug Abuse Act of 1988. He had also seen immigration issues as a judge. He had been on the bench for only six months before hearing the 1991 case *Haitian Centers Council v. Sale*, which challenged the government's emerging policy of indefinite detention of HIV-positive Haitian refugees at Guantánamo Bay.

Although he was a law-and-order judge by nature, Johnson came to view the federal government's policy toward Haitian refugees as racist.[48] Most other refugees—even ones who would be interdicted on the same sea by the Coast Guard at the same time—would be permitted to apply for asylum in the United States. Only Haitians were confined to the overseas prison in Gitmo, where they were subjected to medical screenings for HIV while receiving poor medical care and being denied access to lawyers.

The *Haitian Centers Council* lawsuit unnerved the Justice Department lawyers who thought they had developed a fool-proof way to prevent Haitians from seeking asylum. When local federal prosecutors told Judge Johnson they wanted to bring in Solicitor General Ken Starr to argue the case, the native of the

Bedford-Stuyvesant area of Brooklyn famously replied, "You can bring anybody you want. I'm from Bed-Stuy and I will not be intimidated."[49] Judge Johnson ultimately issued a decision declaring several of the government's policies unlawful and required the government to provide the refugees with access to lawyers.

Several years had passed since the *Haitian Centers Council* case when Judge Johnson received Lefty's petition. And with it, he was confronted with the harsh consequences of the "aggravated felony" term that Senator D'Amato had created. This wasn't the kind of drug trafficking kingpin case that he had in mind back in 1988. And yet Lefty faced the harshest consequences—permanent deportation to China without any assessment of his ties to America. Lefty's case struck Judge Johnson as wrong, but the law didn't seem to provide any path forward—until Lefty, thanks to Robert's handiwork, submitted a supplement to his petition in April 2002. In it, he argued that the law defined an "alien" as someone who is neither a citizen nor "national" of the United States. Most people understood the term "national" to refer simply to people born in US territories. But the law defined it more broadly—as someone who "owes permanent allegiance" to the United States.

That, Lefty argued in his addendum, described him. He was a Brooklyn resident. He had lived there for nearly thirty years. He had attended school in New York, got married in New York, had children and a grandchild in New York. He had registered for the Selective Service and applied for US citizenship. He would have been an American if the consequences of his one and only criminal arrest had not cut everything short.

Lefty's argument—that his single conviction should not overshadow his deep roots in this country—made sense to the judge. Yes, Lefty had a criminal conviction. Yes, Lefty was born outside the United States. But the law seemed to contemplate that "alienage" was not just about one's place of birth, and that a criminal record should not always lead to deportation. On July 15, 2002, Judge Johnson granted Lefty's petition. Lefty, pro se, became the first person facing deportation from the United States to be declared a national.

The local federal prosecutors, who had not paid much attention to the petition of a pro se petitioner from Oakdale, Louisiana, suddenly woke up. They filed a motion with the judge to vacate his decision.

Once again, Judge Johnson was not intimidated. He appointed Lefty counsel. The clerk for the Brooklyn federal court contacted a nearby law school clinic to see if it was interested in taking on the case pro bono. NYU Law School professor Nancy Morawetz answered the call and gave the case to two second-year law students in the Immigrant Rights Clinic. With that, Lefty became my first client.

IIIIIII

GETTING APPOINTED COUNSEL to defend his victory was not the only good thing that happened to Lefty that year. Thanks to the 2001 Supreme Court decision in *Zadvydas v. Davis*, which limited the indefinite detention of immigrants whom immigration officials were unable to deport expeditiously, Lefty was released. Immigration officials couldn't persuade China to accept Lefty, who had an ongoing legal challenge to his deportation and no Chinese passport. In light of the ruling in *Zadvydas*, immigration officials let him go, but promised to deport him the moment the paperwork came from China. Officers at Oakdale used money from Lefty's commissary account to purchase a bus ticket and sent him off on the long journey home to New York. The last sound he heard as he left the Oakdale compound was the pounding of his friends' fists on the walls, happy for his release, saying goodbye.

By the time I met Lefty, he had finally returned to New York. He had been settling back into his home, spending time with Arlene and finding work with a moving company. He had connected with Families for Freedom, a group organizing families facing deportation, and found in them a source of strength and support.

More than anything, Lefty was eager to get on with his life. But the government was equally determined to reverse Judge Johnson's decision.

My clinic partner Melissa Chan and I were daunted by the task ahead. We were two young Asian American women defending an Asian American man who had lived in this country longer than either of us had been alive. And we were standing up for Judge Johnson's decision. We knew the government was going to fight back harder than ever. Lefty had achieved something incredible, not just for himself but for other immigrants who sought to be measured by more than their criminal record.

For a moment, it looked like the government had persuaded Judge Johnson. He questioned his authority to review Lefty's case at all when the government—represented by the US Attorney's Office—pointed to the jurisdiction-stripping provisions of the 1996 laws. We argued against the government's view, and in the end, Judge Johnson sided with us. He rejected the government's motion and reinstated his original decision. Lefty was a US national.

The government appealed. Ultimately, Judge Johnson's groundbreaking ruling collapsed under the weight of its own inclusiveness. Despite our best efforts, in 2005 the appellate court held that the term "national" was indeed confined to those born in US territories. Lefty was rebranded an "alien" once more, subject to deportation for his criminal record.

So we went back to the drawing board. Taking a page from Lefty's endlessly hopeful playbook, we raised every remaining argument that the 1996 laws did not, in fact, apply to him. We challenged his original conviction. We challenged the "aggravated felony" designation. We had to find a way to right this wrong.

I graduated from law school unsure which of these arguments, if any, would succeed. After spending a year working for the wonderful Judge Kermit Lipez of the First Circuit, I joined the Immigrant Defense Project, fighting against the negative consequences of criminal charges and convictions. I pursued that work because of Lefty. And Lefty continued to pursue his legal challenges as well. New teams of clinic students came on the case, litigating our last-ditch petitions. The attempt to challenge his conviction in criminal court failed, soundly rejected by the judge who had taken his initial plea. But the petition to challenge the "aggravated felony" designation had legs—helped in part by a decision by then–Second Circuit Judge (now Supreme Court Justice) Sonia Sotomayor in another case involving a similar conviction. The clinic was able to secure a new shot at the "aggravated felony" argument in front of an immigration judge.

In 2008, I left the Immigrant Defense Project to start a new job—co-teaching the NYU Immigrant Rights Clinic, the same clinic where I learned the law through the lens of Lefty's case. In my first week on the job, I got to stand with Lefty in immigration court as his legal team received an order from his new immigration judge concluding that his conviction was not an aggravated felony, and finally terminating the deportation case against him. "With prejudice," the judge added—meaning that ICE could not reopen the case.

When Lefty heard the judge's decision, he was momentarily stunned. Eight years of fighting for the right to remain in his home with his family had come to an end. As I put my arm around his shoulders, his face crumpled with tears of joy. It was the first time, in all the years I had known him, in all the ups and downs of his case, that I had ever seen him cry.

‖‖‖‖‖

THE TOLL THAT our current deportation system has taken on communities of color is staggering. Roughly three hundred thousand people are formally deported from the United States each year—with at least a million more turned back at or just within the border. That is an exponential increase from the comparatively small number of deportations that took place in the heyday of racial exclusion. Only when the nation's doors opened for people of color did immigration enforcement expand so dramatically.

As communities of color have become increasingly criminalized, racial disparities have become sharply apparent. More than 95 percent of immigrants removed annually from the United States are from Mexico and Central America, a percentage much higher than Latinx representation in the nation's immigrant population.[50]

Immigration detention reflects similar racial disparities. In 2016, 90 percent of immigrants who were detained were from just four Latin American countries: Mexico, Honduras, Guatemala, and El Salvador.[51]

Criminalization has played a significant role in driving these disparities. A three-year study of the Criminal Alien Program demonstrated that 92.5 percent of the people deported through the program were from those same four countries, even though people from those countries make up less than half the nonciti-zen population in the United States. Although people from these countries are not more likely than other immigrants to commit crimes, Latinx people are disproportionately incarcerated in the criminal legal system. By targeting people in jails and prisons, im-migration officials have expanded the racial disparities that led to that incarceration in the first place.[52]

For similar reasons, criminalization also disproportionately af-fects Black immigrant communities. Black people are more likely than any other group in the United States to be arrested, con-victed, and imprisoned in the criminal enforcement system.[53] Be-cause of the intersection of immigration and criminal law, Black immigrants are more likely to encounter the criminal legal sys-tem, and are therefore more likely to confront immigration en-forcement. Although Black immigrants make up 5.4 percent of undocumented immigrants in the United States and 7.2 percent of the total noncitizen population, they made up 10.6 percent of all immigrants in removal proceedings between 2003 and 2015.[54] Further, more than 20 percent of the people facing deportation on criminal grounds in immigration court are Black.[55]

Southeast Asian communities have also been disproportion-ately vulnerable to deportation because of criminalization. Refu-gee communities from Cambodia, Vietnam, and Laos attempted to rebuild their lives in America without the resources and sup-port to heal from the trauma of the killing fields they fled. Under-resourced youth were thrust into a school-to-prison pipeline that left them three to five times more likely to face deportation than other immigrant groups.[56]

The days of formal Chinese exclusion and racist national origins quotas are over. But it is increasingly clear that a vast machinery of crime-based deportation has risen in their place.

ıııııı

TODAY, LEFTY IS a great-grandfather, living with Arlene in their home of nearly forty years. As industrious as ever, he works as the head of custodial services for a city agency, his name on a placard on his office door. Lefty doesn't dwell on what happened all those years ago. He chooses to live in the present. But I often think about everything this country put Lefty and his family through, all in the name of a crime for which he already had served his time.

To this day, I am proud of what we collectively accomplished, fighting tooth and nail for Lefty to find a way out of the 1996 laws. I continue to believe that Judge Johnson's 2002 decision that Lefty should be recognized as an American was right all along. Americanness should mean more than a piece of paper, and belonging should be measured by something other than the existence of a criminal record.

It took me several years to realize it, but in many ways I am still fighting Lefty's case, pursuing the values that underscored his fight to be recognized as an American rather than be cast out of our society after paying his debt to it. Lefty's experience was born of our country's long history of justifying racial and ethnic exclusion through more sanitized labels. Most people take for granted that it is appropriate to deport people for crimes, but few question why we do this or how we got to this point.

These are questions worth asking—something that became abundantly clear in 2008, the year Lefty's case finally came to a happy end. America chose Barack Obama as its next president. With the election of a progressive leader of color who campaigned in part on immigration reform, America had an opportunity to "fix '96" and restore justice in the immigration system. But rather than reverse course on criminalization, America charged ahead—honing criminality as the main justification for ramping up deportations.

By the end of the Obama presidency, the crime-based deportation machine had gained a life of its own. The criminal legal system provided its pipeline; immigration jails provided its cage. When all was said and done, three million people would be gone. It was a record that the Trump administration came in to beat, using and expanding the same machine—a machine designed to exclude, exploit, and punish.

Perhaps understanding our history will give us the courage to confront the cruelty of the machine—and the choices we continue to make that fuel its growth—once and for all.

Chapter Four

THE PIPELINE

AT TWENTY YEARS OLD, MICHAEL HAD THE LOOK AND build of a much younger person. Across the back room of a dusty Harlem police precinct, I could see a mix of defiance and fear in his eyes. I suspected he did not yet understand what was at stake. Deportation was the last thing on his mind.

A few hours earlier, a detective had called Michael, summoning him to the precinct to answer a few questions. My students and I had been representing Michael for a few months, so we went with him. The staff had us wait in a side room, where we learned that Michael's ex-boyfriend had accused him of stealing his cellphone.

As the detective deliberated over whether to arrest him, Michael's anger bubbled over. "It's not true," he said, his voice rising. Michael had paid for the cellphone, and when he and his boyfriend broke up, he had taken it back. Michael began furiously texting his ex.

"You shouldn't contact him until we sort this out," I whispered. I wondered whether Michael's ex realized what he had set in motion by calling the police.

Michael already had a criminal record comprising a handful of minor charges. Shoplifting, for when he and a friend were found with two hats in a department store. Fare evasion, for when he got pulled out of the subway for using a student-rate MetroCard even though he was not in school. Petty crimes had led to two misdemeanor convictions.

Given everything Michael had gone through in his young life, I was surprised his record wasn't more serious. Thrown out of his home as a teenager after his mom found out he was gay, Michael joined the roughly 1,600 gay, lesbian, bisexual, and transgender kids who live on the streets of New York City. Homeless LGBT youth are vulnerable to violence and harassment, cold and hunger, drug addiction and sex work. Six out of ten consider or attempt suicide. With social workers, shelter space, and other interventions in short supply, homeless LGBT youth in New York City are much more likely to come into contact with police than with any other government agency.[1]

Michael's misdemeanors were clearly acts of survival. But rather than getting help, he got a criminal record. So far he had managed to avoid jail time, getting community service or a small fine for his offenses. But this time was different. Stealing a cellphone could be charged as grand larceny—a felony punishable by up to four years in jail. If the police pursued the charges, they would hold Michael at the precinct overnight, and a judge would decide whether or not to set bail in his case the next day. If the judge set bail, Michael would need someone to post it right away. Lacking family to post bail, he would likely be sent directly to Rikers Island, New York's notorious city jail.

The idea of Michael in Rikers, scared and alone, was terrifying. The violent and abusive conditions there are horrific in and of themselves. But that wasn't the only problem Michael would face once inside. For decades, immigration agents had operated a small office at Rikers, scouring the population of pretrial and sentenced individuals alike for deportable immigrants.[2] It was one of many programs that federal immigration officials used to turn the criminal legal system into a pipeline for deportation.

Michael was a green card holder, a permanent resident whose relatives in Jamaica sent him to stay with his mother in the United States when he was just a kid. The convictions he picked up when he became homeless were minor. But immigration officials could consider even petty crimes to be "crimes involving moral turpitude." And two such crimes were all it took to render Michael not only deportable but subject to mandatory detention while he fought his case.

If Michael was sent to Rikers, immigration agents would place a hold on his release known as a detainer. He would remain in Rikers until immigration agents could take him into immigration custody.

In other words, if Michael went to Rikers, the only way he was leaving was in chains. Even if we posted bail in his criminal proceedings, immigration agents would send him to an immigration jail, where he would be ineligible for release. And so there he would stay. Fighting deportation to Jamaica, where being gay is a crime.

।।।।।।

FEDERAL IMMIGRATION OFFICIALS proudly describe the criminal legal system as a force multiplier for deportation. Since the punitive overhaul of immigration law in the 1980s and '90s, the federal government has regularly used local police, prosecutors, criminal courts, corrections, probation, and parole departments to identify and deport more people than federal immigration officials ever could alone.

What emerged was a new infrastructure for deportation. Immigration officials rolled out program after program—the Criminal Alien Program, Secure Communities, and 287(g), to name a few—justifying each on the basis of public safety. These programs, they claimed, would target the worst of the worst. In reality, the programs simply ensured that any immigrant who comes into contact with the criminal legal system gets on a fast track to deportation—including people who never end up being convicted of a crime or who receive only minor records, like Michael.

At the same time that federal immigration officers were developing new ways to use the criminal legal system to deport people, they also used the same system to criminalize those without status. Although the federal crimes of illegal entry and reentry have been on the books since 1929, more recent innovations like Operation Streamline are responsible for filling federal courthouses and prisons with immigrants. A zero tolerance program for crimes of migration that began in 2005, Operation Streamline ensures that people who would have received only civil penalties for crossing the border without inspection now face prison time.

Immigration officials are correct that the criminal legal system is a force multiplier—but not just in terms of the government's capacity to deport and punish. It also multiplies the harms of both the criminal legal system and the deportation system, creating something that is worse than the sum of its parts.

The resulting crime-based deportation machine is designed to extract maximum suffering from someone like Michael. Being Black, gay, and homeless already leaves him vulnerable to severe biases in the criminal legal system. Being all of those things *and* an immigrant extinguishes what little fairness and equity might be left. At every stage of criminal proceedings, the threat of deportation narrows his choices, making it more difficult for him to pursue a just result. And even if he gets through his criminal proceedings without being funneled into the deportation pipeline, the threat of deportation still lurks just around the corner. He faces what criminal justice and immigrant rights advocate Khalil Cumberbatch has called a "perpetual punishment."[3]

Khalil would know. Convicted of a robbery as a young man, he was sentenced to six years in prison. He committed himself to doing everything right: he pursued an education in prison and, upon his release, went back to school. He married and raised two thriving daughters. He gave back to the community, working with the Fortune Society, a program that helps formerly incarcerated people rebuild their lives. Then, a week before he was scheduled to graduate from school with a master's degree in social work, immigration agents came knocking at his door. Four years after his release from prison, he was swept back to an immigration jail. It took a groundswell of support and a pardon from New York Governor Andrew Cuomo to stop his mandatory deportation.[4]

All of this is by design. Ever since the immigration and criminal legal systems merged, escape from the deportation pipeline has been the exception, not the rule. Draconian laws, harsh programs, and human failings weld together to ensure the perpetual punishment of millions. It should come as no surprise that any semblance of justice crumbles in the process.

||||||

THE DETECTIVE WARILY eyed me and the law student who had been waiting with Michael for the past two hours. He had hoped we would have given up by now.

We had been trying to explain to the detective why Michael shouldn't be formally charged. We debated whether to disclose that Michael was at risk of deportation. It was always a calculated risk, and in most parts of the country you wouldn't bring it up. Many officers would simply pick up the phone to call ICE if they thought they had someone who was deportable. But some officers could be sympathetic. It was clear that Michael was young and caught up in a bad situation. The police, like everyone in the criminal legal process, had some discretion.

It was no use. "We're taking him in," the detective finally declared. The charge was, as we feared, grand larceny.

Michael steeled his expression, but his feet kept tapping nervously under the table. "I didn't do anything wrong," he repeated, helplessly.

I put my hand on his shoulder. The waiting had worn on him, and he was still angry at his ex more than anything else. The detective led him away from us, toward the holding cells at the back of the precinct.

"Don't say anything until you see your criminal defense lawyer," we reminded him.

"I know," he replied, quietly. He had done this before.

So had we. We began what was a familiar routine in cases like Michael's: frantic calls and emails to local public defenders' offices to see who might be at the next day's court hearing. We had to make sure the criminal defense attorney understood Michael's immigration history and what was at stake. We knew Michael couldn't plead guilty to grand larceny, and we knew he couldn't go to Rikers.

At the time and place of Michael's arrest—early 2010 in New York City—the biggest deportation threat came from ICE's Criminal Alien Program. The program facilitates partnerships and data collection between federal immigration officials and state and local corrections departments across the country to identify immigrants for deportation. Rikers had partnered with immigration officials for decades. Immigration agents would interview people in the jail, often without identifying themselves, and after gathering the information they needed, the agents would issue a detainer—an "immigration hold" that kept the person in custody for deportation.

The Criminal Alien Program was good at its job. In the five years preceding Michael's latest arrest, Rikers had handed over thirteen thousand New Yorkers to ICE through the program.[5] Nationwide, the number was in the hundreds of thousands. It was the first major program that made the identification and deportation of "criminal aliens" a priority, transforming the criminal legal system in the process. But it would not be the last.

|||||||

THE SPARK THAT lit the fuse for the explosion of crime-based deportation programs came in 1986. Prompted by Senator D'Amato's criticism about the nation's "criminal alien problem," Congress directed the INS to identify immigrants in jails and prisons for deportation. In response, the Criminal Alien Program was born.

Originally called the Alien Criminal Apprehension Program, the initiative took a boots-on-the-ground approach to federal and local cooperation. It sent federal immigration agents to local jails and prisons to check the names of incarcerated people against the federal immigration databases. If they found someone who might be deportable, they would issue a detainer, which directed the local jail or prison to notify the INS of any upcoming release date so that the individual could continue to be held for immigration custody.[6]

These efforts only whetted Congress's appetite for more inquiries into the "criminal alien" problem. At a Senate hearing devoted to the topic in 1995, Delaware Republican William Roth presented a report that concluded that the INS was unable to identify many immigrants with criminal records for deportation despite the Criminal Alien Program. The report estimated that there were 450,000 immigrants in jails and prisons. It described these individuals as having committed serious crimes that were often connected to "their illegal situation." The report ominously theorized about their "'outlaw' status, often leading them into the shadowy realms of criminal lifestyles." Although numerous studies had debunked any correlation between immigrants and increased crime rates, many members of Congress accepted the narrative and demanded to know why more "criminal aliens" were not being deported.

The INS blamed a lack of financial resources, and the report concurred that more federal funding was needed. But the report also blamed the INS's poor record-keeping. Name-based and decentralized, INS records were often unreliable or unavailable, leading agents to miss deportable individuals during screenings. And because those screenings were limited to jails and prisons, people at other stages of the criminal process—such as those sentenced to probation—were often overlooked.[7]

Expanded biometrics became the solution. Whenever the INS encountered an immigrant, federal officials began collecting fingerprints and placing them into a more centralized system. The system allowed the INS to match those records against any fingerprinting systems run by local law enforcement and collected, in part, by the FBI.

In the 1990s, however, biometrics collection was a painstaking process. Millions of older immigration records lacked fingerprint data, and not all local jurisdictions had the capacity or desire to pool their fingerprinting records for deportation purposes.[8]

Those gaps began to close in 2008 when the Bush administration announced Secure Communities, a pilot program in which fingerprints taken during the local arrest and booking process were automatically shared with the Department of Homeland Security. The data sharing triggered a review of immigration records, and if the person was deportable—either because of undocumented status or a criminal record—ICE could issue a detainer asking the local jurisdiction to hold the person instead of releasing her on bail or at the end of her criminal case and any sentence.[9]

Given the number of people who were potentially deportable—an estimated eleven million who were undocumented and some unknown percentage of the fourteen million authorized immigrants who may have been deportable on criminal grounds—not everyone could be detained and processed for deportation.[10] So the Department of Homeland Security prioritized: "criminal aliens" went to the top of the list, and Secure Communities became a way to ensure their deportation. ICE billed the program as a "historic opportunity to transform immigration enforcement and improve public safety by focusing on those aliens who pose the greatest threats to our communities."[11]

When President Obama came into office, he decided to expand Secure Communities. In unveiling ICE's strategic plan for the rollout, federal officials repeated the justification from the Bush administration: expanding Secure Communities would allow ICE to "prioritize enforcement actions on those posing the greatest threat to public safety." By linking local fingerprinting data to federal databases, ICE could better target "criminal aliens" for deportation.[12]

During the initial expansion, the Obama administration suggested that localities could choose whether to join the program. Many signed up. But soon enough, studies began to reveal that a large number of people targeted through the program had minor criminal convictions or none at all—hardly the "greatest threat to public safety." Instead, Secure Communities had become a dragnet for deportation.[13]

Some localities responded by declining to participate in the program. Eventually several larger jurisdictions, including the states of New York, Illinois, and Massachusetts, opted out entirely.[14] That's when ICE revealed that participation was not optional. Localities could not, it argued, pick and choose which federal agencies could have access to their fingerprinting data or for what purposes. Since all localities chose to share their data with the FBI to screen for open cases and criminal history, participation in Secure Communities was part of a package deal.[15] By 2013, Secure Communities was operational in every jurisdiction in the country.[16]

If Secure Communities had been in place in New York City at the time of Michael's arrest, his fight to stay off ICE's radar screen would have been over before it began. That's how Secure Communities works—a fingerprintable arrest is all it takes. It does not matter if the criminal charge is eventually dismissed. It does not even matter if the arrest was illegal—based on unconstitutional racial profiling, for example, or a corrupt police officer. The point of Secure Communities is to piggyback on any arrest, right or wrong.

Many of the localities that had attempted to opt out from the fingerprint-sharing aspect of Secure Communities at the front end now pivoted to challenge the detainer practices at the back end. What authority, immigrant advocates argued, does a city or state have to hold someone after his release date just because ICE has requested it? In such cases no judicial warrant accompanied the detainer, and the detainer provided no process for people to challenge whether it was valid. Once people began successfully suing federal and local officials for what amounted to warrantless arrests, ICE was forced to admit that detainers were simply voluntary requests. It was up to localities whether to honor them and face liability for unlawful custody.

The mounting pressure from immigrant communities prompted some cities and states to pass "sanctuary" legislation, which officially prevented local police or corrections officers from holding immigrants on detainers in the absence of a judicial warrant or other requirements.[17] Some jurisdictions went even further, preventing ICE from gaining access to their jails. The New York City Council, for example, finally kicked ICE out of Rikers in 2015—federal officials would no longer have offices in the city's jails.[18]

True to form, ICE simply changed its tactics. In sanctuary cities, ICE expanded its operations to target "criminal aliens" through more home raids, courthouse arrests, and other forms of immigrant policing.[19] It even launched Operation Safe City, a massive series of community raids targeting sanctuary cities in 2017. ICE made no effort to hide its retaliation. "Sanctuary jurisdictions that do not honor detainers or allow us access to jails and prisons are shielding criminal aliens from immigration enforcement and creating a magnet for illegal immigration," ICE Acting Director Tom Homan said in a statement. "As a result, ICE is forced to dedicate more resources to conduct at-large arrests in these communities."[20]

Despite pockets of local resistance, Secure Communities continues to give ICE what it desires: the name and criminal history of any community resident who comes in contact with the criminal legal system. With that kind of access, even in sanctuary cities, there is no true sanctuary from deportation.

BY GIVING ICE access to people, spaces, and data from local jails and prisons, programs like the Criminal Alien Program and Secure Communities provided the basic structure for an arrest-to-deportation pipeline in the United States. But they are not the only tools in ICE's toolkit. As bad as things have been for immigrants like Michael in places like New York, the situation has been much worse in parts of the country where local police have directly engaged in immigration enforcement of their own.

Immigrants like Juana Villegas saw firsthand how bad it could get. In 2008, she was driving through the small suburban town of

Berry Hill, Tennessee, when a flash of lights and a siren alerted her to a Davidson County police car behind her. Juana pulled over. The officer asked for her license and registration. Being undocumented, she had neither. The officer promptly arrested her for a misdemeanor traffic offense and took her to Davidson County Jail.

Most people would be released from jail to fight a traffic charge in court. But Davidson County had recently entered into a 287(g) agreement. Named after a section of the Immigration and Nationality Act, a 287(g) agreement permits the federal government to deputize local police and corrections officers as immigration agents. Although 287(g) had been on the books since the harsh immigration law reforms of 1996, no locality took the federal government up on its offer to enter into a 287(g) agreement until after September 11, 2001.[21]

Juana had no criminal record before her arrest. But she was undocumented. Armed with their 287(g) agreement, Davidson County officials decided to keep her in custody so that ICE could pick her up for deportation.

Juana was nine months pregnant. Three days into her custody, her water broke. Rather than release her, Davidson County officials continued to honor the ICE detainer request. Police officers took her to a local hospital, shackled her leg to the bed during delivery, and then returned her to jail without her baby or a breast pump. As her baby developed jaundice and she developed a breast infection, local law enforcement continued to keep her in custody. Two days later, she was taken to criminal court, where she was sentenced to time served for unlicensed driving and released pending deportation proceedings.

Juana fought back. She spoke out against her treatment and the practice of shackling incarcerated women during labor. She sued Davidson County, and six years after her arrest, she received a special visa to remain in the United States with her son.[22]

Juana Villegas's treatment shocked the conscience of Davidson County. The county withdrew from the 287(g) agreement in 2012—using Secure Communities as cover for why the agreement was unnecessary—and paid a six-figure settlement for shackling

Juana.[23] Juana's victory was a rare one. If it weren't for legal inter-vention, she would have simply disappeared into the deportation pipeline. Millions of other immigrants have done so—trapped in ICE's dragnet.

Despite federal immigration officials' repeated characteri-zations of their targets as threats to public safety, people with minor criminal records are routinely targeted by the arrest-to-deportation pipeline. A 2011 study of 287(g) programs demon-strated that roughly half of the people issued detainers through the program were convicted of misdemeanors or traffic offenses.[24] A 2012 study of Secure Communities revealed that more than half of people deported through the program were convicted of misdemeanors or traffic offenses, or had no conviction at all.[25] And a 2015 study of the Criminal Alien Program demonstrated that the vast majority of people deported through the program— 80 percent—had either no conviction or a minor conviction.[26]

By piggybacking off the criminal legal system, these programs transform routine encounters with local police into deportation cases for millions of people living in the United States. And con-trary to public messaging, federal immigration officials are well aware that this system has little to do with public safety and every-thing to do with widening the deportation pipeline.

‖‖‖‖

THIS REALITY BECAME clear to me in the summer of 2008 when I joined a gathering of police chiefs and sheriffs from across the country at the annual Police Foundation conference. The con-ference organizers invited me and my colleague Nancy Morawetz to speak about the legal liability that police departments face when they take on immigration enforcement and (inevitably) get it wrong—detaining a US citizen or locking up an immigrant who was not actually deportable.

Blending into the crowd at the beginning of the conference, we sat quietly as Jim Pendergraph, executive director of the ICE Office of Local and State Coordination, stood up to address the large gathering. He opened by offering officers a way to deal with people they wanted out of their communities. He presented the offer in blunt terms: "We can make a person disappear."

I was not the only one in the room to gasp audibly. For years, federal immigration officials had crafted a much more artful crime-fighting rationale for why local police should be involved in immigration enforcement. But the reality is much closer to Pendergraph's unapologetic pitch—deportation is simply a tool to make an unwanted person disappear, whether that person is dangerous or not.

The message resonated with some parts of the country. The majority of jurisdictions entering into 287(g) agreements with ICE were in the South. The common factor among them was not a high crime rate—a majority had a lower crime rate than the national average. The common factor was a change in demographics. Eighty-seven percent of the counties signing up for 287(g) programs had experienced a growth in their Latinx population that outpaced the national average.[27] And 287(g) agreements delivered on their promise—they made unwanted people disappear.

Jim Pendergraph would know. Before joining ICE, he had served four terms as Mecklenburg County Sheriff in North Carolina. The Latinx population in the county grew 81 percent in the six-year period preceding his signing of a 287(g) agreement in 2006. Over the course of the next twelve years, the program would lead to the deportation of fifteen thousand Mecklenburg residents—the vast majority of whom were Latinx.[28]

Mecklenburg eventually joined Davidson County in dropping its 287(g) agreement after community organizers made the program a campaign issue in the 2018 sheriff's election.[29] It was a victory for the community, but a rare and fragile one. As of 2019, ninety localities have signed 287(g) agreements—and the majority are new agreements made since President Trump was elected in 2016.[30]

A similar trend followed the rollout of Secure Communities. When the program was initially billed as voluntary, the majority of jurisdictions that signed up were not the ones with the highest crimes rates but localities in the South that were experiencing growth in their Latinx population. The outcome was predictable. During the first two years of Secure Communities, Latinx people constituted 93 percent of its targets, even though Latinx people constitute only 77 percent of the undocumented population.[31] Profiling was so rampant that a 2011 study demonstrated that at least 3,600 US citizens had been arrested by immigration agents through Secure Communities on the false assumption that they were undocumented immigrants.[32]

Some states were so keen on being involved in the deportation business that they passed their own laws criminalizing immigrants. The most infamous version came from Arizona. SB 1070, known as the "Show Me Your Papers" legislation, created state-level immigration crimes and required police to question people about their immigration status during the course of routine law enforcement.

The Obama administration sued Arizona on the theory that state lawmakers had gone too far into federal areas of responsibility. The case raced to the Supreme Court, which overturned a large portion of the legislation as preempted by federal law. But the Court upheld the provision that required law enforcement officers to question people about their immigration status during otherwise routine encounters.[33] Immigrant rights groups continued to pursue litigation against that provision, resulting in a settlement that permitted rather than required such inquiries.[34] But in the wake of the Supreme Court's decision, many states continue to direct local law enforcement to engage in questioning and to cooperate with federal immigration authorities while prohibiting towns and cities from enacting their own sanctuary legislation.[35]

Between the Criminal Alien Program, Secure Communities, 287(g) agreements, and state-level "Show Me Your Papers" legislation, local law enforcement officers have been more or less converted into immigration agents in many parts of the country. In places where local law enforcement officers embrace the deportation mission, their ability to make immigrants of color disappear is astounding.

But even in places where local police attempt to distance themselves from immigration enforcement, racial disparities in criminal law enforcement ensure that immigrants of color face disproportionate targeting. It is no accident that immigrants of color like Michael repeatedly find themselves targeted for deportation in police precincts in New York City. Like many cities across the country, New York City was an early adopter of "broken windows" policing—going after the small offenses in poor communities of color on the theory that it will deter more serious transgressions. More recent innovations in policing—like "hot spot" policing, which focuses heavily on specific areas like public housing developments and street corners—have a similarly disproportionate impact on poor communities of color. Each of these contacts with law enforcement can thrust people into the deportation pipeline.

That's why even in a sanctuary city, sometimes the only advice I can give an immigrant at risk of deportation is to stay inside his own home. Literally.

I once represented a young Haitian man who lived with his aunt in a housing complex subject to the New York Police Department's Operation Clean Halls.[36] Every Tuesday and Thursday, police would sweep the halls of the building and arrest loiterers along with anyone in sight of a marijuana cigarette or a broken piece of drug paraphernalia, even if it was on the floor and the person was just walking by on the way to work. Because of Secure Communities, I knew that any arrest could derail my client's chances of getting relief from deportation in immigration court. So in the weeks leading up to his immigration court hearing, I advised him about the risks of walking down his own hallway. He didn't need convincing; he had seen the arrests with his own eyes.

For Michael, there was no advice I could give him that he hadn't already heard. Police encounters were a fact of life for him—more reliable than the knowledge of where he would sleep at night. All I could do was hope that we could break some link in the chain from arrest to deportation.

‖‖‖‖‖

THE MORNING AFTER his arrest, Michael was exhausted and jittery. He hadn't gotten much sleep in the precinct. Awaiting arraignment in a holding cell, he watched through glazed eyes as courthouse personnel, guards, and lawyers came and went.

Michael wasn't looking forward to meeting the criminal defense attorney who would be appointed to represent him. The last time he had faced criminal charges—for shoplifting—he had waited in the same courtroom holding area for hours before someone came to speak to him about the case. The man who finally introduced himself as Michael's lawyer had barely looked at him. As the man coldly ran through the shoplifting charges, Michael had struggled to keep up with what was happening.

"Can I fight this?" was all Michael managed to say after the lawyer presented the prosecution's plea offer—plead guilty to shoplifting and go home without jail time.

The lawyer glanced up at him. "Do you want to stay in jail?" he asked. Michael shook his head. The lawyer stood up and put Michael's files back in his briefcase. "Then take the fucking plea." Michael did as he was told. He had no idea he had just made himself deportable.

Michael's experience in court was sadly common. For many years, the right to counsel in criminal cases was cold comfort to immigrants facing deportation. Overworked and underresourced, many criminal defense attorneys prioritized resolving the charges for their clients without considering the possibility of deportation down the line. Even after Congress amended immigration law in 1996 to make deportation practically automatic for a wide range of crimes, many criminal defense attorneys failed to take on the added responsibility of warning their clients about deportation.

For years, courts gave criminal defense attorneys a pass on this score. Although criminal defense attorneys have a duty under the Sixth Amendment to provide "effective assistance of counsel" in criminal proceedings, including advice about the direct consequences of a conviction, courts generally agreed that deportation was a separate process, an indirect consequence, and therefore beyond the scope of a criminal defense attorney's role. And then José Padilla was arrested.

A Vietnam War veteran, José Padilla was pulled over on a Kentucky highway in 2001 while driving a tractor trailer containing a large amount of marijuana. When he told his criminal defense attorney that he was a lawful permanent resident who had lived in the United States for forty years, his attorney told him that he didn't need to worry about deportation because he had been in the country for so long. This advice was, of course, patently wrong. José pleaded guilty and faced mandatory deportation because his conviction was considered a drug trafficking aggravated felony.

You would think that getting the wrong advice from your criminal defense attorney on something so important would be grounds for a new proceeding. Ineffective assistance of counsel is widely understood to be a reason to reconsider whether justice was done in a criminal case. But the state's highest court sided with the prosecutors: José Padilla's criminal defense lawyer had no duty to talk to his client about something as "indirect" as immigration consequences, so no constitutional violation had taken place. The case went to the US Supreme Court.

To the shock and delight of the immigrant rights community, the Supreme Court reversed the Kentucky court's decision in *Padilla v. Kentucky*, concluding that José Padilla could pursue his claim of ineffective assistance of counsel. "Deportation," Justice John Paul Stevens wrote, "is an integral part—indeed, sometimes the most important part—of the penalty that may be imposed on noncitizen defendants who plead guilty to specified crimes."[37] Changes in federal law made deportation virtually automatic—a drastic consequence for José, who had served in the military and built a life here. And so, Justice Stevens explained, "we now hold that counsel must inform her client whether his plea carries a risk of deportation. Our longstanding Sixth Amendment precedents, the seriousness of deportation as a consequence of a criminal plea, and the concomitant impact of deportation on families living lawfully in this country demand no less."[38]

I was in the Supreme Court the day Justice Stevens announced the *Padilla* decision. As he read his decision from the bench, I thought about Michael and dozens of other clients who had pleaded guilty only to learn years later that they had agreed to their own deportation. Justice Stevens's decision could change everything.

It did for José Padilla—after a long battle, he was able to take back his plea. His case was eventually dismissed, and he was sworn into citizenship in 2019, his place in America finally secure. Thanks to his struggle, criminal defense attorneys nationwide now have a constitutional duty to advise immigrant defendants of the immigration consequences of criminal charges before they decide whether to take a plea.

Of course, the gap between constitutional promise and the reality on the ground remains wide. Immigration law is complex, and some attorneys and judges in the criminal legal system are reluctant to address immigration concerns. But winning this uphill battle is no longer the lonely responsibility of immigration advocates. And when immigration advocates and criminal defense attorneys work together, good things happen. Like Michael's release.

Things turned out very differently for Michael this time around. Our calls and emails on the night of Michael's arrest reached the Neighborhood Defender Services of Harlem, one of a handful of public defender offices nationwide that had immigration experts on staff at the time. Its offices modeled the practice that made the decision in *Padilla* possible: one where criminal defense attorneys represented immigrants holistically and zealously, taking the immigration consequences as seriously as the criminal ones.

We spoke to one of the office's immigration experts, who relayed our advice to the public defender who would be assigned to cover Michael's arraignment. When the public defender met Michael in the courtroom holding cell the next morning, their conversation was much different from the one Michael had with his previous criminal defense attorney.

"Michael?" His attorney gave him a sympathetic smile and extended her hand. He hesitated for a moment and then reached out to grasp it lightly.

"That's me," he said cautiously.

"We're going to try to get you out of here," she explained and then went over the plan. She explained that the goal was to get him "released on recognizance"—that is, without bail conditions attached.

It wouldn't be easy. The median felony bail was $5,000, and many criminal defense attorneys would have considered half that sum a victory. But Michael's public defender understood that no amount of bail was an option for him. Michael had no one who could pay it quickly enough to avoid being sent to Rikers, where ICE would find him. His public defender stood her ground as she presented Michael's case, insisting on release. "Your honor, he has every incentive to attend court," she explained, running through the facts of his case.

Ultimately, the judge agreed. Michael was free. But the criminal case wasn't over—and so neither was the risk of mandatory deportation.

‖‖‖‖‖

MICHAEL WAS SAFE from immigration custody, the worst of the deportation machine—but we could not rest easy for long. Bail is just one of numerous decisions made in the criminal legal system that take on heightened significance when deportation is at stake.

Michael still had grand larceny charges pending against him. He faced a potential sentence of up to four years. If convicted and sentenced to prison time, he would be right back in the throes of the Criminal Alien Program, vulnerable to immigration custody. If his sentence exceeded a year, Michael would have a theft aggravated felony on his record. That would mean mandatory deportation—an immigration judge would not have the power to cancel his deportation based on his personal circumstances or to grant asylum in light of his fear of persecution in Jamaica.

The same pressure we felt during Michael's bail hearing followed us into plea negotiations. The vast majority of criminal cases—97 percent of federal cases and 94 percent of state cases—are resolved by guilty pleas.[39] Much of the pressure to plead guilty comes from pretrial detention—a desire to get out of jail as quickly as possible. A sentence of time served or a fine that can be paid later seems like a small price to pay for freedom. People don't necessarily realize that pleading guilty may lead to deportation.

That's why getting people out on bail can be so important—it eases the pressure to plead guilty and gives people time to consider all the consequences. Unfortunately, immigration status can affect bail rights—a criminal court judge might think an undocumented person is categorically a flight risk, even if she has been living in the United States for years and may be more incentivized to show up in court to fight a charge that could prevent her from receiving immigration status one day. Defense attorneys have to fight against those assumptions when seeking bail. And an ICE detainer can prevent release even if bail is posted.

Even when a person is released, the pressure to plead guilty remains. People who don't plead guilty are required to come back to court—again and again and again—going through security, waiting around for hours in a depressing courtroom, only to be called forward as the judge and the lawyers do all the talking and nothing seems to happen. Each date requires getting time off from work or school, paying for childcare, even arranging transportation to get to court—any one of these things can fall apart, resulting in a missed court date and a bench warrant for yet another arrest.

Michael was struggling. He slipped in and out of homelessness even as he had to find a way to attend court appearances and meetings. He eventually secured a temporary space in supportive housing, but finding a job proved more difficult. "They don't want me," Michael mumbled during one of our meetings. Some employers turned him down because of his criminal record. Others were concerned about his immigration status. Friends and relatives would occasionally lend him money, but it never lasted past a few meals. And even in a city with public transportation, most days Michael couldn't afford the subway fare. That's why he had gotten a fare evasion conviction back in the day. Michael was trapped in an endless cycle of poverty and criminalization.

I knew things would have been different if Michael had been provided with social services instead of a criminal record when he was first arrested. Over the years, many people had begun to engage in hard conversations about the criminal legal system. The counterproductive nature of harsh criminal punishment had become so self-evident that defense attorneys, judges, and even some prosecutors had joined forces to champion alternatives. Prisons sentences could be suspended. People who completed rehabilitation could erase their guilty pleas or get their records expunged. People could be diverted out of the criminal legal process altogether and instead receive social services and the support needed to address the root causes of crime.

Great strides have been made to provide these alternatives to many people facing criminal charges who otherwise would have received only jail or prison time. But as significant as these reforms have been, they often fail to reach immigrants. Under immigration law, even suspended sentences count toward the "term of imprisonment" necessary to trigger certain deportation consequences. A guilty plea that is erased or expunged as a result of successful participation in a rehabilitation program still counts as a conviction under immigration law. Once a plea is entered, diversion does nothing to give an immigrant a true second chance.[40]

Immigration law was written this way intentionally. Deportation becomes the most likely outcome of any interaction with the criminal legal system—even when that system would rather forgive than punish.

‖‖‖‖

OVER THE YEARS, the deportation machine's parasitic dependence on the criminal legal system has not only eroded its capacity for reform but has deepened its capacity for harm. Police precincts and criminal courts across the country have been converted into staging grounds for deportation. But nowhere is the capacity for harm more apparent than in the federal courthouses that dot the southwestern border—home to Operation Streamline.

Operation Streamline is the ultimate merger of the criminal and deportation systems. On any given day groups of up to eighty people enter federal courtrooms, chained together with their legs in shackles, subject to mass prosecution for illegal entry. They shuffle into court, sleep deprived from the long journey to the United States and from being penned in cold, overcrowded Border Patrol holding cells for days. They strain to understand what is happening to them. Given headsets and a Spanish translator—the court is often at a loss about what to do when a defendant speaks a language other than Spanish or English—they sit together in rows as the judge begins to read from a script.[41]

Addressing all the defendants together, the judge reads the charges and the defendants' rights, including the right to counsel. The court appoints a defense attorney to represent them en masse, typically forcing the attorney to meet with clients the same day as their criminal arraignment, guilty plea, and sentencing. An attorney for the government also sits by—sometimes a federal prosecutor from the US Attorney's Office, other times a lawyer from Border Patrol with no criminal law experience. This attorney remains mostly silent, pushing paperwork prepared by Border Patrol to establish that the person is not a US citizen and crossed the border evading inspection.[42]

The federal judge, who is constitutionally bound to assess each defendant's understanding of the proceedings and legal rights, instead asks for the defendants' answers in unison. "Do you understand the charges as I have read them?" Defendants, prompted by a nod from the attorney, answer together: "*Sí.*" The proceedings hum along, straight through to the plea, in unison: "*Culpable.*" Then comes the sentencing, anywhere from time served to a few more days or weeks for first-time border crossers. After serving their sentence, the defendants quickly get a deportation order and are expelled from the United States with both a criminal and a deportation record.[43]

No law requires the federal prosecution of illegal entry to proceed this way, and some would argue that the Constitution forbids it. Border Patrol crafted the policy during the Bush administration, and the Department of Justice has embraced it in every adminis-tration since.[44]

For many years, when Border Patrol officers encountered peo-ple entering the United States without authorization, they would fingerprint the individuals and then, if they were citizens of Mex-ico, send them back across the border through a process called "voluntary return." People crossing the border from other coun-tries, however, generally had to be processed for removal because Mexico would not accept them. When detention space was lim-ited, Border Patrol officers would give those individuals notices to appear in immigration court and then do little follow up. Immi-gration restrictionists pejoratively called this process "catch and release."[45]

To limit catch and release, Congress authorized federal officials to create a process of "expedited removal" in 1996. This process gives immigration officers the power to issue a formal order of deportation without referring the case to an immigration court. In expedited removal proceedings, the only way a person can see an immigration judge before getting a deportation order is by ex-pressing a credible fear of persecution. Even then, the person is granted an "asylum only" hearing, with none of the regular ave-nues for other forms of relief from removal and judicial review.[46]

Border Patrol officers were eager to exercise their newfound power. But it took several years for federal immigration authorities to issue the regulations and procedures for expedited removals. Unsatisfied with the status quo, Border Patrol officials approached the US Attorney's Office in the Western District of Texas with a plan, proposing criminal prosecution of all non-Mexican unlaw-ful border crossers in federal court in the border town of Del Rio, Texas. This zero tolerance plan would cure the problem of limited detention space because once the US Attorney's Office brought charges, US marshals could hold the immigrants in their own cells pending criminal prosecution.

At first, the staff in the US Attorney's Office demurred. They were no strangers to illegal entry and reentry prosecutions, which had been on a steady uptick since the 1990s. But the Border Patrol's plan made them uncomfortable. Like all prosecutors, those in the US Attorney's Office exercised some discretion in their prosecutions. They prioritized felonies over misdemeanors and violent felonies over nonviolent ones. Shifting to zero tolerance on all unlawful border crossings would upend the entire system, forcing them to spend resources on low-priority cases.[47]

Putting aside resources, there was another problem with the Border Patrol's proposal. The plan would require federal prosecutors to apply one standard for immigrants from Mexico, who could be summarily returned across the border, and another standard for non-Mexican immigrants, who would have to be prosecuted. The US Attorney's Office pointed out the potential constitutional problems with prosecuting certain groups of people differently based on their national origin.

Undeterred, Border Patrol officials then suggested prosecuting all border crossers, including those from Mexico. To address the resource issue, the officials offered to deputize their own lawyers to serve as federal prosecutors and suggested that the prosecutors and federal magistrate judges could process large groups of defendants in mass hearings.[48]

By December 2005, the federal prosecutors and the federal court in Del Rio had agreed to try it. Dubbed Operation Streamline, the pilot project soon became permanent. Long after expedited removal finally came to Texas, the program remained. Over the next several years, Border Patrol sought to expand Operation Streamline to every federal court along the border.[49] The expansion was met with some resistance. Even with mass hearings, it soon became clear that the relentless flow of new prosecutions had overwhelmed the court system in the Western District of Texas. There is only so much capacity—between the judges, prosecutors, defense attorneys, US marshals, interpreters, court reporters, and other actors in the criminal legal system—to make this system of mass prosecutions work.

Federal defenders were among the fiercest critics. They could see very quickly that their clients did not understand the criminal prosecution process or its consequences, and the speed of the process left defense attorneys without any meaningful ability to investigate the cases or even identify which clients might have a basis to stay in the United States. Nor did it appear that the prosecutions had any meaningful deterrent impact. The factors that were driving people to attempt a costly and dangerous border crossing—constant threats of violence, abject poverty, the desperate hope for a better future—outweighed the consequences of imprisonment and deportation.

Nonetheless, federal prosecutors and judges capitulated, and Operation Streamline spread westward. The Southern District of California in San Diego was the last holdout. For years, the US Attorney's Office in San Diego resisted, stating that it did not want to see its caseload transformed from drug trafficking and violent crime prosecutions to immigration prosecutions. But in 2018, Attorney General Jeff Sessions demanded that the office implement the program. Zero tolerance was now the official policy of the Department of Justice for all unlawful border crossing along the southern border.[50]

In the process, the federal criminal legal system in the Southwest was transformed into what one federal judge described as "assembly-line justice."[51] It was the mass criminalization of migration on overdrive, designed to achieve what the civil deportation process could not do alone: to punish and banish, seamlessly.

||||||

WITH EVERY YEAR that passes, the criminal and deportation systems become more tightly intertwined. Whether in a federal courthouse in Texas or a state criminal court in New York, people of color who lack immigration status find themselves staring down a double punishment, with few safeguards to protect them. The lucky few might find a way to break out of the pipeline—but more often than not, deportation is the end result.

Michael emerged as one of the lucky few. After his public defender secured his release on bail, and after what felt like endless court dates and stalled conversations with the District Attorney's office, the charges against him were dismissed. It was a six-month ordeal, and Michael was devastated by the fear and anger he felt. But he prevailed.

We'll never know why the district attorney's office agreed to dismiss the charges. Did the prosecutor believe that Michael was innocent? Or did he believe that Michael did not deserve deportation even if he was guilty? Maybe both. In *Padilla*, the Supreme Court presented a vision for how both defense and prosecution might consider the harm of deportation during the plea bargaining process. "By bringing deportation consequences into this process, the defense and prosecution may well be able to reach agreements that better satisfy the interests of both parties," Justice Stevens wrote.[52] Perhaps his vision was realized in Michael's case.

Michael was able to avoid a conviction that could have sent him to an immigration prison and eliminated his ability to fight deportation. He escaped the Criminal Alien Program and, if he managed to avoid any future arrests, would escape Secure Communities too. But the fear remained. There is no statute of limitations for deportation. It can come back to haunt a person at any time. A young man like Michael can do everything the criminal legal system expects of him and more—and it still may never be enough.

Only citizenship can truly provide immigrants like Michael with freedom from the threat of deportation. But the process of citizenship, like everything else in the immigration system, requires scrutiny into a person's criminal record. Michael was eligible for citizenship, but in ICE's view he was also deportable. In those cases, you can guess which process the immigration system prioritizes. This is one of the reasons many people delay the process of applying for citizenship—they prefer to wait for a time when they can clean up their record or have a better defense against deportation if necessary. In the meantime, they remain vulnerable to the deportation pipeline.

As a lawyer, I fear the midnight call from clients like Michael, people who are heavily policed because of what they look like or where they live. Another arrest, another charge. The old criminal record comes back to life as a new criminal case begins. The threat

of deportation once again raises its ugly head at every turn, block-
ing the exit paths, making sure the criminal legal system does its
worst. Success depends on the existence of so many actors: a zeal-
ous defender, a sympathetic prosecutor, a reasonable judge. Without them, will we find a way to prevail? If not, the pipeline will
work as it was intended. It will thrust people into cages, just long
enough to banish them permanently.

Chapter Five

THE CAGE

ABA PAUSED ON HER WAY OUT THE DOOR OF HER Bronx apartment, running through her mental checklist. Drop off her four-year-old son, David, at preschool. Take her eleven-year-old daughter, Esi, to a doctor's appointment. Check in with the family of the woman she often cared for as a home health aide. Would they need her this week? If so, arrange for childcare. Between David, Esi, and her two other children, she'd need a good babysitter to look after all four kids.

Aba's husband, Isaac, was visiting relatives in Ghana, so Aba asked her elderly mother to watch Esi. "I'll see you both soon," Aba said as she left with David.

A few blocks away, they strolled into David's preschool. David gave Aba a tight squeeze before running into his classroom. Aba smiled at him, his boundless energy. Summoning her own, she walked back outside, ready to head home and take Esi to the doctor.

Aba had not yet crossed the street outside the preschool when she heard someone call her name. A tall man approached her. A woman joined him from the other side of a van with dark windows that was parked alongside David's school.

Aba hesitated. She did not know them. "Yes?" she said. Then she saw a gun peeking out from under the man's jacket. Her confusion turned to fear.

The man flashed a piece of paper at her. Aba saw typewritten words with a picture of her face. It was a picture from one of the worst days of her life in the United States: the day she had been arrested by the New York Police Department, more than eight years ago. Aba thought she had put that day behind her.

"We're from immigration," the man told her. The woman, who had stepped toward Aba's left, also had a gun. "You have to come with us."

As they approached her, Aba's fear deepened into panic. Her checklist flooded back into her mind. Who would take her daughter to the doctor, pick up her children from school? Would she lose her job? What would her mother do, wondering where she was? And her husband, halfway across the world: who would tell him?

The immigration officers placed Aba in handcuffs. People on the street stopped to stare. The heat of their eyes on her, Aba hung her head in shame.

As the officers led her to the back of the van, Aba glanced back at David's school. Was he watching? Was he scared?

Aba started to cry.

꞉꞉꞉꞉꞉꞉

ON ANY GIVEN night in America, roughly fifty thousand people like Aba are trapped in a form of imprisonment euphemistically described as immigration detention. Through a patchwork of hundreds of profit-driven jails and prisons across the country, ICE uses cages to punish immigrants.[1]

As a matter of law, this form of imprisonment is not considered punishment. Instead, immigration imprisonment is considered civil, not criminal. The legal distinction matters. A person facing incarceration for a crime gets certain rights, including the right to a government-appointed attorney and, if the offense is considered serious, the right to a jury trial. That same person facing potentially years in immigration custody gets none of those things, even when she is held in the same jail or prison designed for punishment in the criminal legal system.[2] Even something as common as the right to bail—called a bond hearing in the immigration system—is out of reach for many immigrants. Mandatory detention laws prohibit immigration judges from holding bond hearings for large categories of immigrants. And for those immigrants who are eligible for bond hearings, securing release remains difficult. In 2018, fewer than half of bond hearings resulted in a grant of bond, the median amount of which was $7,500.[3] Those who cannot afford to post bond in full remain imprisoned.

As a result of these harsh laws and policies, thousands of immigrants languish in jails and prisons each night. Some advocates argue that alternative forms of detention, like electronic monitoring, and alternatives to detention, like community-based supervision, are less punitive and less costly than imprisonment.[4] But for many of those involved in immigration imprisonment, building a punitive, costly system is exactly the point. Private prison corporations and county jails rake in money for each person they lock up on ICE's behalf. To increase their bottom line, they cut corners, sometimes with deadly consequences.

Immigration imprisonment now blends seamlessly into the landscape of mass incarceration in the United States. In small towns and big cities across the country, behind bars and razor wire and chain-link fencing, America trades in the human misery of immigrants.

IIIIIII

TWO HOURS NORTH of New York City, down a desolate stretch of road in the leafy hamlet of Goshen, New York, is the Orange County Correctional Facility. For the hefty price tag of roughly $8 million per year, ICE pays Orange County to imprison immigrants facing deportation alongside their usual population of local residents facing criminal charges and sentences in the county jail.[5]

On a cool September morning in 2016, my students and I piled into our rental car in Manhattan and headed up to Orange County to meet Aba for the first time. After a few wrong turns along the way, we finally arrived. The parking lot was already half full. We squeezed into a spot, gathered our notebooks and papers, and scrambled inside.

A corrections officer glanced up at us as we entered. Seeing three women in plain dark suits, he tapped on the visitor's logbook. "Legal visit?" he asked. We nodded, producing our identification.

While the officer called a supervisor to get authorization for the law students to enter, we sat in the waiting room, with its rows of plastic chairs nailed to the floor. A small bulletin board was tacked to the wall, posting a set of visitation rules and a sign advertising phone cards courtesy of Global Tel Link.

"They'll charge you an arm and a leg," the officer muttered as he saw me looking at the sign. I knew what he meant. We were forced to pay GTL for the courtesy of accepting calls from our clients. It was not uncommon to be charged $20 for a fifteen-minute phone call. This was a fee our law clinic could afford, but our clients' families often could not.

A guard waved us back toward a metal detector as a heavily reinforced door buzzed open. A stream of people walked out. Family visitation hours had just ended. Men and women, a few children in tow, stepped out. Some wiped away tears. Most wore steely expressions, resigned to whatever they had just seen or heard. They had done this before.

We stepped in, led by a guard down the concrete hallway to meet our new client. The door behind us buzzed shut, and another door in front of us opened. A few more doors later in the maze, and we were in the professional visitation area. The guard led us into one of a series of small rooms, each with a long white table stretching from wall to wall, dividing lawyer from client.

We were arranging ourselves in chairs, stacking our papers along the table, when we saw Aba. She was dressed in an orange prison jumpsuit, her hair matted around her head, her face ashen and bare. She seemed shell-shocked.

As she firmly grasped each of our hands across the table, she made her singular need plain: "I just want to be home with my kids."

Four months had passed since the day she had been arrested by immigration officers outside David's school. She had not seen her kids since the morning of her arrest. She didn't want them to visit her in jail. She had seen other people's children in the visitation room, frightened into silence at the sight of their mom or dad in a prison jumpsuit. Or asking unanswerable questions: Why are you in jail? When are you coming home? Nearly always, the children would leave distraught.

"Don't bring them," Aba had told Isaac. He had learned about her arrest while in Ghana and frantically booked the first flight back. Aba worried about him. A taxi driver, Isaac had to take up double shifts to make up for her lost income. She could see how bone-tired he was when he visited, could hear the exhaustion in his voice over the phone.

Isaac abided by Aba's wishes. The children, we would come to learn, did not even know their mom was in jail. No one had the heart to tell them that she was locked up and facing deportation. So they had believed the only thing that made sense to them— Mommy was sick. Doctors were taking care of her, helping her get better.

What else could explain why the woman who woke them up each morning, dressed and fed them, took them to school, read them stories, and tucked them in each night was suddenly not there?

‖‖‖‖‖

IN 2018, PRESIDENT Donald Trump embraced an expanded policy of family separation at the border. Parents who crossed the border with their children would be incarcerated in one facility, and their children would be taken to another. President Trump defended the policy as necessary to deter border crossings. But as the images and sounds of children weeping for their parents quickly spread across social media, Americans were horrified. A few weeks after the program began, Trump caved and scaled back the policy, trying to drum up support for expanded family detention instead.[6]

Many of us in the immigrant rights movement welcomed the public outrage over the Trump administration's inhumane immigration policies. At the same time, we couldn't help wondering, why now? The modern immigration imprisonment system had been separating families for forty years. Not just families at the border, but families within our borders.

The United States revamped its immigration imprisonment system in the 1970s and '80s in response to the rising numbers of Haitian and Cuban refugees. Opening its own federally run facilities while expanding its contracts with county jails and private prison corporations, the United States established a vast network of detention facilities.[7]

As the numbers of Haitian and Cuban refugees began to decrease, some hoped that the rates of imprisonment might drop as well. It had, to an extent, before. The imprisonment of immigrants was not uncommon at the turn of the twentieth century. At the time, detention was brief in most cases, viewed as an aspect of the screening process for newcomers in places like Ellis Island and Angel Island. Those facilities closed, and for a period following World War II, the imprisonment of immigrants became less frequent.[8]

But the political winds soon shifted as crime control captured the mission of nearly every government department—including, quite prominently, the Department of Justice.[9] Haitians and Cubans were labeled as dangers to justify their imprisonment. And as their numbers dwindled, threat-based justification for the imprisonment lingered. In 1988, Congress mandated the imprisonment of people serving time for aggravated felony convictions.[10] In 1996, Congress expanded the aggravated felony definition and added new grounds for "mandatory detention," so that nearly anything from murder to simple drug possession could trigger imprisonment without the opportunity to seek release on bond.[11] It also created expedited removal and mandated the imprisonment of people arriving at the borders without authorization.[12]

Congress had created a monster. Under congressional mandate, federal immigration officials needed massive amounts of jail space. They had long been relying on state and local partners to meet their needs, bargaining for bed space in prisons and jails. As those prisons and jails demanded more compensation, federal immigration officials entered into Intergovernmental Service Agreements specifying per-bed compensation rates.

But the flow of federal dollars attracted more than just state and local prisons and jails. In 1983, Tennessee-based Corrections Corporation of America (CCA), which later rebranded as CoreCivic, was formed. By 1984, it had secured a contract to operate the first privatized immigration facility, in Houston, Texas.[13] Soon Florida-based Wackenhut Corrections Corporation (later rebranded as the GEO Group) and other corporations joined the fray.[14]

Immigration imprisonment was a boon to the fledgling private prison industry. So too was the criminal prosecution of people crossing the border without authorization. When the criminal prosecution of migration began to skyrocket in the late 1990s, the Federal Bureau of Prisons faced its own bed shortage. So it put out requests to meet what it called an emerging "Criminal Alien Requirement." Private prison corporations won the bidding, and they operate thirteen of the immigrant-only CAR federal prisons.[15]

The politicians who expanded the criminal grounds for mandatory detention and criminal penalties for unauthorized migration found a steadfast ally in the private prison industry. Congress even went so far as to adopt a bed quota in some years—essentially requiring the Department of Homeland Security to make tens of thousands of beds available. The provision, quietly written into an appropriations bill by West Virginia Democratic Senator Robert C. Byrd—a longtime statesman and former member of the Ku Klux Klan—was initially enacted with little debate.[16] In no other modern context has there been a bed quota for incarceration.[17]

With all these beds to fill, federal immigration officials did not stop at locking up the people Congress requires them to imprison. They lock up anyone they want. Those who are eligible for bond can try to argue that they're not a flight risk or danger. And those who are not eligible for bond stay imprisoned.

This is how the crime-based justification for immigration imprisonment and its corporate advocates have successfully flipped imprisonment from the exception to the rule. In 1995, on any given day the United States detained 7,400 people in immigration jails and prisons. By 2019, that number had risen to 52,000.[18]

The daily population masks the churn of detention, with some immigrants swiftly deported after a few days while others remain locked away for months or years. All told, the federal government now imprisons more than three hundred thousand people facing deportation over the course of each year.[19] Thousands more, facing charges for criminal illegal entry or reentry, are incarcerated in a separate set of federal CAR prisons.

Behind each number is a human being. Among those imprisoned are those coming to the United States for the first time, seeking asylum or hoping to be reunited with family. And others, like Aba, have lived in the United States for years but become subject to deportation, and thus find themselves imprisoned during the deportation process—separated from their families right here in America.

IIIIIII

WE COULD SEE in our first meeting with Aba that jail had taken its toll on her. She nervously pressed her hands on the table as she spoke, answering our questions about the events leading to her imprisonment.

Slowly, in the clipped, matter-of-fact manner of a person repeatedly forced to share the worst moments of her life with strangers, she spoke. About her childhood in Ghana, how she was cast out of her home by her father and how she walked from town to town in search of work, twice assaulted along the way. About her difficult first pregnancy, which ended with a massive blood transfusion that left her chronically ill. About trying and failing to make ends meet in Ghana, paying for medication and caring for her infant daughter.

Then the opportunity she had been dreaming of finally came. Aba secured a tourist visa to the United States. Her mother had recently traveled to America and had found work. Maybe Aba's luck was taking a turn for the better. Before long, Aba had joined her mother. Time passed, and with no option to extend her tourist visa, her immigration status lapsed. She became one of the eleven million undocumented immigrants living in America.

Still, Aba's life as an undocumented immigrant was better than the hardship and violence she had left behind in Ghana. She found work in the underground economy, paying taxes each year and hoping she could one day fix her immigration status. She fell in love and had three more beautiful children. She married a US citizen, and together they raised their American family. As a wife and mother and worker in the United States, Aba eventually found the safety and security that had escaped her as a child.

And then came the ordinary spring day when Aba was arrested by immigration officers as she dropped off her son at his preschool, the day they called out her name, and showed her a picture from her one and only criminal arrest in the United States.

In the chill of the Orange County Correctional Facility's professional visitation room, Aba recounted the story behind that picture. Eight years earlier, when Aba was pregnant with her third child and the family's bills were mounting, she learned that they were facing eviction. Aba had been working at a small travel agency at the time, but she could not make it to her next paycheck before the rent was due. No bank would help her, and no relative had the funds to cover the difference. So Aba made a life-altering mistake. She took money from the travel agency thinking she could slowly replace the funds with her future paychecks before her boss realized the money was gone. She paid the rent. But her boss found out and quickly called the police, who arrested Aba. She was eight months pregnant.

At the time, the criminal legal system treated Aba with something that resembled compassion. Her circumstances and otherwise spotless record convinced the prosecutor and criminal court judge that no jail time was merited. Probation and an order of financial restitution were deemed to be the appropriate punishment for the crime. Aba spent the next five years repaying her debt to society until every last cent was accounted for and her case was finally over. She put those days behind her—studying to become a home health aide, finding joy in caring for the elderly, and focusing on her family.

It wasn't clear how or why, nearly a decade later, Aba's name appeared on a list of "criminal aliens" for immigration officers to round up and deport. Probation offices across the country routinely share information with federal immigration officials, so perhaps Aba's information turned up that way. Or, given New York City's attempts to clamp down on such information-sharing, some other deceptively mundane method of data collection may have raised a flag on her record. As local and state criminal legal departments have begun to digitize their records and enter them into increasingly sophisticated databases, the federal government has had an easier time sweeping up immigrants with old records as part of splashy "criminal alien" raids.[20]

All that was clear was that Aba's record—a single offense for which she was given probation without having to spend a night in jail—was enough to make her a priority for immigration imprisonment. She was such a high priority that immigration officers went to her home, followed her to her little boy's school, arrested her on the street, and led her in chains to a county jail, where guards swapped her clothes and jewelry for a prison uniform, referring to her by an "Alien number."

By the time we met Aba, immigration imprisonment had turned her into a shell of the woman she had worked so hard to become. Stripped of everything that made her who she was, untethered to the children she loved and was working so hard to raise, Aba felt like she was being punished all over again. But this time, she was locked away in the recesses of a jail in a town she had never heard of before, separated from her children. This time, it was worse.

‖‖‖‖‖

WE LEFT THE Orange County Correctional Facility reluctantly that afternoon, momentarily blinded by the fall sunshine as we walked out the front door. Our time with Aba felt too short. We could not erase her last pained expression from our minds as the guards led her away. She worried about her children, and we worried about her.

Immigration jails are notorious for abuse, neglect, and punitive sanctions. In other words, they are like all prisons. The people inside face the daily indignities that come with mass incarceration.

For many, immigration imprisonment involves a punishment within a punishment. Astrid Morataya, another mother who was locked away pending deportation, learned this the hard way. The mother of three US citizens and a green card holder, Astrid was arrested by immigration officers at her home fifteen years after she received probation for a minor drug offense. Even though she was eligible for a waiver of deportation, she was forced to remain in immigration jail for two and a half years before she won her case. During what felt like endless detention, Astrid was subjected twice to solitary confinement.

Transferred in shackles between county jails in Illinois and Wisconsin, Astrid was punished for breaking the most inane rules—the kind of rules that only exist in prisons and jails. One time, guards sent her to solitary confinement for having a sugar packet in her uniform that she forgot to dispose of at mealtime. Another time, guards sent her to solitary confinement for not being ready to leave her cell; she had begun menstruating and lagged behind her cellmates while trying to secure menstrual pads.[21]

This kind of treatment is a daily fact of life for people facing immigration imprisonment, just as it is for people in prison generally. A few years ago, my students pored over all the incident reports that led to solitary confinement within a single county jail in New Jersey that held eight hundred immigrants. Over a two-year period, guards at the jail sent immigrants to solitary confinement 428 times.[22] The reasons varied widely. One person received a twelve-day sentence for damaging an identification wristband; another received a fifteen-day sentence for refusing to close his food port after he found worms in his meal.[23] Try telling them that immigration imprisonment is not punishment.

Of course, things can get worse. The most heartbreaking stories are about those who lost their lives in immigration jails and prisons:

people like Roxsana Hernández Rodriguez, a transgender woman who fled Honduras only to die in ICE custody in 2018 at Cibola County Correctional Center in New Mexico. An independent autopsy concluded that she died of HIV-related complications because of untreated dehydration.[24] This was indicative of a broader, frightening trend: a 2018 study of detention deaths concluded that half were the result of inadequate medical care.[25] Roxsana's autopsy further revealed that she had hemorrhaging and bruises across her abdomen and wrists, indicating that she may have been abused while in custody.[26] This too is sadly common. Numerous investigations have uncovered rampant physical, sexual, and emotional abuse in immigration jails and prisons.[27]

The immigration system should not provide the US government with license to neglect, abuse, penalize, or kill. But in reality it does. And that's a predictable result of relying on the tools of mass incarceration—which have been abusing and killing people of color in the United States for years—to do the dirty work of deportation.

If immigration imprisonment isn't punishment, our definition of punishment no longer has much meaning in this country.

〰〰〰

THE HORRIFIC CONDITIONS of immigration imprisonment have led advocates to one conclusion: the only way to fix the system is to shut it down. But closing down immigration jails and prisons can resemble a game of Whac-a-Mole. As soon as one shuts down, another pops up in its place.

New York has seen its share of bad immigration jails and prisons. One was even planted in the heart of Manhattan: the Varick Street Detention Facility. Located in a nondescript federal building between the trendy Tribeca and West Village neighborhoods, Varick has long been home to an immigration court for detained people, a processing center for people recently arrested by immigration officers, and a 250-bed immigration prison. Crammed onto the fourth floor of a federal office building, it offered no access to outdoor recreation and had a reputation for poor medical care and chronic overcrowding. Men would languish inside for months and even years, with no access to fresh air, as busy New Yorkers shuffled along the streets below, unaware of the misery of the people locked inside.[28]

ICE announced the closure of the Varick Street Detention Facility in January 2010. ICE would continue to run its immigration court and processing center there, but the 250-bed facility would be closed for good. One would like to think ICE officials closed the facility out of the goodness of their hearts. But the prison was expensive for the federal government, which paid a small security company $253 per person each day to run it, more than twice the going rate of $111 at a county jail across the Hudson River.[29] And as an ICE facility in the middle of Manhattan, it had become the site of massive protests, an easy target for increasingly angry activists.

Immigrant advocates were immediately worried about what would happen to those imprisoned at Varick after the facility closed. In the not-so-distant past, it was routine for New Yorkers to be picked up by immigration agents and sent down to Oakdale, Louisiana, for immigration imprisonment. Under the Obama administration, ICE officials announced a systemic overhaul focused on improving conditions and access to counsel in immigration jails and prisons. As part of the overhaul, ICE officials said, the people locked up at Varick would be sent across the river to the Hudson County Correctional Facility in Kearny, New Jersey. Plans would be made, they said, to secure additional space in the region.

We decided to offer a better plan. "The question," we wrote on behalf of a group of sixteen organizations, "is not where people should be detained, but why they should be detained at all." We offered to review the case of every person imprisoned at Varick to determine if he might be eligible for release on bond, parole, or electronic monitoring.[30]

ICE officials demurred—they didn't have the resources to conduct case-by-case reviews. We went in anyway and screened as many people as we could. That's how I met Paul.

Like Aba, Paul found himself in immigration custody because of a criminal arrest. Unlike Aba, he had a long history of arrests. A large Haitian man with what I later learned was a cognitive disability, he faced constant harassment by police in his neighborhood.

His most recent crime was riding his bike suspiciously on his way home from work. Stopped by the police, he angrily replied to their questioning, insisting that he was doing nothing wrong. They proceeded to charge him with resisting arrest—resisting an arrest for what was not clear. The charges were later dismissed, but not before Paul was sent to jail pretrial, where immigration officers identified him as deportable based on two misdemeanor convictions. One involved an argument with his adult sister, and the other involved riding a bike that someone else had stolen.

On quick review, it was clear to me that immigration officials were acting illegally in this case. Paul should have been eligible for a bond hearing at the very least. His convictions didn't fit the mandatory detention law; he was taken into ICE custody years afterward following a baseless arrest; and—this was the kicker— the government had just suspended deportations to Haiti following the devastating January 2010 earthquake. What purpose would imprisonment serve if deportation was no longer foreseeable?

We presented an array of arguments why Paul shouldn't, and couldn't, remain imprisoned, but they fell on deaf ears. ICE transferred him to the jail in Hudson County. I ran into federal court before the transfer, and after a few weeks of briefing, the judge ordered ICE to give Paul a bond hearing. The judge questioned the constitutionality of Paul's custody, so many years after his supposedly deportable convictions, with no likelihood of deportation to Haiti. The least the government had to do was provide him with an individualized hearing.

We went back to immigration court for his bond hearing, hopeful for a prompt release. Paul explained that he was committed to attending future court hearings and that he planned to work after his release. His mother and girlfriend were in the courtroom, and they promised to help him get back on his feet. The ICE attorney didn't bother to cross-examine the witnesses but instead went straight to closing arguments, claiming that Paul was too dangerous to be released. The immigration judge responded by setting a $40,000 bond.

The sum was outrageous. Unlike criminal bail, which allows partial payment and, in some places, payment by credit card, immigration bonds require you to come up with the money in full. Some bail bond agents will step in, but they generally require property (like a house) as collateral to put up that kind of cash. And because immigration judges don't consider a person's ability to pay when they set bond—yet another constitutional violation we have filed suit to combat—immigrants are routinely kept imprisoned simply because they are poor.[31]

We threatened to go back to court over the sum of Paul's bond, and ICE eventually agreed to lower it to $10,000 and electronic monitoring. It was a rough deal, but we took it. After eleven months of imprisonment, Paul was free. We eventually persuaded ICE to remove the electronic monitor from his ankle after a few months of invasive supervision.

All but a handful of the other men in Varick had, by that time, been sent to Hudson County. By the end of 2010, ICE had announced a new contract to create 2,250 more beds in the region.[32]

||||||

PAUL'S STINT IN ICE custody had pretty much ruined his life. His health deteriorated at Varick and worsened at Hudson. After eleven months of imprisonment, he lost his job, the first good job he had held in a long time. It took years for him to get back on track.

We couldn't let the same thing happen to Aba. Thankfully, in the years since I ran into court to challenge Paul's imprisonment, more and more courts were adopting similar arguments limiting the government's authority to hold people without bond. In 2015, my students and I won a case, *Lora v. Shanahan*, that required the government to provide immigrants with a bond hearing within six months of mandatory detention in the New York region. The decision was short-lived, but over a two-year period it gave hundreds of New Yorkers a shot at a bond hearing.

That, fortunately, included Aba. We used the decision to secure a date for a bond hearing later that fall. The hardest part, though, was preparing her kids. We knew that we needed the judge to see her family in the courtroom. But it meant that they would finally learn the truth—that the US government, *their* government, had been jailing their mother this whole time.

Aba and Isaac agreed on a way to tell their children, who by this point had caught on more than their parents had realized. The older children wrote heartfelt letters to the judge. The littlest one drew a picture. When we showed Aba their letters, her face was a mix of pride and grief.

We carefully went over her testimony in case the judge wanted to ask her questions, and we had frank conversations about how much she and her husband thought they could pay. "The judge will want to hear a number," we explained, noting that $10,000 and even $20,000 bonds were routinely given in cases involving criminal convictions. We knew the family couldn't afford those amounts. We could try to ask for release without bond, but too often we'd seen that strategy backfire, as the judge would set a much higher number than what the person could afford. "I think I could get $3,000 together," Isaac said. We decided to try that.

The morning of the hearing, Aba's children stayed home from school. They brushed their teeth, got dressed, and piled into Isaac's taxi. They arrived at Varick early and gathered in the waiting room, a little breathless. David, the little boy Aba had dropped off at preschool just before she was arrested by ICE, gave me a wide smile and leaned his head on my shoulder as we sat together. Then his smile disappeared. "It's scary here," he whispered.

It *was* scary. I held out my hand. As he grabbed it, I recalled how Aba had clasped my hands when we first met, desperate to get back to her family.

The clerk for our judge poked her head into the waiting room. "355," she called, announcing the last three digits of Aba's "Alien number." We piled into the courtroom. It would be the first time Aba and her children would see one another since her immigration arrest six months earlier.

⁓

MANY ADULTS STRUGGLE to explain the real purpose of immigration imprisonment today. But David's perspective provides as good an explanation as any. Imprisonment is most often used as a scare tactic. It is designed to overwhelm, to punish, to deter.

Over the years, the US government has become more open about its desire to use imprisonment as a deterrent. Deterrence has been a motivating factor since the imprisonment of Haitian and Cuban refugees in the 1980s, and the Obama and Trump administrations both cited it as a reason for their respective family detention and family separation policies.[33] The idea is simple and cruel: make people's lives so miserable that they will give up their rights.

No evidence has backed up the claim that these policies deter migration.[34] But it is clear that immigration imprisonment does have a different kind of deterrent effect. People with good cases will give up their right to defend themselves against deportation just for the chance to feel sunlight on their faces again. Parents will give up their claims just to be able to hold their children—even if it has to be in a foreign country.

Consider the case of Arnold Giammarco, an honorably discharged US Army veteran who faced deportation based on convictions for petty theft and drug possession that he received following his military service. Detained in a county jail, Arnold was separated from his wife and two-year-old daughter by plexiglass, even during visitation hours. "Watching my daughter behind a pane of glass, I still remember her crying that she wanted me to hold her, she wanted me to play with her like I used to. But I couldn't," he recalls.[35]

After eighteen fruitless months of pursuing his challenge to deportation, Arnold gave up and was deported. He was finally able to hold his daughter in his arms again—but only when she was able to visit him in his native Italy. Each visit was bittersweet, and he imagined how his life might have been different if he had been permitted to fight his deportation without being jailed.

Imprisoning people solely for the purpose of deterring them from pursuing their legal rights—to apply for asylum, to pursue status, or to defend against deportation—is illegal. In 2014 a federal court slammed the Obama administration for justifying family detention as a means for deterring asylum seekers fleeing violence in Central America.[36] According to the Supreme Court, the only legitimate purpose of immigration custody is to reduce flight risk or dangerousness. You could compare it to pretrial detention in the criminal context: if a person will show up to court and isn't a danger to society, she shouldn't be locked up pending her trial.

But that hasn't stopped the US government from doubling down on immigration imprisonment. It may not be effective in stopping migration, but it does have the power to coerce immigrants into giving up their cases, and therefore giving up their chances of returning to the United States lawfully. Once deported, people can't come back unless they meet certain requirements, which many people with criminal convictions will never be able to do.[37] They will forever remain "criminal aliens," barred from reuniting with their families in the United States.

Arnold had one of the only kinds of legal claims that could surmount this hurdle. He had applied for citizenship while serving in the military, and lawyers from Yale's immigration clinic took up his cause. In 2017, six years after his deportation case began, he won his right to return to the United States and naturalized as a US citizen.[38]

His story had a happy ending, but those six years of separation took their toll. And none were worse than the eighteen months he spent in immigration jail. Arnold watched a lot of other good people sign away their rights just to regain their freedom, like he did. And unlike him, they remain in exile, permanently separated from their families. They will never know if they might have prevailed in their cases had they stuck it out.

In other words, immigration imprisonment was working exactly as it was designed.

‖‖‖‖‖

THERE ARE A lot of losers when it comes to immigration imprisonment policies. To find the winners, you have to follow the money.

Congress has increased its funding to roughly $2 billion a year to the Department of Homeland Security for immigration imprisonment. But that money doesn't stay with DHS. It flows into the pockets of outside jailers. It lines the pockets of counties like Orange County, which rakes in $8 million each year for its detention contract. One in four immigration facilities is run by a local correctional department, each touting its ICE contracts as a moneymaker.[39]

But it's even more lucrative for private prison corporations like CoreCivic and the GEO Group. Thanks in significant part to immigration imprisonment, CoreCivic and the GEO Group received a combined $4 billion in revenue in 2017.[40] A small number of private prison corporations now operate 60 percent of all immigration jails and prisons.[41]

Cornering the market on immigration imprisonment seems to have only encouraged private prison corporations to, well, cut corners. One can guess who bears the brunt of it.

People like Pedro Guzmán. In 2009, Pedro was loading his car in North Carolina with donation bags to take to Goodwill when immigration officers arrested him in front of his wife, a US citizen, and three-year-old son. Soon Pedro found himself several states away in Stewart Detention Center in Georgia, a private prison operated by CoreCivic. At Stewart, guards put Pedro to work in the kitchen, where his shift began every morning at 2 a.m. If he was late, the guards threatened him with solitary confinement. At one point, he was forced to work while sick with fever. For his work, he was paid $1 a day. The earnings went straight back into the coffers of the private prison, since he had no choice but to purchase food, basic hygiene products, and phone cards to call his family from the prison-run commissary.[42]

CoreCivic denies that its guards ever forced Pedro Guzmán to do anything, but he's not alone in raising these claims. Since 2014, no fewer than six class action lawsuits have been filed alleging forced labor and human trafficking at CoreCivic and GEO Group prisons across the country. As it turns out, private prisons negotiate with the federal government to take advantage of what they call a voluntary work program, which purports to permit private prisons to pay people $1 a day for certain jobs. Their contracts also permit guards to require immigrants to clean their immediate living areas for no pay.[43]

It's an ugly business, and if labor and antitrafficking laws are applied, it's illegal. In case it needs to be said, coercing immigrants into working under the threat of solitary confinement isn't voluntary, and tidying immediate living areas doesn't mean cleaning the whole prison.

But that's the private prison business model. It's how the GEO Group got away with hiring just one janitor for its entire Aurora Contract Detention Facility in Colorado: a 1,500-bed prison.[44] Why pay workers the prevailing wage when you can force someone locked inside to work for $1 a day or, better yet, for free? Immigrants are literally forced to do the dirty work while private corporations increase their profit margin.

Using immigrants to drive down labor costs isn't the only way that private prison corporations are accused of cutting corners. Roxsana Hernández Rodriguez, the transgender woman who died with signs of abuse and medical neglect in immigration custody, was held in Cibola County Correctional Center in New Mexico.[45] Years ago, CoreCivic ran Cibola as a "Criminal Alien Requirement" facility for the Federal Bureau of Prisons. After receiving repeated complaints about medical negligence and preventable death at the facility, the Bureau of Prisons ended its contract there with Core-Civic. But the Department of Homeland Security was only too happy to pick up the contract and give it right back to CoreCivic, medical complaints and all, to become a civil immigration jail.[46]

Some of the worst examples of medical neglect come from the privately run CAR prisons, where the majority of inmates are held for illegal entry, reentry, and other immigration crimes. After investigative reports into these "shadow prisons" revealed several cases of medical abuse and neglect, the Department of Justice finally launched its own investigation in 2016.[47]

In the words of Sally Yates, then serving as deputy attorney general, the audit of CAR facilities made clear that private prisons "do not maintain the same level of safety and security" that federally operated prisons do.[48] Much to the outrage of the private prison industry, Yates announced that the Bureau of Prisons would phase out its contracts for private facilities in the criminal legal system.

Soon after Yates's announcement, all eyes turned to the Department of Homeland Security. Following the lead of the Bureau of Prisons, the Homeland Security Advisory Council formed a subcommittee to advise it on DHS's use of private prisons for immigration imprisonment. Immigrant rights advocates were skeptical. Reliance on private prisons was much more deeply ingrained in the immigration imprisonment industry. To no one's surprise, the subcommittee concluded that, despite the faults of private and county contract facilities, DHS's reliance on them was necessary to meet the so-called need for immigration imprisonment. Only one person dissented, urging DHS to phase out private prison contracts despite the practical difficulties.

To everyone's surprise, the council voted to override the subcommittee in support of the lone dissenter. The members believed that a shift away from private prisons was possible. They also criticized DHS's reliance on county jails, noting that such arrangements also ensured an overly restrictive penal model.[49]

Private prison corporation stocks took an immediate plunge. It might have been the death of the industry, but they had an old trick up their sleeves.

For years, private prisons had been pouring millions into politics: paying lobbyists, donating to political candidates, and hiring former senior immigration officials to become new executives. It was a revolving door of money, political favors, and pro-imprisonment policies.

CoreCivic, for example, had been a longtime sponsor of the American Legislative Exchange Council (ALEC), a collective of elected officials and pay-to-play corporations that creates model legislation on everything from immigration to gun rights. With active participation from CoreCivic, ALEC infamously worked on the draft legislation for Arizona's SB 1070 law, and Core-Civic promptly donated to elected officials who sponsored the legislation.[50] After journalists exposed CoreCivic's role in pushing the controversial "Show Me Your Papers" legislation, CoreCivic left ALEC. But it did not leave politics.

In 2016, as the Obama administration announced the rollback of private prison contracts, CoreCivic and the GEO Group donated heavily to the campaigns of several candidates, including Donald Trump.[51] His election sent the stocks of CoreCivic and the GEO Group skyrocketing.[52] Within days of his inauguration, President Trump announced that he would be disregarding the recent decisions of the Bureau of Prisons and the Homeland Security Advisory Council.[53] Private prisons—at least for the time being—were here to stay.

Corporations like CoreCivic and the GEO Group deny that they lobby for legislation that extends the number of people imprisoned or their length of time there. But CoreCivic and the GEO Group spent a combined $2.55 million in fiscal year 2017 on federal lobbying for something.[54] Even when legislators admit they received proposals and ideas for anti-immigrant legislation from these lobbies, the corporations still dispute their involvement.[55] But it's ludicrous to believe that they go behind closed doors with members of the Trump administration and Congress and have nothing to say about proposals to expand immigration imprisonment across the United States.

CoreCivic and the GEO Group cast such a long shadow over the industry that they sometimes mask other bad actors in the system. The business of imprisonment doesn't stop with the contract itself. Private corporations profit off lucrative subcontracts to provide services like food, medical care, commissary, and phone access.

Kickbacks abound. For years, the NYU Immigrant Rights Clinic worked on a campaign in New Jersey to end kickbacks on prison phone contracts for people incarcerated in state, local, and privately run correctional and immigration detention centers. Before advocates got the state to change the practice, the cost to call someone in jail was out of control. Families often paid $20 for a fifteen-minute phone call with a loved one. County jails that held residents on criminal charges and deportation grounds alike were some of the worst offenders. Instead of negotiating the lowest phone rates for families trying to connect with their incarcerated loved ones, they would accept contracts with prison phone corporations like Global Tel Link or Securus, which paid the counties as much as 60 percent commissions for the calls made—costs that were borne by the families least able to afford it.[56]

This is typical. When any part of the prison system is up for sale, jailers will always drive down their costs and ratchet up their kickbacks from corporations to improve the bottom line. When those corporations mix money with politics, the result is the explosive growth of the immigration imprisonment system. Winner takes all.

|||||||

AS THE DATE of Aba's bond hearing approached, she called us more and more frequently. I'd pick up my phone to hear the chipper recorded female voice representing Global Tel Link. "You have a call from an inmate at Orange County Correctional Facility! Press 1 to accept the call." I pressed 1.

Aba was understandably anxious about her hearing. She had been waiting for six months, pressing Isaac on the details of their children's lives. Esi never did make it to the doctor's appointment; her headaches were getting worse. David, whom they had potty-trained, had started wetting himself again. Their older children's teachers had noticed that something was wrong—one was acting out, and the other no longer spoke in class. The kids wanted the hearing to come even more than Aba, but they were worried about what the judge would do.

When we walked into the courtroom that day, we took comfort in the stacks of papers representing all the time that Aba, Isaac, and her children had spent preparing for the hearing. We saw the judge marking up our documents: the stack of marriage and birth certificates; letters of support; work, tax and medical records, all demonstrating the nearly two decades of ties Aba had built with her family in the Bronx.

Aba had been prepared to answer the judge's questions, and to hear the government's ugly defense of its position: she should not be given bond. The ICE attorney observed that Aba shouldn't have been able to get a bond hearing at all. ICE had no interest in agreeing to release. We told Aba to pay ICE no mind, reminding her that the judge would be the one making the decision and that Aba had a right to the hearing.

Though Aba had prepared herself as much as she could, nothing could prepare her for the sight of her children. As the guards led her into the courtroom, the tears spilled across her cheeks. And as her children saw their mother in a prison uniform, shackled at the hands and feet, their own tears met hers. For a moment, no sound could be heard. But then David, the little boy who had not seen his mother since she dropped him off at preschool six months earlier, began to sob. Louder and louder, he cried out, struggling against the arms of his father as he tried to reach for Aba across the room. David sobbed so loudly that the judge ordered Isaac to take him out of the courtroom.

We all stood there, stricken. The judge turned to my students, who were forced to somehow get through our argument for release even as we heard David's cries echo from beyond the courtroom doors. Aba deserved bond, they explained, walking the judge through the papers we presented.

Minutes felt like hours. "Bond granted," he said, setting bond at $3,000 so that Aba could be released that day. Detention was unnecessary, he concluded as her family wept tears of joy. We know exactly where she'll be.

⁞⁞⁞⁞⁞

THE HEARING THAT Aba received no longer exists. In 2018, the Supreme Court vacated the decision that required bond hearings for immigrants within six months of their mandatory detention. The Court didn't like the way that lower courts interpreted the statute to include a bright-line bond hearing requirement, but it left the door open for other arguments. We continue to assert that imprisonment without bond is unconstitutional.

What would have happened if Aba never received a bond hearing? The damage of six months of separation from her family was devastating enough. And not just for her. We took her children to meet with child psychologists. The diagnoses were unequivocal. Post-traumatic stress disorder. Depression. Anxiety. You can't take a parent from a child and expect that no harm will be done.

You would think we already learned that lesson, having studied the burden that mass incarceration places on the children of incarcerated parents.[57] Instead we replicate the mistakes of mass incarceration for immigrants and their families.

More than two million people are caged in the United States on any given day. We have the largest system of mass incarceration in the world, and civil immigration imprisonment is an increasingly large piece of the pie.[58] In addition, one in five people in federal prison on criminal charges is an immigrant, often locked away for illegal entry or reentry.[59] All of it is the direct result of the choices America has made to criminalize immigrants.

The purpose seems transparent: to make it easier to banish immigrants while punishing the ones who remain.

A system this cruel is simply unjustifiable. It is easy to imagine a world where people are asked to show up in court to address immigration issues without being locked up in the process—the way we treat so many other civil processes. If Aba was never imprisoned, she still would have had every incentive to attend her immigration court hearings—to figure out a path to status, to remain with her husband and children. And she would have done so while continuing to care for them, in their home, together.

As a free woman, Aba did pursue her rights. After two more years of immigration court appearances, she received her green card with a waiver of her conviction. Her deportation case was finally over. But the emotional scars of her imprisonment remain.

Years have passed, but Aba will never forget the sound of her son's sobs as he stretched out his thin arms to her in the courtroom. And her children will never forget the image of their mother in chains, knowing that their own country chose to do this. To lock her in a cage, like so many others, in the hope that she might disappear forever—another casualty of the crime-based deportation machine.

Chapter Six

THE "LOSS OF ALL THAT MAKES LIFE WORTH LIVING"

"I—I CHOOSE NOT TO REMEMBER." LUISA BLINKED TWICE, looking up at the ceiling. Her lip trembled. Tears spilled down her cheeks as she began to rock slowly back and forth in her chair.

Luisa was our client, and she faced a hearing in immigration court later that month. My students and I had gone over her testimony a few times in preparation, but we never quite got through it. Whenever we approached the subject of her ex-husband—a man she had met years ago, charming and handsome, who accepted both her and the little boy she had given birth to as a teenager—the panic attack would begin.

"How would you describe your relationship with him?" The innocuous question brought ugly memories to the surface. Her oldest son, now a grown man with a child of his own, remembered the violence even though she had tried to hide it from him. "He beat her with a door guard, a large metal beam, and an ambulance had to come," he told us. "You never forget something like that."

Luisa had tried. She had tried to forget everything. It had taken her years to escape the relationship and even longer to put the past behind her.

By the time we had met her, Luisa was a grandmother, caring for a large and adoring family, and focused on battling a very different kind of enemy. Luisa had been diagnosed with Stage IV breast cancer. Chemotherapy and a mastectomy had bought her some time—how much, she did not know. She was making the most of her time with her children and, especially, her grand-daughter. The last thing she wanted to think about were the years she had spent with her abusive ex-husband.

But here we were, carefully threading through a patchwork of traumatic memories, poking and prodding where we did not belong. "I'm so sorry. Do you feel like you could be ready to try again?" Pause. "We could come back tomorrow."

Luisa shook her head. "I can't do this. Do we have to talk about this?"

I hated it. I hated having to dredge up the worst moments of her life. We weren't even sure if the judge would let her talk about her past. Immigration officials had argued that she was not eligible for a hearing to contest her deportation. But we knew if we could convince the judge that she was eligible for a hearing, her relationship with her husband would be front and center. No one had ever bothered to ask her before, but it was the reason she had a criminal record. And her criminal record was the reason this grandmother with Stage IV breast cancer was facing deportation to a country she had left when she was four years old.

The crime-based deportation machine had blindly banished millions of people like Luisa from the United States over the years. Criminal bars to relief from deportation strip immigration judges of the power to consider the lives of the people who stand before them. Deportation becomes the end result even in the face of extraordinary harm to the people who are deported and the loved ones who are left behind.

Luisa didn't want to relive her painful past in immigration court. She knew it might not even matter in the scheme of things.

The law required the judge to ignore what was right in front of him. It was the ultimate punishment for a survivor of domestic violence who, like so many others, had already been punished far more than she had ever been protected by the law.

‖‖‖‖‖

A CENTURY AGO, the Supreme Court described deportation as the "loss of all that makes life worth living."[1] Those words have stuck with me from the moment I read them in law school. Everything that makes life worth living—family, community, work—is rooted in the place we call home. Termination from a job, eviction from a home, separation from a spouse, the loss of one's children—any one of those events would be enough to throw a person's life into a downward spiral. Deportation is the equivalent of all those devastating events wrapped together, with the added consequence of being exiled to a place where one faces isolation at best, persecution at worst. It is an uprooting from which few recover. Yet America forcibly deports roughly three hundred thousand people from its borders each year.

I am reminded of the Supreme Court's words every time someone I know is deported or loses a loved one to deportation. I think of my client Thomas, a gay man deported to Jamaica. Shortly after his deportation, he called to let me know he was OK. But I knew he wasn't. Thomas had seen the violence against gay men in Jamaica firsthand, a country that *Time* magazine had once labeled "the most homophobic place on earth."[2] As we talked about his safety, his voice became strained. "I'm just going to hide that part of me," he said. Deportation had trapped him in a life he could not recognize.

I also think of the young woman I met in a holding cell in a police precinct in New York City. I met her the day the Trump administration announced the end of DACA. Thousands protested across the country that day, myself included. A group of us, arms linked, led a peaceful march that stopped traffic leading to the Brooklyn Bridge. We were arrested and paired up in holding rooms as officers processed us for disorderly conduct charges.

In the hours that followed, I asked the young woman in the cell with me why she had participated in the march. Her story came tumbling out. Her father had been deported when she was just a little girl, a casualty of the roundups in Muslim communities following September 11. A decade had passed since they said their goodbyes, but with every birthday and graduation the pain would return fresh once more. He ached to be with his family, and she felt it every time they spoke. She led the march to protest the end of DACA because she did not want others to go through what her family had gone through. She did not want eight hundred thousand people and their families to bear the pain she felt every day.

We often think of deportation as the end of something, but it is also the beginning of something else. A life outside the one we chose for ourselves. A life haunted by loss.

With deportation comes stigma. In *Deported Americans*, former public defender Beth Caldwell writes of those who lived in the United States for most of their lives before being deported to Mexico. In Mexico, they are often unable to get identification or jobs, forced to live the lives of the undocumented even after being deported to the country of their birth.[3] In *Banished to the Homeland*, sociologist David Brotherton and criminologist Luis Barrios examine the trajectories of people deported from the United States to the Dominican Republic. Their fellow citizens often blame them for the country's crime rates even though those who are deported tend to fall victim to crime and discrimination themselves.[4] They are strangers in the land of their birth.

For those whose roots in the United States run deep, deportation also brings betrayal. Howard Bailey, a Navy veteran who came to the United States from Jamaica as a teenage green card holder, was deported in 2012 after he disclosed a 1995 marijuana conviction on his citizenship application. After he was deported, his trucking business closed shop, his family's home went into foreclosure, and his marriage fell apart. With a sea between him and his children, he became despondent. He could return to the United States in death but not in life, his right to be buried on US soil secured by his military service. Howard is one of thousands of deported veterans questioning how the country they risked their lives for could discard them so easily.[5]

For some, deportation means persecution and even death. The Department of Homeland Security does not track what happens to the people it deports. Their stories are revealed only when anguished family members come forward. As Sarah Stillman reported in *The New Yorker*, she and other journalists with the Global Migration Project at Columbia University tracked down more than sixty cases of people who were harmed or killed after federal immigration officials deported them during the Obama and Trump administrations. The federal government had refused to grant asylum to many of these people, ignoring the threat of targeted violence that eventually took their lives.[6]

Juan Coronilla-Guerrero's wife predicted her husband's death after federal immigration agents entered a Travis County, Texas, courthouse to arrest him in 2018. ICE made the arrest in retaliation for the Travis County sheriff's refusal to hold immigrants on detainers in low-level cases. His wife pleaded for his life, telling a judge that he would be killed by gangs if he was sent back to Mexico. ICE deported him anyway. Three months later, armed men entered the family's home in San Luis de la Paz and dragged Juan out of his bed at gunpoint. "Don't worry, my love," were his parting words to his terrified son. His body was found on the side of the road the next day, a homicide.[7]

Separation from family, deprivation of identity. Stigma, betrayal, even death. The Supreme Court was right. With deportation comes profound and undeniable loss.

I thought about Luisa, my client with Stage IV breast cancer, whose life was focused on caring for her children and granddaughter. She sometimes worked as a car service dispatcher, when she was feeling up to it, to help keep a roof over her family's head. She sometimes made visits to the doctor for cancer treatments. She simply wanted to live and die in peace, surrounded by the people who loved her.

After a lifetime of living in the United States, Luisa had everything to lose.

WHEN LUISA WAS four years old, her mother left their native Costa Rica for the United States to work as a domestic servant for a wealthy New England family. The family eventually helped her mother sponsor their entire family for migration to the United States in the 1970s. It was a rough transition, growing up as an Afro-Latina girl in a mostly White neighborhood without cultural context, but Luisa was happy that her family was together.

After her mother's contract ended, the family moved to Brooklyn. Luisa's parents supported her throughout her teenage years, including after she became pregnant as a junior in high school. She managed to receive her high school equivalency degree and eventually enrolled in community college while working nights at a law firm.

Then she met Walter. Smooth-talking, charming, he showered Luisa with compliments. He was impressed with her intelligence and beauty. He told her he would support her dreams of finishing school and pursuing a career. He said he would love her son like his own. The photos from their wedding day show the fading images of a man and woman in love.

But before long, the marriage became, in Luisa's understated words, "too much to handle." On some nights Walter would explode with anger, fueled by alcohol or drugs. In his rage, he would beat Luisa, sometimes with his fists, other times with any object he could find within arm's reach. Trying to shield her children from violence, she often agreed to whatever demands Walter made of her.

One of those demands was financial. Walter had amassed huge debts and learned to forge money orders and checks to get around them. Banks and post offices would look at him with a skeptical eye when he came in with large deposits. So he turned to Luisa. She had the "right look." The polished way she dressed and talked, he thought, would shield them from scrutiny.

Not so. Soon after Walter sent Luisa to do his dirty work, she was arrested. With makeup barely covering her bruises, she faced police officers and judges who never asked her why she was doing what she was doing. She might have been too scared to tell them anyway. Instead, she accepted the punishment—at times, stints in prison—and hated every minute of it.

Years passed before she gathered the strength to leave Walter. By then, Walter had weakened from drug abuse and did not fight their divorce. Luisa moved on, no longer under his direct control but still haunted by what he had done to her.

She worked odd jobs to support her family but rarely landed anything steady because of her criminal record. After a few years on her own, she was arrested once more—this time when a co-worker used a customer's credit card to purchase some items at the concession stand where she worked. She didn't do anything wrong, so her defense attorney encouraged her to plead "no contest" as a way of ending the case without admitting guilt. She was numb to the idea of more punishment and just wanted to bring her legal troubles to an end.

She moved on with her life. Then her father passed away. His ties to Costa Rica were strong, and he had wanted to be buried there. His death came at a rough time for Luisa. She had twice been diagnosed with breast cancer, and despite chemotherapy and a mastectomy, she worried that the cancer had returned. But she wanted to honor her father's wishes, so she went back to Costa Rica for the first time in forty years to bury him.

Her flight back to the United States landed at JFK Airport. Customs and Border Protection ran her information in their system. She had green card status, but she also had a criminal record. After questioning, they referred her case to ICE.

In a matter of moments she had become one of the hundreds of thousands of immigrants facing deportation each year. She didn't realize it yet, but her life now depended on her ability to navigate an impenetrable system designed to deport her without reprieve.

|||||||

WHEN AMERICA DEPORTS people like Luisa, it is punishing survival. People like Luisa—whose criminal records are a reflection of years of abuse and poverty—rarely receive protection in the US legal system. In response to their acts of survival, our legal system simply locks them up or locks them out. It's little wonder that many women in prison are survivors of domestic violence, just as many women and children who journey north to enter the United States are survivors of sexual assault and other forms of violence.[8] Their acts of survival lead not to intervention or support but to criminalization and deportation.

Operation Streamline throws this dynamic into stark relief. In theory and by law, people fleeing violence and persecution in their countries of origin must be provided an opportunity to apply for asylum. But in reality, they are punished for their attempt to seek safe haven by crossing the US-Mexico border.

I saw this firsthand in November 2018 while visiting a makeshift refugee camp in Tijuana, where thousands of people waited for their turn to seek asylum at the border. The camp was filled with youth and families—each one more desperate than the next. The violence and instability they were fleeing were the bitter harvest of seeds sown by US foreign policy—everything from military interventions that propped up brutal dictatorships to trade deals that decimated farmworkers and textile industries in the Global South. But when they arrived at our doorstep, our government told them to wait—as if they posed a threat to us, and not the other way around.[9]

Sabrina was among those who hoped for something different. Too desperate to wait for months in one of the camps, she crossed between checkpoints into the United States in the summer of 2018 and then quickly presented herself to Border Patrol. She was taken to an *hielera*, or "icebox," as the frigid Border Patrol holding stations are called, where she spent two days without access to basic necessities, unable to shower or call her family or even brush her teeth. From there she entered Operation Streamline.

Armed men led her into the basement of a federal courthouse. There a man introduced himself as her lawyer. He asked a series of questions, taking down her information to send away for her records from Mexico. And then he walked her quickly through what was about to happen. She would go before a federal judge that afternoon to face criminal charges for illegal entry, and the only way to get out of prison quickly would be to plead guilty.

Sabrina answered each question and nodded her head as the man explained the process. The armed men reappeared at her side, leading her to join a line of shackled women and men shuffling into a large courtroom. There sat an older man in a black robe, his eyes buried in paperwork, reciting a script in monotone.

Sabrina looked up at the judge and then at the men and women to her right and left. No one looked back at her. She gingerly picked up the headset that rested on a nearby bench and heard a soft Spanish voice interpreting the judge's script. Listening to the words, she repeated what the other men and women said.

"How do you plead?" the judge asked.

"*Culpable*," she said, her voice small in the courtroom. Guilty.

A few days later, her paperwork came back from Mexico. Sabrina's attorney read it twice to be sure. There had been a mistake. She had given him the wrong birth date. She was a minor—which meant that she should not have been prosecuted under Operation Streamline. Rather than face criminal prosecution, she should have been sent to the Department of Health and Human Services. She still would have been imprisoned, but she would have been with other minors and would have had a shot at being screened as a youth for asylum and Special Immigrant Juvenile Status.

Her attorney raced over to the federal court to file emergency paperwork to vacate her conviction, but it was too late. Sabrina was already gone, deported as a criminally prosecuted adult, back to Mexico.[10]

Sabrina didn't just fall through the cracks—America's crime-based deportation machine pushed her through. The entire legal system moved too fast, just as it was designed to do.

It doesn't surprise me that people like Sabrina and Luisa were both targets in a callous deportation system. Were they victims or criminals? America has a choice in how it sees those whose survival conflicts with what we call our rule of law. We can protect, or we can punish. Time and again, America chooses punishment.

||||||

AFTER LUISA'S TRIP home from her father's funeral put her on ICE's radar screen, ICE officers arrested her and sent her to York County Prison in Pennsylvania. There the prison guards processed her, stripping her of her clothes and jewelry, her undergarments, and the hair scarf she used to cover her patches from chemotherapy. They issued her a prison uniform and sent her for an initial medical screening. She told them about her cancer from the beginning, and the medical staff could see the mastectomy scars.

Her family tried to post bond, but it was no use. "She's an arriving alien. No bond," her deportation officer told them. The paperwork ICE gave her used the same words: "arriving alien." Luisa struggled to make sense of them. She had lived in the United States since childhood. She didn't know that the simple act of traveling to her father's funeral would convert her into something else.

Desperate, her family eventually found a group of advocates at Families for Freedom in New York. Led by people who had faced deportation themselves, the group encouraged Luisa and her family to fight back. One strange upside of being considered an "arriving alien" was that ICE might be willing to release her on humanitarian parole. Had she been charged as merely deportable based on her criminal record, she would not have been eligible for release.

After four months of advocacy, her health was in a nosedive. ICE granted parole. Dozens of immigrants had died in detention in recent years. "They were probably afraid of the bad publicity if a grandma with breast cancer died on their watch," one of the Families for Freedom organizers guessed.

But even after Luisa left, ICE did not drop its deportation case. It ordered her to appear in immigration court to face charges. The notice ICE gave her listed her name and her old convictions, but that was all she could comprehend without a lawyer's assistance. The rest of the notice was laced with legalese, with terms like "arriving alien," "removal," and "moral turpitude" glaring from the page.

The words made little sense to her. "But I have cancer," she tried to explain when an ICE officer handed her the notice in detention.

After she was released, she showed up to immigration court in New York as required, but still without a lawyer. She didn't know what to expect. The immigration judge listened to her explain her situation. "You need to find a lawyer, ma'am," he stated on the record. "You have an aggravated felony." She was confused. The notice didn't say anything about an aggravated felony, and she wasn't sure she understood why it mattered. "You have a serious criminal record," the judge tried to explain. "The law ties my hands. I'm not sure what I can do. But you need to find a lawyer." He gave her time to find one.

Families for Freedom reached out to our clinic, and I took a team of law students to meet with Luisa at her home. We knew right away that we would defend her right to stay. We just didn't know how we would pull it off.

||||||||

IMMIGRANTS HAVE FACED deportation based on past crimes for decades, without the right to counsel and with limited access to the courts. But in the past, they had something on their side: the right to ask for mercy. Several laws gave immigration officials and judges the power to grant relief from deportation. This power was put on the chopping block in the 1990s, a casualty of the punitive turn in immigration law.

The color of immigration had changed during the post–civil rights era, and sympathy for immigrants who committed crimes had disappeared.[11] The 1996 overhaul of immigration law removed many forms of relief from deportation. The options that remained on the books were filled with onerous eligibility requirements. Just unpacking their meaning required a high level of legal training and the will to follow a dizzying maze of cross-references. Some had to do with a person's status, or the length of time the person had lived continuously in the United States, or qualifying relatives who met a certain threshold of hardship, or some complex combination of varying factors. And nearly all forms of relief were unavailable to people like Luisa because of their criminal records.

For Luisa, the old form of relief that she would have easily qualified for before 1996 was called 212(c) relief. For decades it allowed immigration judges to waive deportation wherever the "good" outweighed the "bad." A lawful permanent resident like Luisa could explain to an immigration judge why she had received her criminal record, how her situation had changed since then, and why she deserved to stay.

But Congress repealed 212(c) relief in 1996 and replaced it with something called "cancellation of removal." At first, federal immigration officials took the position that the repeal was retroactive: a person with a conviction from the 1980s, for example, could not apply for 212(c) relief even if she had been eligible when she pleaded guilty to the offense. After years of litigation, courts rejected the government's position and concluded that 212(c) relief had to remain available to people who would have been eligible when they were convicted.[12] But such relief was not available in cases where the conviction occurred after the law went into effect.

Cancellation of removal offered a new form of relief to green card holders with post-1996 deportable offenses. It too let judges consider the factors when deciding whether to cancel deportation. But there were limitations, including a permanent bar if a person had been convicted of an aggravated felony. To tighten the screws, Congress lengthened the list of crimes that could qualify as aggravated felonies, no matter how long ago they occurred.[13]

Luisa was in a bind. The lingering impact of the abuse she had faced from her ex-husband did not neatly map onto Congress's timeline. She could have gotten 212(c) relief except that she had one post-1996 conviction listed as a deportable offense. And she could not get cancellation of removal because one of her pre-1996 offenses was deemed an aggravated felony thanks to the 1996 laws.

It was a mess of Congress's own making. The reforms had prevented judges from judging, rendering a domestic violence survivor with breast cancer ineligible for relief.

|||||||

ELIMINATING THE SAFETY valves in the deportation pipeline has had enormous consequences. Many of the people targeted by the 1996 laws had lived in the United States for years and even decades. They had families and communities that depended on them. It was their voices—the voices of husbands and wives, sons and daughters, employers and employees, friends and colleagues—that were silenced when Congress eliminated the main forms of relief for immigrants with criminal convictions.

The impact has been staggering. According to Human Rights Watch, in the first decade after the laws were enacted, nearly nine hundred thousand people had been deported based on their criminal records. Human Rights Watch estimates that these deportations—more than 70 percent of which involved nonviolent convictions—have left more than one million spouses and children behind, struggling to pick up the pieces of a life torn apart.[14]

If deportation is the "loss of all that makes life worth living," that loss is shared with the people left behind. My friend Kathy lost her partner to deportation more than a decade ago when their son Josh was only six years old. The loss of her partner plunged her and her son into homeless shelters and welfare, an endless struggle to make ends meet. Their lives became so unstable that Kathy was afraid she might lose Josh to the child welfare system—a fear only too real when one or both parents are detained or deported. A 2011 study estimated that there were 5,100 children in the child welfare system because their parent or parents had been detained or deported.[15]

Kathy and Josh had no right to be heard when Josh's dad was deported, but they refused to stay silent. As longtime members of Families for Freedom, they fought tirelessly for families like their own, advocating for federal legislation to require immigration officials to consider the best interests of a child when a parent is deported, no matter what the parent's criminal record may be.

Deportation is a collective loss. In America's fervor to eliminate discretion, the country is harming itself.

⁑⁑⁑⁑

THE LACK OF a meaningful hearing in cases involving criminal bars has transformed the immigration court process. Stripped of the ability to share their stories or call upon loved ones to speak on their behalf, immigrants are forced into a far more complex fight. They must first find a way to argue that their criminal convictions do not fit into the categories Congress created as bars to relief.

What is required is a complex analysis of what courts call the "categorical approach": a comparison of the elements of a person's offense with the definition of the criminal bar at issue. It demands attention to how terms like "aggravated felony," "crime involving moral turpitude," and "controlled substance offense" are defined under the Immigration and Nationality Act. Then those definitions must be compared to the minimum conduct punishable under the federal or state criminal statute under which the person was convicted.[16] If a person's convicted conduct does not categorically fit the relevant criminal bar, then one can make the case before a judge that federal immigration officials are overreaching. Only after successfully making this argument will the person receive her day in court on relief from deportation.

The idea that we require someone facing deportation—imprisoned without counsel, perhaps with limited English proficiency—to make these legal assessments just to defend herself is offensive to basic notions of fairness. That she must do so while pitted against a contrary assessment by an attorney representing ICE is ludicrous.

Even worse, ICE attorneys often argue that the categorical analysis of the person's crime represents the floor, not the ceiling, of the negative immigration consequences that should flow from an old conviction. ICE attorneys routinely ask immigration judges to consider what they think "really happened"—essentially forcing a retrial of the underlying crime. They will try to pull in police reports and charging documents and suggest the case involved something far worse than the conviction indicates. Imprisoned, unrepresented immigrants, without access to the evidence from their old criminal cases, are left to defend themselves with only their word and an uneasy understanding of criminal and immigration law.[17]

One might hope that immigration judges would reject arguments by overzealous government attorneys and help unrepresented immigrants figure out the law—and sometimes they do.

But immigration courts are badly underresourced and increasingly under political pressures that challenge any semblance of independence or neutrality. Former Attorney General John Ashcroft infamously gutted the Board of Immigration Appeals, which oversees immigration courts, of its more progressive members in 2003.[18] And subsequent attorneys general, including Michael Mukasey, Jeff Sessions, and William Barr, have stepped in to issue their own immigration decisions, sweeping away decades of favorable precedent with a stroke of a pen.[19]

The implications are not limited to immigration courts. Before a case even begins its winding path toward an immigration judge, frontline deportation officers look at criminal records to decide whether a detained immigrant is eligible for bond or subject to administrative removal. As summary removal procedures increase, immigration judges play a diminishing role in deportations. The majority of removals never involve an immigration judge—it's all paperwork, with the deportation officer acting as judge, jury, and executioner.[20]

At every turn, criminal bars are designed to block immigrants' paths to justice. Even if a person is lucky enough to be released from immigration custody, lucky enough to see a judge, and lucky enough to find a lawyer, it still may not be enough. As the deportation system has grown more complex, the power of judges to stop deportations has diminished. A person can try her best to navigate the system, but at some point the law itself becomes a wall.

﹏﹏﹏

THE COMPLEXITIES OF criminal bars to relief were enough to make anyone's head spin. We tried our best to explain the law to Luisa. She did not miss a beat: "So we'll do what we have to do. I've been through worse." She was confident that the judge wanted to help her. "He was kind to me," she said.

Armed with her optimism, we got to it. We hunted down each conviction record, researched every criminal statute. In a forty-page brief, we explained to the judge why none of Luisa's pre-1996 convictions were aggravated felonies and why her single post-1996 offense was not deportable. The ICE attorney, unsurprisingly, opposed our position. We sent the attorney a packet including details on Luisa's equities, letters from her children, and the reasons she needed relief from deportation. I wonder if the attorney winced when she skimmed through Luisa's medical records.

The judge wanted to hear our arguments in court. So my students donned their suits and marched him through the dizzying array of arguments. No, no, no: the judge saw no hope in our aggravated felony arguments. Luisa's face fell. Her optimism was starting to falter under the pressure of the courtroom.

We then turned to the single post-1996 offense, relating to the credit card. It's not a deportable offense, we offered. The judge grimaced. Luisa had pleaded no contest, we continued. She had not admitted any underlying guilt, and she had been convicted under an exceptionally broad statute covering offenses that involved no moral turpitude.

The silence in the room was thick. Luisa kept her eyes downward. I spied her rocking slowly back and forth. A panic attack was beginning.

The judge finally glanced up. "I'm going to rule that she's 212(c) eligible," he said. The no-contest plea was the hook he was looking for. "Just don't come back here in another case," he added, "and tell me that I've ruled this conviction can never be a deportable offense."

My students and I glanced quickly at one another. His ruling meant that Luisa would finally get a hearing. "Thank you, Your Honor" was our only response. I caught Luisa's eye and gave her a small smile, willing her to understand that this was good news.

We got out of the court. Luisa was quiet. When she finally spoke, her voice was small. "So I'll have to testify," she said sadly.

EVEN IN THE best-case scenario, the preparations for a hearing of this sort can be agonizing. As a lawyer, I hate having to counsel clients on how to, more or less, beg for the dignity of being able to stay in their homes with their families instead of being deported for something they've already been punished for. It is always painful.

For Luisa, the pain was amplified. We knew that every time we forced her to go through her testimony, we were retraumatizing her. But like all of my clients, Luisa was far more resilient than I could imagine myself being under the same circumstances. She arrived at court with her family in tow—a veritable army of men, women, and children who would put their lives on the line for her if that's what was demanded.

We arrived early for the long wait outside the courtroom. When the door opened and Luisa's family walked in, the government attorney absorbed herself in her case file. The judge walked in and greeted everyone briskly, ready to begin. We went over the paperwork, a massive stack of documents my students had prepared detailing Luisa's life here. School records. Birth certificates. Immigration paperwork. The letters from her children. Photographs of graduations and birthday parties. Prison records. Taxes and employment history. Medical records of surgeries and chemotherapy. Life's paper trail.

After evidence was formally entered into the record, it was time for the testimony to begin. We asked Luisa's family to step outside the courtroom. Luisa didn't want them all to hear her describe everything she had been through.

My students walked Luisa through questions about her children and her breast cancer diagnosis and treatment, and then finally shifted to talk about her ex-husband. "How would you describe your relationship with him?"

Luisa took a deep breath. She brought her hands to her face, running them across her forehead, her eyes, her cheeks, as if to wipe away the tears before they came.

"Violence. That's what I remember. The violence." The tears came flooding down. But she shook her head, as if to tell us that she could do this, and began to explain.

By the time she was done, the judge had seen what we had seen all along. Luisa was a survivor. She wanted nothing more than to live her life in peace, with the family she had fought so fiercely to protect. The judge granted 212(c) relief, and the government attorney did not appeal. Luisa walked out of the courtroom into the arms of her family, now with tears of joy. The agony was finally over.

ııııııı

WHAT WAS IT all for? I think of a postscript that her youngest son wrote in his letter to the judge in support of her 212(c) relief application: "I didn't lose my mom to cancer. I don't want to lose her to deportation." The conclusion—that she should not be deported—was so obvious from the beginning. Yet she and her family came very close to losing everything.

It's difficult to pinpoint what problem Luisa's deportation would have solved. Deportation isn't a deterrent for crime. Luisa committed her crimes while living in fear for her life at the hands of an abusive husband. It's unfathomable that some future threat of deportation would have stopped her from ceding to his demands. If one were really trying to solve that problem, there are real solutions. Diverting even a fraction of the resources spent on her incarceration, immigration imprisonment, and deportation case toward the prevention of domestic violence and support for survivors would have saved her, her family, and her community from the suffering that was to come.

It may be hard to pinpoint what problem Luisa's deportation would have solved, but it is very easy to see what problems her deportation would have created. The family matriarch—gone. Instead of receiving her care and support, Luisa's children and grandchild—all US citizens—would have had to figure out how to care for her in Costa Rica. The disruption in her cancer treatment would have been deadly. For whatever time she had left, her family would be torn apart. All as a second punishment for things that happened long ago.

Luisa survived the deportation process, drawing from the same reserves of resiliency that enabled her to survive everything else. She was lucky enough to secure release from immigration imprisonment before her health deteriorated past the point of no return. Her case was heard by a judge who gave her time to find a lawyer. The hearing she received no longer exists in the law; we had to move mountains to convince the judge that she was entitled to it, but it worked. She could have died alone if she had been deported. Instead she returned to her family.

Yes, she was "lucky." But the process was designed to punish her. And although she escaped the worst outcome, the process was punishment enough.

Chapter Seven

POLITICS OF FEAR

IT HAPPENED QUICKLY. ONE MOMENT, KATHRYN STEINLE was walking along a popular San Francisco pier with her father, taking in the sights and sounds of a beautiful summer day in 2015. The next moment, she collapsed in her father's arms when a .40-caliber bullet struck her in the back. She died within hours at a local hospital.[1]

The shooting was traced to Jose Inez García Zárate. When prosecutors and the Steinle family learned that he not only had a lengthy criminal record but was undocumented and had been deported to his native Mexico five times, they were outraged. Their outrage only deepened when they learned that the San Francisco Sheriff's Department had custody of Jose Inez García Zárate only months before the shooting on marijuana charges but had ignored a request by ICE to inform federal immigration officials when he would be released. To the family and much of the public, it was clear that he should not have been on the pier that day, or even in the country.[2]

The San Francisco Sheriff's Department's choice to release Jose Inez García Zárate was based on its broader policy banning communication with ICE about individuals in local custody absent a warrant or court order.[3] The policy, among others, made San Francisco a sanctuary city. It limited the city's involvement in immigration enforcement in order to preserve trust with immigrant residents.

Proponents of stricter immigration enforcement seized upon Kathryn Steinle's death, urging an end to sanctuary policies across the country. They pointed to Jose Inez García Zárate as the quintessential example of failed immigration policies at the border and within the country. Donald Trump, then a Republican presidential candidate, led the chorus. Jose Inez García Zárate was an "animal," a vicious and dangerous man who exemplified the "bad hombres" Trump railed against in speeches.[4] After Trump became president he continued to follow Jose Inez García Zárate's trial closely and signed an executive order that attempted to strip sanctuary cities of federal funding.[5]

As it turned out, some of what people assumed had led to Kathryn Steinle's death was wrong. The gun that fired the bullet had belonged to a federal agent who apparently kept it loaded in his car. An unknown person had broken into the car, stolen the gun, and stashed it in a bundle on the pier. Jose Inez García Zárate, a homeless man with mental health issues, came across the bundle and picked up the gun. At some point the gun fired, sending a bullet into the pavement twelve feet away, where it ricocheted seventy-eight feet to strike Kathryn Steinle. What happened was horrific, but it was not murder. The jury in Jose Inez García Zárate's case agreed, acquitting him of both murder and manslaughter charges in light of the evidence.

But the condemnation from politicians like President Trump, who criticized the jury verdict as a "travesty of justice," echoed more loudly than any acquittal could have. The blowback was swift. The sheriff who had defended the city's sanctuary policy lost his reelection, and the city narrowed its policy. A wave of state and local governments prohibited sanctuary policies across the country.

The episode was one of many "Willie Horton" moments that have fueled the growth of America's crime-based deportation machine. People hear these stories and think the targets of this machine are "animals." They believe what they are told: as one journalist described President Trump's trope, "immigrants are coming over the border to kill you."[6] Fear overshadows truth.

The truth is that immigration is not associated with higher crime rates. Immigrants commit crimes at lower rates than native-born Americans. Border towns, which tend to have high rates of both authorized and unauthorized immigration, are among the safest in the country.[7]

The truth is that when immigrants do commit crime, they do so for the reasons that people generally commit crime, and not because they are immigrants. Even putting aside the fact that the majority of crimes that lead to deportation are nonviolent and victimless, sensationalizing any crime as an "immigration problem" is disingenuous.[8] Even in cases of terrorism and gang violence—the favored examples of anti-immigrant restrictionists—treating such crimes as an immigration issue is a dangerous distraction from real solutions.

Despite these truths, people are still afraid. Fear drives policy and chases us toward deportation. In the process, an actual threat to public safety emerges—one posed by the crime-based deportation machine itself. Home raids, imprisonment, abuse: over the last several years, new forms of state violence have largely gone unchecked by courts or Congress.

By embracing a "foreign threat" narrative and allowing the crime-based deportation machine to grow, we are making ourselves less safe, not more.

〽〽〽

IN THE FALL of 2018, a group of refugees from Honduras began the roughly 2,800-mile trek to the border between Tijuana and San Diego. As their journey crossed through neighboring countries, more people joined the group. Their numbers grew to roughly seven thousand men, women, and children. There was safety in numbers. Their plan, like that of others who had made the journey in similar "caravans" in recent months, was to apply for asylum at a port of entry, as permitted by US law.

The timing could not have been more perfect for Republicans in the lead-up to the 2018 midterm elections. President Trump labeled the group an "invasion" during a series of speeches and social media posts, much to the delight of his base. And who was invading our country? "Gang members and many bad people," Trump tweeted. In one speech, he claimed that the caravan included "criminals and unknown Middle Easterners."[9]

The Department of Homeland Security echoed Trump's sentiments. Without citing evidence, DHS officials stated that they had confirmed that some of the caravan participants were "gang members" or people with "significant criminal histories."[10]

Immigrant rights groups widely condemned the fearmongering. One of those groups was HIAS. Founded in 1881 as the Hebrew Immigrant Aid Society, HIAS spent many years helping Jews across the world flee from anti-Semitic persecution and resettle in America. Over time, HIAS broadened its mission to help all refugees, following religious teachings to "welcome the stranger."[11]

With Trump, HIAS's mission became much more difficult. In 2015, after a US-born citizen of Pakistani descent and his wife shot several people in San Bernardino, California, Trump issued a press release calling for a "total and complete shutdown of Muslims entering the United States."[12] Stating that "Islam hates us," he repeatedly warned Americans of the dangerous threat that Muslim immigrants posed.[13] Within days of taking office in 2017, President Trump issued his first Muslim ban, preventing people from several Muslim-majority countries from entering the United States and placing a moratorium on refugee admissions.

Condemning Trump's policies as Islamophobic and cruel, HIAS became one of the first refugee rights organizations to sue the administration over the ban.[14] HIAS leaders never forgot the dark periods in history when the United States turned back Jewish refugees to perish in Nazi-occupied Europe. The organization would not let Muslims fall victim to religious intolerance and discrimination now.

When Trump began vilifying Central American refugees in 2018, HIAS denounced the administration's fearmongering just as readily. Ahead of the midterm elections, as Trump leaned into his condemnations of refugees as "bad people" bringing violence with them, HIAS organized a National Shabbat encouraging Jewish worshipers to consider the plight of refugees during their religious observance.[15]

And then, just before the midterm elections, Trump's prediction of violence and terror came true—but not in the way that he had suggested.

On October 27, 2018, US citizen Robert Gregory Bowers posted a message on Gab, a social media site popular with White nationalists, in which he wrote, "HIAS likes to bring invaders in that kill our people. I can't sit by and watch my people get slaughtered. Screw your optics, I'm going in."[16]

Minutes later, Bower entered the Tree of Life Synagogue in Pittsburgh, Pennsylvania, and shot eleven people dead.

〰

AMERICAN POLICY ROUTINELY conflates immigration, public safety, and national security. This reflex carries serious costs to our safety and security.

For starters, the conflation of immigration, public safety, and national security turns immigrants into threats. It creates an us-versus-them mentality, excluding immigrants from a public that we must keep safe and secure. By doing so, it gives "us" permission to take stark and defensive actions against "them" (and those who support "them"). Taken to extremes, this mentality provides a depraved justification for the actions taken by people like Bowers.

The Tree of Life massacre became the worst attack on the Jewish community in American history. Sadly, it was not an isolated incident. From the Oak Creek massacre of six Sikh worshipers in 2006 to the murder of Srinivas Kuchibhotla in Kansas in 2017 to the mass shooting of Latinx shoppers at an El Paso Walmart in

2019, an increasing number of violent crimes in the United States have been perpetrated by individuals espousing some mixture of anti-immigrant and White supremacist rhetoric.[17]

These acts point to another fact: immigration status—or a violation of immigration law—is simply not a good proxy for figuring out who poses a threat to our public safety and national security.

For starters, terrorism in the United States is, by and large, homegrown.[18] As the Cato Institute has documented, 78 percent of terrorist homicides on US soil from 2002 to 2017 were committed by native-born Americans.[19] The ideological motivations behind the majority of attacks today are far-right, White supremacist views.[20] Not exactly a foreign threat.

But what of the minority who are foreign terrorists? It's not clear what immigration screening can do to identify those who are threats at the time they come to the United States. According to national security reports, most attacks by immigrants involve individuals who came to the United States legally and were radicalized after they arrived.[21] The conclusion is that "nationality is a poor predictor of later terrorist activity, and vetting people coming to the United States, no matter how rigorous, cannot identify those who radicalize here."[22]

Take, for example, Sayfullo Saipov. An immigrant from Uzbekistan, Saipov plowed a rented vehicle into pedestrians and cyclists along a busy stretch of highway in New York City in 2017, killing eight. President Trump was quick to point out that Saipov, a lawful permanent resident, had come to the United States through the "diversity lottery," a program that Congress created to diversify visa entrants. Trump's solution was to call for an end to the program, which primarily benefits immigrants from Africa, eastern Europe, and Asia.[23]

Trump's political choice to label this act of terror as an immigration problem may have played well with his base, but it has dangerous consequences. It takes our eyes off the ball. What caused Sayfullo Saipov to become radicalized? What would have prevented him from becoming radicalized? Those are the questions the incident should have provoked. Instead, immigrants take the blame, shutting the conversation down.

The evidence indicates that Sayfullo Saipov was a so-called lone wolf, isolated from much of his community. He became radicalized well after he came to the country, influenced by terrorist ideology espoused online. No red flags emerged when Saipov entered the country through the diversity lottery program—not because of a failure of the immigration screening system but because there were simply no notable indicators at the time.[24]

If the screening system was not at fault, something else must have been. Terrorism experts suggest that lone wolf radicalization may occur when individuals become socially isolated and exposed to extremist ideology that incites them to acts of hate and violence.[25]

But rather than focus on identifying and disrupting the forces that put people like Sayfullo Saipov on a path to radicalization, government actors too often turn to tools of mass surveillance. For years, the New York Police Department secretly surveilled Arab and Muslim communities throughout New York and even across state lines in a breathtaking example of Islamophobic profiling. But NYPD's mass surveillance program not only failed to produce any leads into terrorism; it actually disrupted the very community bonds that are effective tools in the fight against radicalization.

The NYPD's surveillance, for example, even reached the Masjid Omar, the mosque where Sayfullo Saipov was worshiping before his 2017 attack. Although the Masjid Omar once encouraged its congregants to commune with one another at the mosque following religious services, that all changed as the disclosures of NYPD surveillance came to light. No one was there to witness, let alone prevent, Saipov's descent into extremism. Mass surveillance tactics can isolate those who truly seek to do harm, while saturating terrorism investigations with unfocused and irrelevant data— building a larger and larger haystack in which to bury the needle.[26]

Nonetheless, immigration law adopts a similar approach. As far back as 1990, Congress enacted what became a long list of "terrorism-related inadmissibility grounds" (TRIG) in immigration law. The hope was that federal immigration officials could curb terrorism if they repeatedly screened people for terrorist connections as they went through the immigration system, even long after they'd entered the country.

Today, the State Department and the Department of Homeland Security manage various lists of terrorist groups, some of which are undisclosed. When federal immigration officials discover that an immigrant is tied to one of these groups, they can deny status and deport the person. However, these lists are notoriously broad.

I think of my former client Francois. Growing up in Congo-Brazzaville in the years leading to its 1997 civil war, Francois and his schoolmates joined a swelling prodemocratic youth movement. Affiliated with their regional party, they organized nonviolent demonstrations against Denis Sassou-Nguesso, whose militia responded with a violent crackdown. At the age of seventeen, Francois joined his neighbors in a peaceful demonstration in the capital city of Brazzaville and soon found himself locked away at the notorious Maison d'Arrêt. Amnesty International intervened to secure Francois's release from the prison, and he eventually received a visa to come to the United States, where he sought asylum.

Francois's road to an asylum hearing was long, and he struggled to study and work in the United States with his status in limbo. But when the day finally came, he was granted asylum. It was, he would later tell us, the happiest day of his life. "It was the first day of my life that I felt truly safe and like I belonged," he explained. He continued to build his life in the United States, finishing school and operating a small business. And when he became eligible to apply for a green card, he worked with a local chapter of the Quaker organization American Friends Service Committee to submit his paperwork.

Then the wait began. Days turns to months, and his lawyer submitted an inquiry to the US Citizenship and Immigration Services. An answer arrived in shorthand: "TRIG hold." Francois was confused, and when he looked up the term online that evening he was thunderstruck. His case was on hold while US officials decided whether to apply a terrorism-related inadmissibility ground to deny his case.

"There must be some mistake," he thought. He loved America— it protected him, it was his home. He was not a terrorist.

As it turned out, the very actions that had qualified him for asylum—organizing peaceful prodemocracy protests—were grounds for a terrorist designation. Each of the main political parties in Congo-Brazzaville, including the one that organized nonviolent student protests in Francois's neighborhood, was affiliated with a political candidate, who in turn hired personal security forces to protect the candidate during the civil war, some of whom became affiliated with militias. According to the US government, that string of affiliations was enough to raise the specter of terrorism. Never mind that such a broad definition would exclude any peaceful prodemocracy activist fleeing persecution from Congo-Brazzaville from getting status in the United States.

The American Friends Service Committee responded to the TRIG hold by contacting the NYU Immigrant Rights Clinic. We challenged the hold in Francois's case. Our expert witnesses explained the political structure of Congo-Brazzaville, noting how the prodemocratic youth movement was peaceful and distinct from any of the acts of violence that overtook some of the political candidates' security forces. After years of negotiation, our efforts were ultimately successful: federal immigration officials lifted the TRIG hold.

It was a bittersweet victory for Francois. He got his green card, and his life moved on. But his friends and colleagues wondered why it had taken him so long to receive one. He did not dare explain the circumstances. A terrorist label lingers long past the time it is discredited. He could not take the risk that someone would not believe his story, so he bore the burden of his case alone. He continued to love America, in the deep and devoted way so many asylees do. It was just no longer clear to him that America loved him back.

IIIIIIII

INDISCRIMINATE LISTS OF terrorist groups are just one of many programs that the US immigration system uses to police immigrants. But rather than prevent terrorist attacks, these programs simply terrorize communities, sweeping more and more people into the deportation system who have no ties to terrorism.

In 2002, federal officials launched the National Security Entry-Exit Registration System (NSEERS), which targeted immigrants from twenty-five countries, twenty-four of which are Muslim-majority countries.[27] Under NSEERS, also known as Special Registration, immigrant men over the age of sixteen were required to register their presence with the US government.[28] More than ninety thousand people were registered under NSEERS. Those who failed to comply with the program were placed into the National Crime Information Center (NCIC), described as "a national database utilized daily by state and law enforcement" in order "to enable local enforcement officials to apprehend such individuals."[29]

Within the first two years of the program, 2,870 Muslims were detained and 13,799 were placed in deportation proceedings.[30] In addition, those who did not comply were denied immigration benefits and deported.[31] Those who were told to register and discovered to be out of status were also deported.[32] Yet the program did not produce a single terrorism prosecution.[33]

In 2002, the same year Attorney General John Ashcroft launched NSEERS, the deputy attorney general launched the Alien Absconder Initiative. This program gave law enforcement agencies access to the names of 314,000 immigrants who allegedly had old orders of deportation.[34] The attorney general authorized "fugitive operations" task forces to go after the absconders, initially focusing on nearly six thousand men from largely Muslim and Arab countries.[35] Former INS Commissioner Doris Meissner commented that the Alien Absconder Initiative had "marginal security benefits, while further equating national origin with dangerousness."[36] As with NSEERS, no one deported under the Alien Absconder Initiative was ever linked to terrorism.[37]

As these track records indicate, it is improbable that the immigration system itself will identify a terror suspect. And even if it did, it's not clear that we would ever want civil immigration law to take care of the problem. Deporting someone engaged in terrorism hardly feels like a good move for national security.

Many experts are attempting to understand why people commit acts of terror, how and when they are motivated by political or religious ideologies, and how previously apolitical people become radicalized. No one denies that would-be terrorists who are radicalized outside the United States may take advantage of US immigration laws, just as they may take advantage of US gun laws, tax laws, and other laws to aid their violent pursuits. But the solution is to prevent and identify and respond to radicalization—in all of its forms—before it is too late.

Terrorism, and the radicalization at its root, transcends immigration. So it shouldn't be a surprise that focusing on immigration policy as the problem puts the cart before the horse. It redirects our focus onto vast swaths of immigrants who have not done and will do no harm to our country. By doing so, it misses the vast majority of people who commit terrorist acts in the United States: native-born White supremacists. We're left with what one law enforcement officer calls a "Bermuda Triangle of intelligence"—with no sense of homegrown radicalization, we ignore the very people in our midst who pose the greatest threat.[38]

Terrorism crosses over citizenship and immigration status lines, and we endanger the safety and security of communities across the country when we assume differently.

ALONGSIDE TERRORISM, GANG violence is an increasingly popular theme among immigration restrictionists. Episodic but brutal violence by Mara Salvatrucha (MS-13), a gang with roots in the United States and El Salvador, has fueled claims that gang violence, like terrorism, is an immigration problem with a deportation solution.

"Crippling loopholes in our laws have enabled MS-13 gang members and other criminals to infiltrate our communities," President Trump announced in a 2018 speech in Long Island, New

York, following the brutal murder of two teenage girls in 2017.[39] Under his administration, ICE has expanded its operations to deport gang members, issuing press release after press release lauding its arrests.[40]

Some law enforcement officers welcomed President Trump's focus on MS-13. When Fresno County Sheriff Margaret Mimms complained about California law limiting her efforts to turn over suspected MS-13 gang members to ICE if they didn't meet a certain threshold of criminal activity, President Trump infamously replied, "We have people coming into the country, or trying to come in—and we're stopping a lot of them—but we're taking people out of the country. You wouldn't believe how bad these people are. These aren't people. These are animals."[41]

Although Trump's comment drew widespread criticism—people are people, after all, and dehumanization is the first step in every historical account of genocide—it did not change his approach. Trump doubled down, releasing a White House memo on MS-13 that used the term "animals" ten times.[42]

The focus on MS-13 came long before the Trump administration. The gang had been on ICE's radar screen since 2005, when the agency began Operation Community Shield. An immigration policing initiative dedicated to combating the proliferation of transnational gangs, Operation Community Shield combines the work of ICE with other federal and local law enforcement agencies that target gangs.[43] Claiming responsibility for more than forty thousand arrests and the seizure of property worth nearly $100 million since its inception, Operation Community Shield relies heavily on federal and state gang databases to ensure the deportation of members of MS-13 and similar transnational gangs.[44]

The program enjoyed wide support from the Bush and Obama administrations. By 2012, the Obama administration had declared MS-13 a "transnational criminal organization" in hopes of dismantling its financial infrastructure and deporting its members.[45] Trump's fixation on MS-13 served only to pour more law enforcement resources into arresting and deporting its members, affiliates, and anyone else who happened to be around during an immigration raid. The effort was necessary, Trump claimed, in light of MS-13's "bloodstained killing fields" in places like Long Island.[46]

Police departments in Long Island were quick to point out that their communities were, by and large, safer than much of the country. Many welcomed the intensified focus on MS-13—the gang's crimes were violent, to be sure—but questioned the motivations. After all, there was no evidence that MS-13 was new or growing. By all accounts, the number of MS-13 members in 2018 was ten thousand. The number of MS-13 members in the United States a decade ago? Ten thousand.[47] These numbers paled in comparison to other gangs operating in the United States that failed to draw comparable attention from a sitting president, much less a windfall of law enforcement dollars.[48] Of the 1.4 million gang members in the United States, focusing on MS-13 started to feel a bit contrived.

Regardless, most people would say that ten thousand gang members is still ten thousand too many. To those people, it might seem reasonable to close whatever loopholes may be permitting these gang members to enter the country. For Trump, however, the loopholes are laws that protect children who flee to the United States from violence and abuse in Central America. Pointing to the fact that unaccompanied minors were responsible for some of the more heinous Long Island murders, Trump vowed to clamp down on laws that protect children and close the borders.[49]

But treating MS-13 as a foreign threat—particularly one stemming from unaccompanied minors entering the country as gang members in disguise—is a strange characterization. Experts who study MS-13 observe that the gang operates and recruits locally. As one Long Island police commissioner described it to Congress:

> MS-13 sustains itself by constantly recruiting new members. MS-13 gang members recruit in our schools and communities. They prey on the vulnerable, frequently targeting young people who recently immigrated to this country. They often target individuals who lack the support of close relatives and healthy social networks, using threats and acts of violence to coerce those

reluctant to join. Several factors lead individuals to become members of MS-13, including, but not limited to, social alienation, the need to be part of a group, a sense of cultural unity, the promise of protection, and economic gain.[50]

In other words, there's no reason to think that MS-13 is actively sending more of its people across the border when it can simply recruit people who are already here.[51] And even though some unaccompanied minors might be particularly vulnerable to recruitment, in reality they make up only a tiny fraction of MS-13 members.[52] A meaningful response to youth recruitment would necessarily involve youth-focused gang prevention tools—like resources for after-school programs and social supports for youth. These tools would go much further in disrupting MS-13 than closing down the border or depriving immigrant youth of social services.

The difficult work of gang prevention does not, however, get the attention and resources that gang policing does. When the police encounter an MS-13 gang member, the instinctual reaction is to remove that gang member from the community as quickly as possible. That sometimes means working with ICE to deport MS-13 members who are foreign-born. The instinct is dangerous. Deportation—and the harsh border policies that precede it—is exactly how we ended up in this mess.

MS-13 was not founded in Central America. It was founded in Los Angeles after the Reagan administration backed the right-wing military government in El Salvador during its civil war. Refugees fled for the United States, but they were labeled as "economic refugees" and denied asylum. Many found themselves living under the radar in Los Angeles, where they faced an American-born gang problem. Without economic support and stability, a small number responded by forming their own gangs, including MS-13.

As MS-13 members began committing crimes, the US government responded with mass incarceration followed by mass deportation—returning members (and others falsely labeled as members) to El Salvador and surrounding countries. The ongoing economic deprivation and civil war allowed the US-born MS-13 members to flourish, gaining a stronghold in Central America that had been unimaginable before.

The history of MS-13 is now repeating itself. People are fleeing the gang violence in Central America for the United States. The government's response has been to make it harder for refugees to get asylum status and, in some cases, basic social services. The New York attorney general had to remind schools in Long Island, for example, that they are constitutionally required to provide children with a public education regardless of immigration status.[53] Isolating vulnerable children doesn't weaken MS-13; it strengthens MS-13.

As for the cases in which an individual *does* join MS-13, deportation doesn't solve the problem. If a person is actively engaging in violence, deportation fuels and spreads that violence and danger, often in countries where prior and current US policies have already contributed to massive instability. Ending gang violence requires a different approach—often focused on youth intervention, helping young people flee violent situations and receive the educational and economic opportunities they need to achieve a different life. By persisting in labeling gangs as an "immigration problem," we become co-conspirators in gang recruitment and proliferation.

⸻

UNDERLYING ALL THIS is the assumption that law enforcement agencies are good at figuring out who is actually a gang member. But as communities of color in the United States have long known, law enforcement officers rely on notoriously broad criteria to decide who is a gang member. One officer enters a name into a gang database, and suddenly gang affiliation is set in stone, regardless of accuracy.

For years, immigrant rights organizations have tried to get their hands on ICE's criteria for and definition of gang membership. With press release after press release, ICE has announced the results of the newest versions of Operation Community Shield, like Operation Matador and Operation Raging Bull, apparent references to one of MS-13's symbols, a horned bull. Someone at ICE even created a mascot for Operation Raging Bull, announcing the program with a cartoon of the mounted head of a blue bull with smoke streaming from its nostrils, the words "RAGING BULL" written in red letters.[54] But the definition of who is targeted by these aggressive operations is murky. Some are immigrants, others are not. Some are adults, others are not. Some have committed crimes, others have not.

Take, for example, ICE's November 2017 press release about Operation Raging Bull. ICE, in a coordinated international operation led by its Homeland Security Investigations division in cooperation with a long list of federal agencies and departments, made 267 arrests of "gang members," "gang affiliates" and others.[55] Of the 214 arrests in the United States, ICE reported that "93 were arrested on federal and/or state criminal charges" and that "the remaining 121 were arrested on administrative immigration violations." ICE further reported that, of the 214 people arrested, sixteen were US citizens and 198 were noncitizens. Sixty-four of those arrested had come to the United States as "unaccompanied alien children," and most are now adults.

Although ICE did not break down the statistics by the number of gang members, affiliates, and collateral arrests, it provided some definitions. First, ICE defined "gang members" as individuals who "admit membership in a gang; have been convicted of violating Title 18 USC 521 or any other federal or state law criminalizing or imposing civil consequences for gang-related activity; or if they meet certain other criteria such as having tattoos identifying a specific gang or being identified as a gang member by a reliable source." It further defined "gang associates" as "individuals who exhibit gang member criteria but who are not formally initiated into the gang." Who decides whether a person falls under this definition? "Law enforcement officers encountering these individuals will determine whether indications of gang association are present by referring to the gang membership criteria."[56]

When the criteria for gang membership or affiliation are this broad, it's hard to avoid getting on a list. The overbreadth takes its biggest toll on kids, many of whom come to the United States fleeing gang violence only to be at risk of being falsely labeled a gang member.

I remember one of my former clients, Santos, who fled gang recruitment after his father was murdered in Central America. Santos joined his mother, who had fled for the United States a decade earlier. His first months in America were challenging. A shy kid, years behind his peers in school, he begrudgingly got himself out of bed in the morning to attend bilingual classes with much younger children. His mother confessed to us her worries that he would not listen to her admonitions to go to school. We intervened on more than one occasion, reminding him that any lapse at school could put his immigration status in jeopardy and offering to connect him with counseling and support.

We were so focused on making sure Santos got to school each morning that we didn't think to warn him about tattoos. The day we met with Santos to get his photos taken for his immigration application, we saw a bright red tattoo on his neck. It would have been comical—this lanky, quiet boy, who hardly said a word to the girls in his class, choosing of all things to get a highly visible cartoonish tattoo of a kiss. I'm sure his mother was furious. But we were just plain worried. On the long list of signs of MS-13 gang involvement: a kiss tattoo.

When we looked up examples online, we breathed a sigh of relief. The MS-13 version of a kiss tattoo was much different—thin lips shaped not-so-subtly like the number thirteen—not the rounded Betty Boop–like pucker Santos had chosen. He blanched when he learned our concerns. It never occurred to him that a tattoo could mean the difference between his new life here and a quick deportation. Deportation is not on most people's list of reasons to regret getting a tattoo at age seventeen.

Though our fears were misplaced in Santos's case, they were not unfounded. Over the years, cases of mistaken gang affiliation have proliferated. They are born from human bias and the heightened fears politicians provoke when they, for example, describe your hometown as a "bloodstained killing field."

Surely that was the idea when Andrew Fiorillo, the school resource officer at Long Island's Huntington High School, reported gang activity by student Alex Ulloa Martinez. The school suspended Alex, then nineteen, for doodling "504," the country code for Honduras, in his notebook and sketching horns onto his calculator. It didn't matter that Huntington High School's mascot was a horned blue devil, or that Alex had not been accused of doing anything other than doodling. His sketches were enough to get him suspended for gang activity, enough for Fiorillo to report Alex to ICE, and enough for ICE to deport him back to Honduras—the country he had fled in 2015 when gangs killed his cousins, shot his uncle, mugged his mother, and then turned their sights on him.[57]

Alex became one of the statistics in ICE's anti-MS-13 Operation Matador. In a June 2017 press release covering the Operation Matador surge in Suffolk County, Long Island, ICE claimed that all of the forty-five people arrested were confirmed to be gang members by reliable sources. But Alex was not a gang member, and Fiorillo was not a reliable source. Alex's classmates and neighbors demanded answers. At a 2019 school board meeting following Alex's deportation, five hundred people gathered to hear the school's plans to protect their students. A recent graduate spoke at the podium through tears. "It's very hard to be Latino here," he said. "Something has to change." Fiorillo had been pulled from the school, but it was unclear what could be done to prevent ICE from continuing to deport their students based on false gang allegations.[58]

Over the years, reports and studies have repeatedly questioned the reliability of gang criteria and databases used for criminal and immigration enforcement alike.[59] In 2016, a scathing audit of Cal-Gangs, California's long-standing gang database, discovered that it included widespread errors, including more than two dozen babies who were listed as admitting to gang membership.[60] In 2018, four Chicago residents sued the city based on their wrongful inclusion in its massive gang database, which notoriously includes many dead people.[61] Two Chicago men also sued after facing deportation when the police department incorrectly included them in the database, prompting an immigration arrest.[62]

These errors are a predictable outcome of relying on immigration enforcement to address gang violence: building a crime-based deportation machine that embraces an ends-justify-the-means mentality. As the Suffolk County police commissioner admitted, "Although it is often our objective to arrest and prosecute MS-13 gang members for federal criminal offenses in order to prevent them from merely reentering after deportation, circumstances do arise when we are not able to effectuate a criminal arrest, and the Department of Homeland Security is able to utilize its immigration enforcement tools to remove these dangerous people from our streets."[63] These "dangerous people"—i.e., Central American immigrants for whom there is no probable cause to arrest for actual crimes—are vulnerable to deportation. The policy is a boon to law enforcement because according to ICE, no probable cause is needed to arrest them for immigration purposes. But what happens next?

Conflating gang violence and immigration policy is dangerous. Even when we get the labels right, we're not disrupting transnational criminal organizations when we deport people who may be gang members. We are creating them.

‖‖‖‖

A BY-PRODUCT OF our unquestioning acceptance of terrorism and gang violence as immigration problems is the unchecked growth of a highly armed deportation force. The Department of Homeland Security now receives more federal funding than all other federal law enforcement agencies combined. With every operation it launches in the name of public safety, more federal dollars flow. The result is a highly militarized agency ready to be deployed against immigrant communities for a wide array of civil immigration violations.

The evolution of the Alien Absconder Initiative is a prime example of this phenomenon. After failing to identify actual terrorists, the program morphed into the National Fugitive Operations Program, or FugOps. Targeting people with old deportation orders, FugOps aims to "remove criminals from our communities." Claiming to prioritize "aliens who present a heightened threat to national security and public safety, such as transnational gang members, child sex offenders, and aliens with prior convictions for violent crimes," FugOps uses SWAT-style, heavily armed teams to arrest immigrants for deportation. More than 129 such teams operate across the country, working with other divisions of ICE to carry out raids.[64]

Like other crime-based deportation programs, FugOps works much differently in practice than its messaging projects. In its first five years of operation, 73 percent of people arrested under FugOps had no criminal conviction. They weren't so much fugitives as people who may never have received their deportation orders or were merely bystanders in the places where FugOps came knocking. Even so, FugOps still managed to grow its budget twenty-three-fold, more than any other immigration enforcement program in its first five years.[65]

It's hard to measure the harm that the aggressive growth of this program has wrought on communities in the United States. Whether they are active targets or merely collateral damage, many immigrants—and their US citizen families—brace themselves for the worst.

Alicia Carmona was caring for her daughter's four children when ten federal officers burst into their apartment in Heber City, Utah, in 2017. Waving assault weapons and pistols, they demanded Alicia tell them the whereabouts of her husband, who had been charged with illegal entry six years earlier. Her grandchildren, whose ages ranged from three to six, clung to the folds of her clothes and sobbed as Alicia stepped between them and the officers.

Alicia explained as best she could that she didn't know where her husband was. So ICE officers arrested her instead. ICE announced that she would be taken to an immigration jail and threatened to place her grandchildren in state custody. When one of her sons, Eduardo, rushed to her apartment, ICE arrested him too, cuffing him so tightly that he had marks around his wrists for over a month, despite the fact that he had DACA status and could not be detained. The ICE officers responded to Eduardo's requests to see a warrant by saying, "Don't worry about it," and then took Alicia into custody.

The next night, ICE returned. This time the officers used a battering ram to break down the apartment door while Alicia's daughter and grandchildren were sleeping. Pointing guns at the children, they forced Alicia's daughter out of the apartment for questioning about her father-in-law. They also forced out members of the family who lived in other apartments in the complex. When Alicia's son Carlos arrived in the middle of the raid and saw his apartment door broken down, he too asked the officers if they had a warrant. One of the officers laughed at the question, telling Carlos that ICE didn't need a warrant to break down a door and that Carlos was watching "too much Univision." The officers left with the apartment in disarray. It was several weeks before the family was able to bail Alicia out of immigration jail.[66]

The use of such aggressive, military-style tactics are the rule rather than the exception for interior immigration enforcement. They are part of the blueprint for street-level operations by ICE, the threat of which sparks fear in immigrant communities.[67]

The violence seems only to be amplified when ICE locks people away in immigration jails. Sexual and other forms of physical abuse are rampant, with little accountability. Dozens of people die in detention each year, many reportedly because of medical neglect. And those who survive the violence and abuse are rarely able to hold ICE accountable for its actions—even when ICE employees and contractors are caught red-handed.[68]

When CCA (now CoreCivic) employee Donald Dunn pleaded guilty to sexually assaulting women held at ICE's infamous T. Don Hutto Residential Facility in Taylor, Texas, the women hoped that ICE, its private contractor, and the county that facilitated the contract would be held responsible for their part in the assaults. According to ICE's own protocols and its contract with CCA and Williamson County, Texas, women like the plaintiffs were not supposed to be left alone with men on transports to and from the facility—but that's exactly what happened here.

Despite the duty that the government and private prison corporations have to protect those whom they imprison, the federal appellate court tossed this lawsuit against each party, one by one. The court held that ICE did not violate a "clearly established constitutional right" when it failed to enforce a policy intended to prevent sexual assault against people in detention. The court also gave the private prison corporation a pass, concluding that CCA was not acting "under the color of state law" just because it was contracted with ICE through Williamson County. Finally, the court held that the county itself could not be held responsible for CCA's actions because it did not show "deliberate indifference" in monitoring the facility.[69] This was a typical outcome in such lawsuits. When corporate and government defendants pull out all the stops to avoid liability, they usually get off scot-free.

If courts won't step in, it is up to Congress to ensure some oversight. In 2002, Congress created an Office of the Inspector General to oversee the workings of DHS. In addition to exposing fiscal waste and fraud, the inspector general also investigates misconduct by ICE and Customs and Border Protection (CBP) officers, and has the authority to audit immigration prisons operated by or contracted with DHS.[70] The question is whether these investigations lead to any meaningful change.

At times, the inspector general has been a harsh critic of the treatment of immigrants at the hands of ICE and CBP. A 2017 report of immigration jails, for example, exposed the public to a number of problems that "undermine the protection of detainees' rights, their humane treatment, and the provision of a safe and healthy environment."[71]

But the inspector general's ability to effect change is limited. Its reports, scathing as they may be, leave DHS with the responsibility of implementing any changes. To "resolve" an inspector general report, DHS may simply submit an acceptable "corrective action plan ... that addresses the findings and recommendations."[72] Nothing actually requires ICE to implement the plan.

The result is a vague, sanitized exchange between bureaucracies that does little to address the underlying violence. For example, after intensely criticizing the treatment of immigrants in one of its reports, the inspector general proposed only a single recommendation for ICE to "develop a process ... to conduct specific reviews" of the areas of deficiency.[73] ICE concurred—after all, it was hard *not* to concur with a recommendation that it investigate the deficiencies. But very little actually changed.

The inspector general's own reports at times simply reidentify the problems the office has previously reported.[74] It's so bad that the office itself questions the value of its own process: "Neither the inspections nor the onsite monitoring ensure consistent compliance with detention standards, nor do they promote comprehensive deficiency corrections."[75] Immigrant advocacy groups echo these concerns. "Every 'authorized' ICE facility has passed every inspection since 2012, even those where multiple people have died, some later reported to be as a result of medical neglect," as the National Immigrant Justice Center reported.[76]

In the name of public safety, there is real violence being done every day by the crime-based deportation machine, and no one is being held accountable.

〰〰〰

IN THE END, all the heated rhetoric around immigration and crime raises an important question: who gets to be counted as part of the public when we talk about public safety? My public includes immigrants. My public isn't defined by citizenship or paperwork; it's defined by the people I live with, my family, my neighbors, my colleagues, my community.

The public that the Department of Homeland Security serves seems to be more limited. "With honor and integrity, we will safeguard the American people, our homeland, and our values," reads the DHS mission statement. What is meant by "American people"—whether it refers to all the people who live in America or only those who are US citizens—remains ominously unspoken.

And regardless of how one defines the public, it has become increasingly clear that the tactic of deportation doesn't promote safety. Deportation does not prevent a person intent on harming others from committing that harm. The mass deportation of suspected gang members allowed gangs like MS-13 to expand transnationally. The rapid expansion of militarized deportation forces allowed SWAT-like home raids to take down whole families. And the demonization of some immigrants as "terrorists" and "animals" has led to spikes in hate crime and acts of domestic terrorism right here at home. The conflation of crime and immigration often misdirects our focus from the solutions that might actually prevent such tragedies from happening in the future.

This conflation also serves as a justification for harsh immigration policies. ICE gets the upper hand because of the inflammatory labels it deploys. After Kathryn Steinle's tragic death on the San Francisco pier in 2015, Jose Inez García Zárate remains a murderer in the minds of many—even though he was acquitted. Immigration agencies issue press releases describing their efforts to capture "aggravated felons," gang members, and terrorists. The more these labels are repeated and the connection between immigrants and crime is made, the more we think the hard cases justify harsh policies.

But as someone who represents immigrants with criminal records, I know that the labels are often wrong. For every reference to gang members, I think of a client like Santos, with his cartoonish kiss tattoo. For every reference to terrorists, I think of a client like Francois, the prodemocracy activist from Congo-Brazzaville. The term "aggravated felon" brings to mind clients like Ely, Aba, and Luisa—all of whom are struggling to build better lives for themselves and their families in America. Somehow immigration law is designed to deliver the harshest labels to people who are the survivors of harm, just when they believed their second chances were secure. We owe them more than that.

We owe more to all those who have strived for redemption. I once represented a man who had, twenty-five years before I met him, killed another person in a fight as a teenager. He spent his entire adult life behind bars, atoning for the life he took, seeking forgiveness, teaching others not to follow his path. I cannot say what was in his heart twenty-five years ago, but I can say that the man he is today is not the boy he was. He was ultimately deported, and upon his deportation, he wrote to us expressing his hope that in his new life he could continue to help others learn nonviolent responses to violence. His deportation did not make us safer. To the contrary, I can only imagine how much we could have learned had he been permitted to remain in the United States with his family.

And for those who are actively perpetrating harm, deportation does not promote safety in any meaningful sense. Too often, it makes things worse. I don't feel safer when I see an ICE press release about a deported gang leader. My own fears of terrorism and violent crime are not put to rest knowing that immigrants live with a target on their backs. Instead, it's the dogged focus on these issues as "immigration problems" that scares me. It sucks the oxygen out of the room. We can't have a real conversation about guns, education, youth intervention, and social services. We can't have a real conversation about White supremacy. Instead we distract ourselves by calling everything an immigration problem, and the crime-based deportation machine feeds off those fears.

Safety and security start when we stop thinking we can deport ourselves out of harm's way. There is a better path forward, and it doesn't involve building a bigger deportation machine.

Chapter Eight

JUSTICE FOR ALL

"YOU CAN'T BRING HIM IN." THE CORRECTIONS OFFICER barely glanced up from his post at the Hudson County Correctional Facility as two visitors approached. He missed the shocked expression of the woman standing expectantly at the visitor's desk and the bright, eager smile of the toddler she had in tow.

Gabrielle couldn't believe it. She had been telling Alex all week that he would finally get to see his son. The little boy who shared his name, his dimples, the curl in his hair. Alex would be crushed.

It felt like a lifetime had passed since the cold November morning when she and Alex, her fiancé, had awoken to a phone call. Gabrielle remembered the edge in Alex's voice as he spoke to his brother Benito on the line. A warrant squad was at his mother's house, waving around a picture of a Black man whom they claimed was Alexander Lora, saying they had a warrant for his arrest. "I told them it wasn't you," Benito said. Benito handed the phone to one of the officers, who agreed to meet Alex outside Gabrielle's house in Queens.

"I better clear this up," Alex said that morning, pulling on his clothes, asking Gabrielle to wait for him inside. Alex was three years into probation for a drug conviction. He had been working at a deli when the police found drugs in the cash register and arrested everyone present. Alex told them the drugs weren't his, but his defense attorney encouraged him to take a plea in exchange for probation—a slap on the wrist that would let him get on with his life.

The regular grind of probation appointments had left Alex numb to interactions with law enforcement. Just another mistake, he thought, when he got Benito's call. At least this one would be easy to fix.

Alex left to meet the officers across the street. A few minutes passed before Gabrielle called Alex on his cellphone. No answer.

She would later come to learn that Alex was not met by the officers of the New York Police Department, as he had been led to believe. Instead, he was surrounded by unmarked cars and at least ten officers out of uniform. Without identifying themselves, they drew their guns and forced him to the ground to cuff him. Alex was confused until they told him he would be deported. He suddenly realized that they were immigration agents, not the police.

The sun had risen, and neighbors were beginning to leave their homes for work, stopping to stare at the spectacle on their quiet block. Embarrassed, Alex begged the officers to just take him into one of their cars. They left him shackled on the street. "Fucking immigrant," one muttered.

Back at home, Gabrielle grew more anxious by the minute. Then came a loud banging on the door as officers demanded to see Alex's papers. Scared, Gabrielle wouldn't let them in. It would be a few hours before Alex could call her. "It was immigration," he said. "I'm in New Jersey. They're saying they're going to deport me."

Alex had never served time in jail before. The place left his skin crawling; the food was inedible. The night was punctuated by the sounds of men sobbing. "You wanna leave, then sign," an immigration officer told Alex. Sign a deportation order. Give up your fight. After two weeks had passed, Alex began to lose hope. Too many of the men he met inside had been in there for months, or years, only to lose their case.

And then there was his little boy. Alex had shared joint custody with the little boy's mother. She suffered from mental health issues and, to Alex's horror, was hospitalized shortly after his detention. In came child services to take away the child. He was eventually placed into kinship foster care with Alex's sister, which gave Alex some comfort. But it was still too much—losing both parents in the span of a couple of weeks—for a toddler to understand.

Gabrielle, who had cared for the little boy alongside Alex every weekend for the past year, hoped that reuniting them would give them each the reassurance they needed to get through the next few days. She didn't expect to be turned away because she wasn't his biological mother.

As she heard the corrections officer's words, she peered through the window in the door that separated the visitation area from the jail. All she saw was a vast emptiness, a series of doors that were closed to them.

Gabrielle blinked back her tears as she left the jail, tugging Alex's son with her across the parking lot and back to their car. "Momma, don't cry," little Alex said. Gabrielle's heart broke at his words. She summoned the strength to put the key in the ignition and start the long drive home.

Their story could have ended, as so many have, with deportation. Alex's drug conviction, though minor enough to receive probation, was considered a drug trafficking aggravated felony by immigration authorities. That meant no eligibility for release from detention or for cancellation of deportation.

But Alex's family was ready to fight. And New York was willing to fight at his side. The New York City Council had just funded a small pilot project to give New Yorkers who were detained a free public defender. As a result, Alex's attorney, Talia Peleg, worked with him and his family to fight for his release from immigration jail. Five long months after ICE arrested Alex, he received a bond hearing and was released.

When the federal government appealed the decision that authorized his bond hearing, Alex's attorney reached out to my clinic, and together we defended his rights on appeal. In 2015, with the support of the ACLU, we won the right to bond hearings for all immigrants like Alex in the region. Those hearings—hearings for immigrants within six months of their detention—were called Lora hearings. Knowing that his fight had helped more than 150 other people secure their freedom through hearings in his name made Alex feel just a little bit better about everything he had suffered.

Eventually, the Supreme Court overturned the detention case, sending us all back to the drawing board to find other ways to ensure that immigrants could have access to freedom. But by then it was too late for ICE to come after Alex. He had already been granted cancellation of deportation. His freedom had cleared his path to remain in the United States with his family, reunited with his son, able to marry Gabrielle and grow their family together.

None of this would have happened if New York City officials had looked the other way, if they had continued to devote resources to collaborating with ICE rather than collaborating with the community. Stories like Alex's helped turn the New York Immigrant Family Unity Project from a pilot program into the country's first universal public defender system for detained community residents. Thanks to the program, New York City has improved the chances that detained New Yorkers will win their cases four times over. The program has also spurred similar initiatives across the country, and it helped solidify New York City's reputation as a sanctuary city.[1]

But New York City was never truly a sanctuary city. The scope of sanctuary has always been a matter of degree: some immigrants receive protections, but not all. And now even the model for inclusive justice that the New York Immigrant Family Unity Project offered was about to be tested—not just from outside forces like ICE but also from city leaders who thought that only some immigrants deserved to have the access to justice that public defense could provide.

Good versus bad immigrants: this is a recurring theme, even in one of the most progressive cities in the country. It echoes the rhetoric that has fueled America's crime-based deportation machine since the beginning.

Ensuring justice for all takes work. In the immigrant rights movement, there is much more work to be done. We share culpability for the crime-based deportation machine when we reinforce the lines that divide our communities into good and bad. A new path forward would start with erasing the dividing lines altogether.

||||||

FOR MANY YEARS, "humane" immigration enforcement has been equated with the concept of prioritization. The question is not why we deport but who deserves it. We prioritize "bad" immigrants for deportation while giving "good" immigrants a reprieve through prosecutorial discretion.

In a world where the resources and political will for deportation are scarce, a system of prioritization may bring some comfort. So long as there is a hierarchy of people subject to deportation, at least some will benefit from prosecutorial discretion.

For decades, the federal government has embraced its power to exercise this discretion. The same person who presided over one of the darkest chapters in deportation history, Operation Wetback, also used his powers of discretion to allow thousands of people—from adopted orphans to Hungarian and Cuban refugees—to enter the United States despite visa caps.[2] Every president since Eisenhower has exercised some measure of discretion, including the discretion to prevent deportation. Presidents Ronald Reagan and George H. W. Bush, for example, both supported the Family Fairness Program, which spared as many as 1.5 million people from deportation while Congress legislated reforms.[3]

Prosecutorial discretion of this nature did not come under serious attack until President Obama announced the DACA policy in 2012. Pundits denounced Obama's actions as an unconstitutional power grab and a dereliction of his duty to enforce immigration laws. The president—and many legal scholars—defended this use of discretion. In 2014, President Obama issued a new set of immigration enforcement priorities, celebrated by many as a more humane approach to deportation. On the top of his deportation list were people with aggravated felony convictions, convicted gang members, people with other felony records, and people who had recently crossed the border without authorization. People with minor criminal records were lower priorities, and undocumented immigrants with clean records were at the bottom of the list.

Importantly, the Obama administration clarified that immigration officials should exercise prosecutorial discretion regardless of these categories if the person was eligible for relief from deportation or other special circumstances were present.[4] The list of factors immigration officials were to consider was long: "extenuating circumstances involving the offense of conviction; extended length of time since the offense of conviction; length of time in the United States; military service; family or community ties in the United States; status as a victim, witness or plaintiff in civil or criminal proceedings; or compelling humanitarian factors such as poor health, age, pregnancy, a young child, or a seriously ill relative."[5]

When President Trump stepped into office, he issued an executive order within days that swept away the prioritization system. In his new system, nearly everyone was a priority, with "criminal aliens" at the top of the list. Gone was the encouragement to consider discretion in cases involving special circumstances.[6]

Immigrant rights groups were quick to denounce the elimination of prosecutorial discretion. Some even critiqued the expanded definition of criminality, which now includes anyone who has been convicted or charged or who has committed a criminal offense. But no one critiqued the hierarchy itself.

Perhaps the immigrant justice movement ought to take a page from Trump's playbook. If Trump can include everyone in his priorities for deportation, why can't we include everyone in our priorities for justice?

INSTEAD, WHAT WE have is the "carve-out." We carve immigrants with certain criminal records out of the rights and protections we provide. We defend immigrants with timidity: protections for some, not all.

These limitations were built into the first local laws that attempted to safeguard immigrants. Some of the first modern examples of these laws date back to the 1980s, as the humanitarian crisis in Central America led thousands to flee the Northern Triangle for the United States. When the Reagan administration declined to recognize Central Americans as political refugees, the rise in deportations prompted churches to provide physical sanctuary to immigrants and highlight their plight. Confronted with these daily reminders of the harshness of immigration policies, localities began to question their involvement in immigration enforcement. Some cities began to pass what we now describe as sanctuary policies, limiting their information- and resource-sharing with federal immigration authorities.[7]

As important as these first forays into protective policies were, they universally contained a gaping exception. Places like San Francisco and New York City didn't want their local public benefits office turning over an undocumented immigrant to federal immigration agents. But they had no problem with their local police department turning over a criminal suspect for deportation. Local laws prohibiting information-sharing during this period almost always had an exception for law-enforcement purposes.[8] This happened at the same time that Congress directed federal immigration agents to use the criminal legal system to identify people for deportation.

Prominent immigrant rights organizations were slow to come to the defense of these so-called criminal aliens, choosing instead to make them bargaining chips in the federal fight for legalization for undocumented immigrants more broadly. America's Voice, for example, defended legalization policies for undocumented immigrants by suggesting that immigration officials should instead "focus on removing immigrants who are actually dangerous or who have committed serious crimes."[9] The National Immigration Forum similarly advocated for legalization as way of fulfilling America's "labor needs" while allowing "law enforcement agencies to focus on apprehending individuals with criminal records."[10] The danger of the "criminal alien" is so ingrained in the debate that even those who advocate for immigrant rights frame their messaging around whom to deport rather than why we deport our community members at all.[11]

At the grassroots level, however, the massive deportation dragnet forced a growing awareness of the harms of this approach. As more immigrants were deported, more communities organized to fight deportation policies, and more people became aware of the role of criminalization as a pipeline to deportation. A new sanctuary movement emerged, this one more inclusive than the last.

People began demanding change, and by 2011 several cities and counties with large immigrant populations had adopted laws limiting detainers in their local jails.[12] Some policies, like one in Cook County, Illinois, were sweeping; without reimbursement from the federal government, the county would not honor any detainers.[13] Others policies were incredibly narrow: a 2011 law in New York City prohibited correctional officers from honoring detainers but only in cases where the individual had a spotless record (i.e., no ongoing criminal case, no open warrant, no prior conviction, and no prior deportation order).[14]

Grassroots immigrant rights groups pushed for more inclusive framing. In 2013, the #Not1More campaign demanded a moratorium on all deportations.[15] ICE responded by pressuring cities to continue cooperating. But when it came to legal liability for unlawful detention on ICE detainers, localities were left holding the bag. Federal courts slowly began to issue orders that awarded monetary damages to the detained, concluding that localities had no probable cause for holding people.[16]

Organizers used the court victories to push for more progressive legislation. In 2013, the New York City Council expanded its protections, prohibiting correctional officers from honoring detainers in cases involving a specified set of minor past convictions and pending charges. This was an improvement over the previous law, but not by much—it continued to permit the city to honor detainers for many cases even though there was no lawful basis for detention. Advocates pressed on, and in 2014 the New York City Council finally passed legislation that included a judicial warrant requirement.[17]

It was a huge victory—but there was a catch. The new legislation included a list of 170 crimes for which the city's Department of Corrections would honor a detainer, but still only if a judicial warrant was presented.[18] ICE never obtained judicial warrants, so advocates concluded that the list wouldn't have any meaningful impact. Advocates brushed off the list as a political device to signal that New York did take public safety seriously while ensuring that no immigrant would be handed over to ICE without a warrant.

But as the fight over the New York Immigrant Family Unity Project would soon reveal, even the nominal existence of carve-outs had an impact. It reinforced the message that ICE's pursuit of deportation against some people with criminal records was justified in the name of public safety. By doing so, it made it easier for the country's first universal representation program for detained immigrants to come under attack.

||||||||

BY THE TIME Alex Lora met Talia Peleg, who was then with Brooklyn Defender Services, he was about to give up.[19] But Talia sat down with him in the jail and explained that there was a light at the end of the tunnel. She could try to get rid of his old conviction, which would give him a chance at eligibility for relief. She could try to get him out of detention, even if it meant filing a federal lawsuit. Alex didn't know what his chances were. But he knew he had a shot with someone in his corner. He hung on to that hope.

Alex became one of the first success stories from the New York Immigrant Family Unity Project. Shortly after his release from immigration jail, the New York City Council voted to provide $4.9 million in funding to support universal representation for all indigent people facing imprisonment by ICE in the jurisdiction.[20]

The Vera Institute of Justice, an early supporter of the program, studied its impact carefully. In 2017, it released its findings. Before the launch of the New York Immigrant Family Unity Project, 60 percent of detained immigrants in the city were unrepresented. Only 3 percent of unrepresented detained immigrants won their cases, and 18 percent of represented detained immigrants won their cases.[21] In the months since the project launched, 95 percent of detained immigrants were represented, with a remarkable 48 percent success rate for the project's clients.[22] By providing universal representation, New York City ensured that hundreds of people who would have been deported—like Alex Lora—were instead released from immigration jail, rejoining their families and winning their right to stay in the United States.

The time came to secure New York Immigrant Family Unity Project's place in the mayoral budget. It was not expected to be a hard sell. Voters had elected a progressive Democratic mayor, Bill de Blasio, who championed New York's role as a sanctuary city. Surely he would jump at the chance to ensure the long-term success of the project.

But in the spring of 2017, proponents of the project began to hear the first murmurings of dissent. City Council members began warning community leaders that funding for the project was in jeopardy. Sure enough, the commissioner for immigrant affairs announced that Mayor de Blasio would put the New York Immigrant Family Unity Project into the city budget but only with carve-outs. No one with a criminal history involving any of the 170 crimes in the city's detainer law would receive a public defender in immigration court.

Things got ugly quickly. In a packed City Council budget hearing that summer, public defenders and other advocates sat row to row, flashing unsexy but to-the-point "Due Process for All" signs every time mayoral officials defended the carve-outs. At first, advocates assumed de Blasio's position was motivated by fiscal constraints. But he soon made it clear that he saw this issue as a matter of public safety. People who commit "serious crimes that threaten public safety" don't deserve city funding for legal representation, a mayoral spokesperson said.[23]

Advocates cried foul. Pointing to the 170 crimes listed in the city detainer law, they noted, was disingenuous because the exclusions go into effect only if ICE shows up with a judicial warrant—something it never does. The exclusions were largely symbolic.

But de Blasio, in his quest to distinguish good immigrants from bad, gave the exclusions teeth by applying them to eligibility for free legal services. It was painful to watch—and not just for those who would be deprived of a lawyer.

Immigration advocates knew that once the New York Immigrant Family Unity Project ceased to be universal, even immigrants who did receive public defenders would be harmed. All the cases of people jailed by ICE in the region were heard by the same handful of judges. An unrepresented person, presenting an important legal issue to a judge without the assistance of a lawyer, can forever affect the way that judge views the legal issue. Once a judge issues a decision on a matter of law, it's hard to get that same judge to change his or her mind. That's why the power of universal representation rests with its universality. If every immigrant has a lawyer, the chances that any one immigrant will get an unfair shake decreases.

Those nuances were somehow lost on the mayor. But thankfully the City Council sided with the immigration advocates. City Council Speaker Melissa Mark-Viverito went toe-to-toe with Mayor de Blasio all the way through the budget process.[24] Still, the mayor insisted that the city would not fund representation for people whose crimes were on the list. But an anonymous donor stepped in to fill the gap, saving, for the time being, the universal nature of the country's first public defender program for detained immigrants.

Even with the donor stepping in, the mayor's pursuit of the carve-outs took its toll. In the uncertainty over the project's budget, an untold number of immigrants who were detained that

summer never received legal representation.[25] They became casu-
alties of a divisive debate in which the mayor was only too willing
to throw some immigrants under the bus.

||||||||

A PROGRAM LIKE the New York Immigrant Family Unity Project expresses a value: due process for all. It also represents a significant investment in our communities, giving people tools so
they can fight for their right to remain with us. But exclusions like
the one Mayor de Blasio proposed—which exist in many different forms of otherwise pro-immigrant policies across the country—diminish that value and the impact of the investment. We
give license to federal immigration officials to take our loved ones
away, naming them as public safety threats who do not deserve
due process. In doing so, we cycle power back into the crime-
based deportation machine and exhaust our best resources for
combating it.

Imagine what would have happened if no one stepped in to fill
the void Mayor de Blasio created. The data suggest an answer: the
deportation of as many as one in five people who otherwise would
have received an attorney.[26] To those who believe these individuals are dangerous, that's one in five fewer people threatening our
communities. But to those of us who work with immigrants with
criminal records, that's one in five fewer people left to fight the
system.

Some of the fiercest immigrant rights leaders in the movement
have criminal records. People like Ravi Ragbir and Jean Montrevil, leaders of the New Sanctuary Coalition in New York City,
which mobilizes faith communities for immigrants. Or Alejan-
dra Pablos, a fiery Arizona-based activist who is organizing communities around immigrant and reproductive rights. I think of
Ny Nourn, a California activist with the Survived and Punished
Coalition, Asian Prisoner Support Committee, and Advancing
Justice-Asian Law Caucus, who advocates on behalf of criminalized survivors of violence. And Khalil Cumberbatch, chief strate-
gist for New Yorkers United for Justice, a leader in the movement

for criminal legal reform. Their experience with the criminal legal system didn't make them threats; it made them assets in intersectional movements for social justice.

Carve-outs carve up our communities. We have already lost many great leaders, Jean Montrevil among them, to deportation. And what rationale do federal immigration agents use to justify these actions? Public safety. In other words, the exact same rationale that the mayor of New York City used reflexively to deny justice to people in our communities.

Many people in power, Mayor de Blasio included, want to do right by immigrants. One of the most important things they can do is adopt proposals that avoid the politics of division. Rather than divide our communities into good and bad, deserving and undeserving, truly pro-immigrant policies invest in the whole community. They rest upon universal values—values that unite rather than divide. Like due process for all.

||||||

LONGTIME IMMIGRANT RIGHTS activists understand these principles. In particular, activists who work in intersectional spaces across race, ethnicity, religion, and gender lines have done much to redefine sanctuary to be more inclusive of those who are often targets for state violence, including Black, Latinx, indigenous, LGBT, and Muslim people, to name a few, citizen and immigrant alike. They are the ones who are pushing for a more inclusive vision of public safety. It starts with proposing immigrant rights policies without carve-outs. But it doesn't end there.

For starters, community activists seek to end the use of the criminal legal system as a pipeline for deportation. Programs like Secure Communities ensure that this pipeline begins as soon as a person is arrested. As long as data-sharing programs are in place along with broken windows policing and other racially biased criminal enforcement, there can be no sanctuary. Data sharing is the way ICE targets people like Alex Lora, a green card holder who was flagged for deportation only because of a years-old drug arrest.

Ending Secure Communities at the federal level would go a long way toward breaking the chains that bind bad criminal enforcement policies locally with bad immigration policies federally. The program has only been around since 2008 and is something that a future president could end without Congress. President Obama reformed the program in 2014, replacing it briefly with the Priority Enforcement Program, which limited the circumstances in which an arrest would trigger an immigration detainer. But because the new program collected data for every person arrested and fingerprinted at the local level and issued some detainer requests—literally asking for unconstitutional detention—it was hardly real reform.

As long as programs like Secure Communities exist, and criminal records are in any way, shape, or form used as a proxy for deportability, the fate of the immigrant rights movement will remain intimately tied to the fate of criminal law reform. Local efforts to end stop-and-frisk policies and broken windows policing; to decriminalize acts that disproportionately target communities of color, LGBT communities, and poor communities; to change the way we handle harm overall—these are intersectional efforts that can move the needle for immigrants and citizens alike.

We see these trends in Chicago, where organizers have long been working to end carve-outs while pushing for real sanctuary. Although Cook County had one of the most expansive anti-detainer policies in the country, Chicago adopted a policy that carved out large groups of people from its protections—allowing the Chicago Police Department to hold them unconstitutionally for immigration agents to pick them up. Those groups included anyone who has a felony conviction or is a defendant in a felony case, anyone who has an open criminal warrant, and anyone who is a "known gang member" by admission or database.[27] The policy contained no additional universal judicial warrant requirement to soften the blow from these exceptions.

For many organizers who work with immigrant communities in Chicago, dropping the carve-outs to the policy has been a top ask for years. But it's not the only one. During the Trump administration, organizations like Black Youth Project 100, Mijente, and Organized Communities Against Deportation have come together not only to push to amend the welcoming policy but to tackle broader issues—from rampant police brutality to Chicago's notorious gang database. When ICE arrested Wilmer Catalan-Ramirez based on the Chicago Police Department's erroneous inclusion of him in its gang database, organizers took aim at the database as a whole. The effort became part of their broader Campaign to Expand Sanctuary, centering the shared harms that Black and Latinx people, regardless of citizenship status, face under long-standing policing practices.[28]

This kind of intersectional organizing works. When organizers from Comunidad Colectiva in North Carolina took aim at the Mecklenburg County Sheriff Office's long-standing 287(g) agreement to enforce immigration laws during the 2018 county sheriff election, they didn't make it a one-issue election. Instead, they joined with Charlotte Uprising and the Southeast Asian Coalition to raise issues about solitary confinement of youth and the restoration of in-person visitation at the county jail.[29] Electing a new sheriff meant finding an elected official willing to support a broader platform for reform.

Broader movements to reform criminal law and policy—particularly those aimed at decriminalization—are among those with the greatest potential to reduce harm to immigrants. Reforming state and local drug law and policy, for example, is a major priority for many communities of color, which have been disproportionately targeted by the war on drugs for years. But such reforms also have the potential to help immigrants, who have been similarly targeted and who face the double punishment of deportation. Legalizing drug use—truly treating it as a public health issue rather than as a crime—achieves both these goals. And although marijuana legalization once felt like an impossibility, several legalization campaigns have been successful and may open the door for broader drug reform.

But not all drug reform proposals protect immigrants. Some proposals would lower criminal penalties, allow for expungements of old records, or expand access to court-mandated treatment. These are laudable changes. But because the definition of "conviction" is so sweeping in immigration law, and because a conviction for a violation of any law relating to controlled substances can trigger deportation consequences, these steps do not necessarily protect immigrants from deportation.

The good news is that, with a careful eye to the federal deportation consequences for drug offenses, reforms can be written in a way that reaches citizens and immigrants alike. Full legalization works. But even measures short of that can help immigrants: summons reform that avoids fingerprinted arrests, treatment alternatives that divert people from the criminal court process pre-plea, expanded opportunities to erase old convictions on legal defects—these are steps that can make a huge difference for immigrants and citizens. Organizations such as the Immigrant Defense Project are advising policymakers on how to do decriminalization the right way so that immigrants are not left behind.

The fact that we have to be so careful about how we craft criminal law reform points to the huge gap in access to second chances for immigrants. At the federal level, a change to the definition of "conviction" that honors state and local choices to expunge or erase records for any reason—not just legal defects— would be a huge leap forward in equitable criminal law reform. This kind of amendment, which has on occasion shown up in comprehensive immigration reform packages over the years but has never been enacted, should be included in comprehensive criminal reform packages as well. It's a small, eminently reasonable change. If a state or locality wants to erase a conviction because a person has demonstrated rehabilitation, why should federal immigration agents get to swoop in and banish that person from the very same community that is trying to ensure that she can stay?

The same goes for pardon power. Federal immigration officials recognize that a full and unconditional pardon can erase some immigration consequences. But some categories are inexplicably left off the list. I've represented clients who have received pardons for drug crimes, erasing the consequences of a drug trafficking aggravated felony but leaving the controlled substance consequences intact under immigration law. These pardons can still be helpful because those who are lawful permanent residents may now be eligible for relief from deportation. But why should they have to go through the deportation process at all? A pardon should do what it's supposed to do: erase all consequences.

Federal law should be amended to clarify that pardons of any kind should erase all immigration consequences for that offense. Until that happens, it's on the states to expand their own pardon power to do what they can. Some states offer full and unconditional pardons under extremely limited circumstances. Other states offer full and unconditional pardons without exceptions but rarely exercise that power. Broadening pardon power and exercising it more regularly would help citizens and immigrants alike. Forgiveness and redemption are powerful values, and they should include everyone.

ıııııı

WHEN NEW YORK City gave Alex Lora a lawyer, it opened a world of possibilities for him. It also gave him the one thing he desperately needed: hope. Before the city stepped in, Alex was close to signing his deportation order. That's what immigration jail did to him. It is why the abolition of immigration imprisonment is such an important step in disrupting the crime-based deportation machine.

Alex still remembers what it felt like to be arrested so publicly on the street in Gabrielle's neighborhood in Queens, handcuffed and driven to a processing center, questioned and harassed, and finally jailed across the river in Hudson County Correctional Facility. At the jail, guards stripped him and bagged his clothes and possessions, handed him a uniform, and led him to the dorm where he would bunk with dozens of other men. The depressed, haggard looks on their faces—and the constant sound of crying at night—were enough to extinguish what little hope Alex had of returning to his fiancée or son again.

Because of his drug conviction, Alex was subjected to mandatory detention—imprisonment without the right to a bond hearing. When he was arrested years ago, he had gotten a bail hearing in the criminal legal system right away and never had to spend time in jail. As he quickly learned, the deportation system is different. Even though he was facing a civil deportation charge for the same drug crime that had led to probation without jail time, he could spend months and even years in immigration jail if he chose to fight his deportation.

Within two weeks of detention at the Hudson County Correctional Facility, Alex was ready to sign out. His son had been put into kinship foster care. His mother and fiancée were inconsolable. Deportation officers told him that he'd be deportable no matter what he did. Day after day he did nothing but lose himself in these thoughts, staring up at the peeling paint, pushing away the inedible food, and thinking he could take it no more. But then Alex met his lawyer, who convinced him that there was a way to fight. Five and a half months later, Alex was released on bond. It was a nightmare, but he was finally free.

Eighty-six percent of the people in civil immigration custody in this country don't have a lawyer fighting in their corner.[30] The system is designed to isolate people from their families, legal services, and the outside world. It is designed to make people like Alex give up on their right to be here. It is emblematic of the destructive role of mass incarceration in this country.

Ensuring that every imprisoned person has a lawyer would give them all a fighting chance. This is a minimum step toward expanding access to justice. So too is ending mandatory detention—every immigrant, at a minimum, deserves the right to a bond hearing. These are key components to build the kind of procedural justice that is sorely lacking when immigrants are locked away.

But these reforms are just placeholders until we can achieve the real goal: the abolition of immigration imprisonment. Immigration imprisonment—which, by definition, is a form of preventative civil incarceration—serves no legitimate, nonpunitive purpose in the law. It felt like punishment to Alex because that's exactly what it was. And it was not just punishment for him but for his little boy, his fiancée, their entire family, and their community.

Years ago, community groups felt uncertain about calling for an end to immigration detention. They wondered how they could advocate for the release of people with serious criminal records. Perhaps the more politically prudent course would be to limit their demand to the right to a bond hearing or to focus on reforming the conditions inside immigration jails and prisons.

But year after year, these groups watched as their calls for modest reforms left greater space to expand the imprisonment system as a whole. In response to some of the older, more cautious advocacy, the Obama administration announced sweeping reforms to ensure civil conditions in immigration custody. To achieve this, however, the administration contracted with the same private prison corporations that had held people in carceral settings generally.[31]

The number of people in custody skyrocketed. As the Obama administration was quick to point out, many were "criminal aliens." But community organizations were less willing to take those records at face value. Behind every "criminal alien" was someone like Alex, a hardworking father who had put his past behind him and was caring for his family. Imprisoning him years after his conviction didn't make anyone safer; it simply tore his family apart.

Community groups are uncertain no longer. Umbrella organizations like Detention Watch Network, which has been bringing community organizations together for years to advocate for imprisonment, are unequivocal. There is no way to reform immigration imprisonment that will make it anything less than a cage, and caging people for immigration purposes is unacceptable.

To accomplish such a broad goal will take hard work. At a national level, the federal budget for immigration imprisonment has expanded steadily since the 1980s to more than $2.8 billion in 2019. This money is used to imprison more than fifty thousand people on any given day. Congress holds the purse strings, making it a target for political pressure to defund imprisonment. At critical times, Detention Watch Network and its members have been successful in reining in excess. But so far no one has been able to get Congress to reverse course and seriously downsize its financial support for locking up immigrants. It will take a massive campaign, which groups like Detention Watch Network are trying to build, to make that happen.

On the other side of the funding stream are the local counties and private prison corporations that contract with ICE to imprison immigrants. These entities, in the business for the profit or revenue boost, have strong incentives to keep detention going. But each is vulnerable.

Counties are answerable to their constituents. In Hudson County, New Jersey, where Alex was imprisoned, concerned residents have been organizing with their local county executives to drop their ICE contracts. Reports about practices ranging from inadequate medical care to the rampant use of solitary confinement have raised serious questions about how these jails are run. And when public attention intensified following reports of President Trump's family separation policy, the demand was no longer to improve conditions but to drop the ICE contract entirely. After an outpouring of protest, Hudson County agreed to change its contract with ICE from an indefinite term to a two-year term, allowing for the possibility of dropping or renegotiating the contract—and providing an opening for more organizing.[32]

States also have a role to play. In California, groups like the Immigrant Legal Resource Center and Freedom for Immigrants mobilized Governor Jerry Brown to sign the Dignity Not Detention Act in 2017. The act placed a moratorium on detention contracts in California, prohibiting counties from expanding beds or entering into new contracts with the federal government or private prison corporations for the purposes of civil immigration detention. It also required public notice of land conveyances, ensured that facilities are covered by open public records law, and authorized the state attorney general to inspect all detention facilities.[33] Subsequent legislation banned private prisons, and soon other states, like Illinois and Washington, adapted versions of its model.[34]

Reform at the federal level is not without hope. Just before the 2016 election of President Trump, both the Bureau of Prisons and the Homeland Security Advisory Council concluded that it was time to roll back reliance on private prisons.[35] Because approximately 73 percent of immigration jails and prisons are privately run, a move away from private prisons would mark a dramatic scaling down of immigration detention.[36] President Trump rejected these policies after taking office, embracing private prisons. But that position can easily be reversed.

The Bureau of Prisons' position was particularly remarkable because it applied to federal prisons, and the only federal prisons that contracted with private prison corporations were "criminal alien requirement" prisons: those designed to hold immigrants on crimes of migration, like illegal entry and reentry. Over the past several years, people convicted of federal immigration crimes became the majority of people incarcerated within the federal system, outpacing even those with drug crimes. Ending their incarceration in private prisons could have marked the beginning of the end of mass incarceration in the federal criminal system. The Bureau of Prisons was on board in 2016, and it can be again.

We collectively recognize the harms that come with mass incarceration. As we make strides toward scaling back mass incarceration, we must include immigrants in that struggle.

‖‖‖‖

THE ELEPHANT IN the room is the enormity of criminal prosecutions for migration crimes. Over the past several years, the criminal prosecution of people for immigration-related offenses, particularly illegal entry and reentry, has skyrocketed even as drug prosecutions have dropped. Illegal entry and reentry prosecutions are propping up the federal prison system.

These prosecutions rely on federal laws that have been on the books in one form or another since 1929, when White nationalists demanded a tool to punish and deter Mexican immigrants from entering the United States. Although nominally colorblind in application, modern programs like Operation Streamline ensure their discriminatory and aggressive application at the southern border, just as the original drafters intended. Operation Streamline, which requires complicity by Border Patrol, US Attorney's Offices, US marshals, the federal court system, and ICE, has led to mass hearings where as many as eighty people plead guilty in a single setting. The criminal records they receive not only set the stage for quick deportation in many cases; they also ensure that any subsequent attempt to return to the United States will result in felony charges, a lengthier prison sentence, and fewer avenues to be reunited with family or protected from persecution abroad.

Operation Streamline was further weaponized in 2018 when the Trump administration used it to separate criminally prosecuted parents from their minor children. When public protest of this cruel tactic reached a fever pitch, and after immigrant rights groups sued the administration for violating long-standing agreements governing the incarceration of children, President Trump relented. But, he argued, this was all the more reason to imprison whole families. And the zero tolerance criminal prosecutions of adults traveling without children continued.

Advocates responded largely by attempting to maintain protections for children, reunite separated families, and fight family and child imprisonment. In other words, faced with an onslaught against basic human rights, advocates were forced to stand their ground.

Pushing the movement forward requires more. It requires the immediate abolition of Operation Streamline—a purely administrative program that DHS and the Department of Justice could end immediately without congressional action. But ending Operation Streamline through executive action would not prevent the next administration from reviving a similarly discriminatory and draconian program. That will take an act of Congress. Congress should repeal 8 US Code 1325 and 8 US Code 1326—the illegal entry and reentry statutes within the Immigration and Nationality Act. Criminalizing migration was racist back in 1929 when it was initially placed on the books. It remains racist today. It enables a system of discriminatory and harsh prosecutions that fuel our system of mass incarceration even as we recognize the time has come to end it.

‖‖‖‖‖

ENDING IMMIGRATION IMPRISONMENT, civil and criminal, dismantling the arrest-to-deportation pipeline, eliminating criminal immigration offenses—where does this leave agencies like ICE and CBP? Admittedly, with very little to do. And there is nothing wrong with that. Federal agencies come and go. The predecessors of ICE and CBP were created to police our borders in order to exclude and deport people of color. Their modern versions, reorganized under the banner of homeland security, achieve the same results but on overdrive, with millions deported to Mexico, Central America, the Caribbean, Southeast Asia, Africa, and beyond.

Meaningful change requires more than reorganizing the agencies, as some have proposed. It starts by recognizing that immigration imprisonment and deportation do not enhance public safety. They destroy it, harming people and families while distracting us from the hard work that comes with safeguarding communities. This doesn't mean that there would be no laws to enforce. Immigrants in general, and America as a whole, may certainly benefit from orderly processes by which newcomers are welcomed and supported. Interior enforcement, then, would become about facilitating immigrants' access to rights and services. Border enforcement similarly would become about humanitarian aid.

This is far from a radical vision. These changes would simply place immigration on equal footing with other areas of administrative governance. We do not typically need an armed force to enforce administrative laws and policies. Nor would we need an armed force to address those parts of our immigration system that have been thrust into our criminal system.

This would change the face of criminal prosecutions as well. Without border prosecutions, the workload of the Department of Justice's Criminal Division, like CBP, would dramatically drop. As groups like Mijente have advocated, this would open up space to reimagine the Department of Justice's role altogether.[37] What if the Criminal Division protected people from abuses and exploitation?

Such a change in focus certainly would be more in line with the Department of Justice's core mission than what it has done in recent years. Its capacity for cruelty was on full display in 2018, when it fully participated in President Trump's family separation program by engaging in thousands of zero tolerance prosecutions. Amid that debacle, the department also found time to prosecute humanitarian aid workers at No More Deaths for leaving water in the desert so people would not die on the journey north. That the prosecutions came after the aid workers released footage of Border Patrol agents emptying water containers only added to the indignity of these prosecutions.[38]

Putting the "justice" back in the Department of Justice does not diminish the rule of law; it restores it.

⸻

ON JANUARY 4, 2018, Alex Lora finally received his day in court. His legal team, led by Talia Peleg, felt cautiously confident. It had been more than three years since his release from immigration jail. The first thing Alex did when he was released was reunite with his little boy and start the process of regaining legal custody. He married Gabrielle. He found work in construction and joined his local union. He returned to the hardworking life he had before he had been detained.

No purpose would have been served by his deportation. If anything, his family and community would have been irreparably harmed. The immigration judge agreed, granting his cancellation application the same day at his hearing. ICE did not appeal. It was as if everyone understood that deportation was pointless here.

And not a moment too soon. The next month, the Supreme Court overturned the decision that had secured Alex's release, concluding that Congress had written a statute that did not require the bond hearing he received. Had the Supreme Court's decision come earlier, or had we been unable to secure the earlier release, Alex might have been imprisoned throughout his fight to challenge his deportation.

Had Alex remained in immigration jail, it is difficult to predict what would have happened. Alex sometimes thinks back to those nights in the jail, when all signs pointed toward deportation. When the overwhelming feeling of hopelessness would settle in. When the voice in his head repeated the callous admonition of the ICE officers: "Sign your deportation papers. End this." What if he had given up?

And what if he had no access to a hearing to cancel his deportation? That was at the core of the Fix '96 campaigns—restoring discretion in the immigration system for all, not just for some. Another reform at the federal legislative level that falls in the category of the very least we should do.

For too long, the politics of fear have dominated our vision for justice. We are ready for a new chapter in the fight for immigrant rights in this country. Where we embrace people like Alex. Where we champion his right to stay in his home, with his family, in America. Where we stand by our values, knowing that nothing justifies the destruction of the life he has built here for himself and his family.

It is time for inclusive immigrant justice, and it starts by disavowing the criminalization of our communities.

EPILOGUE

A FEW WEEKS AFTER PRESIDENT TRUMP TOOK OFFICE, immigrant rights activist Ravi Ragbir stood in a plaza outside a federal immigration building in New York, speaking to a large crowd. He paused, searching for the right words to explain how it felt to face the constant threat of deportation. It was like living, he said, under a guillotine.

Someone from the crowd shouted, "We are with you, Ravi!" Ravi nodded, his emotions overcoming him.

A year later, Ravi would be back in that same plaza, having barely survived ICE's attempted deportation. An even larger crowd had gathered to celebrate their collective victory in securing his freedom. "We Are All Ravi," their signs proclaimed. "You Can't Deport a Movement."

The immigrant rights movement has come a long way from where we were a decade ago, when the most common sign at rallies bore a different statement: "We Are Not Criminals." Our messaging back then often left out those like Ravi who had contact with the criminal legal system. Three million deportations under President Obama demonstrated the pitfalls of dividing ourselves into "good" and "bad" immigrants. But it was the rise of President Trump that truly brought people together to fight the criminalization of all immigrants.

Where will the movement be after Trump? The guillotine of deportation will pass into the hands of a different executioner. Is our condemnation about the man or the deportation machine?

Politicians have faltered on this score. In 2018, a small cadre of Democrats put forth a bill that would have disbanded ICE. But when the Republican House leadership sought to bring the bill to a vote, Democrats withdrew their support. Democratic leadership did not want a roll call of where their party stood on abolishing ICE in an election year. The House instead passed a resolution praising the work of ICE officers, with the majority of Democrats voting a tepid "present" instead of no. It was easier to take aim at the president's anti-immigrant rhetoric than it was to try to dismantle the machinery of deportation itself.[1]

Nor have politicians made progress in addressing the laws that fuel the machine. During the Democratic primary debates in 2019, a growing list of presidential hopefuls recognized the necessity of repealing the laws that criminalize illegal entry and reentry. In response, pundits—including former immigration officials who came out of the woodwork—condemned the move, urging the Democratic Party to focus its criticism on Trump's policies of family separation rather than on the laws that make such policies possible.[2]

But there is reason to believe that the tide is turning. These conversations, about abolishing ICE or repealing the laws that criminalize illegal entry and reentry, had not so much as grazed the mainstream debate before. The credit belongs to movement leaders—people who have put their safety and security in this country on the line to expose the evils of the crime-based deportation machine. Their work has been effective, so much so that they have become the new priorities for persecution by the Trump administration. Scores of immigrant activists like Ravi found themselves targeted for imprisonment and deportation after speaking out against ICE.[3] Humanitarian aid workers faced criminal prosecution for giving people water and medical attention in the desert.[4] Lawyers, journalists, and clergy were detained and questioned after exposing the harsh treatment of refugees who were prevented from seeking asylum at the US-Mexico border.[5] These people have been targeted because the Trump administration knows that the deportation machinery operates best in the shadows.

After Trump, we will be tested. Some may be tempted to declare victory and return to the days of protecting the "good" immigrants and deporting the "bad" ones, more comfortable with the people who are drawing the lines. Some will be willing to accept the rhetoric of public safety as a justification for deportation if it comes from a different voice, even as deportation continues to threaten the safety of the public.

America has a collective responsibility to resist a return to the status quo. If we repeat the mistakes of the past, the cycle of criminalization will continue to divide and conquer our communities. If we recommit ourselves to ensuring justice for all, we can break free from this cycle and finally dismantle the machine.

ACKNOWLEDGMENTS

I must begin by thanking the many individuals whose wisdom and resiliency inspired this book, and whose stories are interwoven in these pages. To Ravi, Lefty, Alex, and my many clients who shared their stories under names not their own: thank you.

I also wish to thank Families for Freedom, New Sanctuary Coalition, and the Immigrant Defense Project, three organizations whose leaders have especially shaped my views on the injustices in the immigration and criminal legal systems. I thank the many organizers, activists, faith leaders, and lawyers affiliated with these groups and groups across the country who continue to push for a more inclusive immigrant rights movement. I am similarly indebted to the Soros Justice Fellowship, which gave me my start as a young lawyer and influenced the way I see the world through the expertise of leaders directly affected by mass incarceration.

I express deep and humble gratitude to my colleagues at New York University School of Law's Immigrant Rights Clinic: Nancy Morawetz, Jessica Rofé, and Noelia Rodriguez. I couldn't imagine a more brilliant, passionate, and supportive set of colleagues. I also thank the many other incredible advocates who, from deep in the trenches of deportation defense, have co-taught the clinic during my time teaching there, including Sarah Gillman, Ruben Loyo, Talia Peleg, and Jessica Swensen. I am dearly grateful for the support of NYU Law School's Dean Trevor Morrison and our Faculty Research Committee. This book would not have been possible without this support.

Many of the stories I describe in this book involve the beautiful and creative advocacy of law students. I thank all of the amazing students whom I have had the pleasure of teaching since I began teaching at NYU in 2008. I want to give a special thank you to the then-students who worked with me on behalf of the clients whose stories I profiled in the book. While I avoided identifying those students in each story, at times to help protect the identity of our clients, I wish to collectively thank them here: Elizabeth Carlson, Brittany Castle, Carolyn Corrado, Cody Cutting, Colleen Duffy, Semuteh Freeman, Tsion Gurmu, Kevin Herrera, Rebecca Hufstader, Wonjun Lee, Ruben Loyo, Nunu Luo, Kulsoom Naqvi, Dami Obaro, Josh Occhiogrosso-Schwartz, Rhiya Trivedi, Connie Tse, Martha Saunders, Luis Angel Reyes Savalza, Meredythe Ryan, and Samah Mcgona Sisay. And there are many more former students whose ideas and hard work helped get us to the points in time described in the book. I am in awe of the entire NYU Immigrant Rights Clinic community, past and present, and the lengths they have gone to leave no stone unturned for the people we represent and work alongside.

My own teachers and mentors have given me the courage to take on these issues over the years. I am especially grateful to Derrick Bell (in memoriam), Nancy Morawetz, Manny Vargas, Devesh Kapur, Judge Kermit Lipez, and so many others who have mentored me over the years at various stages of my education and career. It is a lifelong goal to emulate their guidance through my own teaching and mentorship.

Once I decided to write this book—during a moment of outraged disbelief at the state of the progressive world in 2017—I needed the encouragement of those more familiar with the process of writing and publishing a book of this nature. I am grateful to the many people who took the time to give me their frank advice, including Jane Isay, Deepa Iyer, Erin Murphy, Tony Thompson, and Kenji Yoshino. I am also grateful for the editorial assistance of Bailey Georges in the early stages of this project.

Thank you to my agent, Gail Ross, who put this proposal in the hands of the wonderful Katy O'Donnell at Bold Type Books of Hachette Book Group. I couldn't be more grateful to Katy and the entire team who made this possible, including Johanna Dickson, Lindsay Fradkoff, Evan Malmgren, Brandon Proia, Mark Sorkin, and Melissa Veronesi. Your belief in this project sustained me through the process.

This book, more than two years in the making, was supported by the excellent research assistance of Juan Bedoya, Whitney Braunstein, Elizabeth McLean, Ryan Mendías, Meena Oberdick, and Gerardo Romo. It was also informed by writing that I've done over the years, including law review articles and essays that I have published with the University of California–Davis School of Law, the NYU School of Law, the University of Chicago School of Law, and others. I have explored many of these themes and stories in Supreme Court amicus briefing on prolonged immigration imprisonment, co-written with Anthony Enriquez, Terry Ding, Rachel Levenson, Ryan Mendías, and Jessica Rofé.

My dear circle of friends cheered me on throughout this process, and I am grateful for all of them. I must share a special thank you to those who bravely read my first full manuscript: Mizue Aizeki, Amy Gottlieb, Ian Head, and Nancy Morawetz. I am indebted to them for their insightful feedback, given so generously even in the midst of all that they do in the struggle. The flaws in the book are, of course, my own.

Most importantly, I thank my loving family. I thank my parents, Mala and Dilip Das, who crossed oceans to make America our home. I owe them everything for what they have done to give me the opportunity to thrive here. I thank my wonderful husband,

Nafees Tejani, for his love and support for this project and my life's calling. I thank our extended family: Shamik, Anne, Caleb, Evelyn, Yas, Ba (in memoriam), Nabyl, Emily, Aria, Rafiq, and so many more who have supported my endeavors over the years.

For Isha and Naya, my two incredible daughters, I save my deepest gratitude and the final word. They are my greatest blessing. They inspire me to believe that a more loving and compassionate world is within reach. Time after time, my daughters give me hope.

NOTES

PROLOGUE

1. The Sentencing Project, Americans with Criminal Records, November 2015, www.sentencingproject.org/wp-content/uploads/2015/11/Americans-with-Criminal -Records-Poverty-and-Opportunity-Profile.pdf (noting that one in three adults in America has been arrested by age twenty-three).

2. Mark Joseph Stern, "The George W. Bush Advice Obama Should Have Taken," *Slate*, January 5, 2017, slate.com/news-and-politics/2017/01/obama-didnt-follow -bushs-pardon-advice-bad-move.html.

3. Rebecca Morin, "A Quick History of Trump's Evolving Justifications for a Border Wall," *Politico*, January 8, 2019, www.politico.com/story/2019/01/08 /trumps-evolving-reasons-border-wall-1088046; Richard Wolf, "Travel Ban Lex- icon: From Candidate Donald Trump's Campaign Promises to President Trump's Tweets," *USA Today*, April 24, 2018, www.usatoday.com/story/news/politics/2018 /04/24/travel-ban-donald-trump-campaign-promises-president-tweets/542504002; "Donald Trump: Deport 'Bad Hombres'—Video," *The Guardian*, October 20, 2016, www.theguardian.com/us-news/video/2016/oct/20/donald-trump-bad-hombres -us-presidential-debate-las-vegas-video.

4. Muzaffar Chishti, Sarah Pierce, and Jessica Bolter, "The Obama Record on Depor- tations: Deporter in Chief or Not?" *Migration Policy Institute*, January 26, 2017, www .migrationpolicy.org/article/obama-record-deportations-deporter-chief-or-not.

5. Barack Obama, "Remarks by the President in Address to the Nation on Immigra- tion," The White House, Office of the Press Secretary, November 20, 2014, obamawhite house.archives.gov/the-press-office/2014/11/20/remarks-President-address-nation -immigration.

6. *Id.*

7. Beth Fertig, "Arrests and Protests Follow Detention of an Immigrant Activist," *WNYC News*, New York Public Radio (WNYC), January 11, 2018, www.wnyc.org/story /arrests-and-protests-follow-detention-immigrant-activist.

8. Ragbir v. Sessions III, No. 18-cv-236 (KBF) (SDNY January 29, 2018), at 1–2.

9. "Devil in the Details," *On the Media*, New York Public Radio (WNYC), February 15, 2018, www.wnycstudios.org/story/on-the-media-2018-02-16.

10. Jake Offenhartz, "Ravi Ragbir Was Freed by the Movement He Helped Build," *The Nation*, January 29, 2018, www.thenation.com/article/ravi-ragbir-was-freed-by-the -movement-he-helped-build/.

11. Advancement Project et al., to Speaker Pelosi, Majority Leader Hoyer, and Minority Leader McCarthy, June 19, 2019, www.searac.org/wp-content/uploads/2019/06 /Open-Letter-to-Congress-FINAL.pdf.

12. The history of this transformation is described in detail in Chapter 3.

13. The origins of the immigration system's reliance on criminality are described in detail in Chapter 2.

14. Migration Policy Institute, "U.S. Spends More on Immigration Enforcement Than on FBI, DEA, Secret Service and All Other Federal Criminal Law Enforcement Agencies Combined," press release, January 7, 2013, www.migrationpolicy.org/news/us-spends -more-immigration-enforcement-fbi-dea-secret-service-all-other-federal-criminal-law.

15. Nicholas Kulish, Caitlin Dickerson, and Ron Nixon, "Immigration Agents Discover New Freedom to Deport Under Trump," *New York Times*, February 25, 2017, www.nytimes.com/2017/02/25/us/ice-immigrant-deportations-trump.html.

16. *Id.*; Julie Hirschfield Davis and Michael D. Shear, "How Trump Came to Enforce a Practice of Separating Migrant Families," *New York Times*, June 16, 2018, www.nytimes .com/2018/06/16/us/politics/family-separation-trump.html; Anne Flaherty, "More Than 260 Migrants Died Trying to Cross the US Southern Border: Report," *ABC News*, December 14, 2018, abcnews.go.com/International/260-migrants-died-cross -us-southern-border-report/story?id=59832675; David Nakamura, "Trump Administration Announces End of Immigration Protection Program for 'Dreamers,'" *Washington Post*, September 5, 2017, www.washingtonpost.com/news/post-politics/wp/2017/09 /05/trump-administration-announces-end-of-immigration-protection-program-for -dreamers.

CHAPTER 1: THE "CRIMINAL ALIENS" AMONG US

1. Dana Leigh Marks, "Immigration Judge: Death Penalty Cases in a Traffic Court Setting," CNN, June 26, 2014, www.cnn.com/2014/06/26/opinion/immigration-judge -broken-system/index.html.

2. Ingrid V. Eagly and Steven Shafer, "A National Study of Access to Counsel in Immigration Court," *University of Pennsylvania Law Review* 164, no. 1 (December 2015): 1–90, scholarship.law.upenn.edu/cgi/viewcontent.cgi?article=9502&context =penn_law_review (14 percent of detained individuals nationwide have counsel); Peter L. Markowitz et al., New York Immigration Representation Study, *Accessing Justice: The Availability and Adequacy of Counsel in Immigration Proceedings*, December 2011, www.ils.ny.gov/files/Accessing%20Justice.pdf (comparing rate of success in cases with and without counsel).

3. American Immigration Council, "Removal Without Recourse: The Growth of Summary Deportations from the United States," April 28, 2014, www.american immigrationcouncil.org/research/removal-without-recourse-growth-summary -deportations-united-states.

4. 8 USC. § 1101(a)(3).

5. US Immigration and Customs Enforcement, *FY 2018 ICE Enforcement and Removal Operations Report*, www.ice.gov/doclib/about/offices/ero/pdf/eroFY2018 Report.pdf.

6. "Immigration Now 52 Percent of All Federal Criminal Prosecutions," TracReports, November 28, 2016, trac.syr.edu/tracreports/crim/446.

7. Michelle Alexander, *The New Jim Crow* (New York: New Press, 2012), 47–53.

8. *Dillingham Commission Report, Immigration and Crime*, vol. 36, 1911, 1.

9. *Wickersham Commission Report, Enforcement of Deportation Laws*, 1931, 171.

10. Herbert Hoover, State of the Union address, December 2, 1930.

11. Alex Wagner, "America's Forgotten History of Illegal Deportations," *The Atlantic*, March 6, 2017, www.theatlantic.com/politics/archive/2017/03/americas-brutal -forgotten-history-of-illegal-deportations/517971.

12. "Police to Round Up Criminal Aliens Here; New Bureau to Get Evidence for Mulrooney," *New York Times*, December 20, 1930, 1.

13. "Drop the I-Word," Applied Research Centre, accessed August 8, 2019, www .raceforward.org/practice/tools/drop-i-word.

14. The legislative changes made in 1988 are discussed in greater detail in Chapter 3.

15. The legislative changes made in 1996 are discussed in greater detail in Chapter 3.

16. Lopez v. Gonzales, 549 US 47 (2006).

17. Carachuri-Rosendo v. Holder, 560 US 563 (2010).

18. Alexander, *supra*, 12–15.

CHAPTER 2: ORIGINS OF CONTROL

1. Mijente, "After DACA Announcement, Immigrants Name Jeff Sessions a Living Monument to the Confederacy," press release, September 5, 2017, www.latino rebels.com/2017/09/05/after-daca-announcement-immigrants-name-jeff-sessions -a-living-monument-to-the-confederacy/.

2. Sharon LaFreniere and Matt Apuzzo, "Jeff Sessions, a Lifelong Outsider, Finds the Inside Track," *New York Times*, January 8, 2017, www.nytimes.com/2017/01/08/us /politics/jeff-sessions-attorney-general.html.

3. United States Department of Justice, "Attorney General Sessions Delivers Remarks on DACA," US Department of Justice Office of Public Affairs, September 5, 2017, www .justice.gov/opa/speech/attorney-general-sessions-delivers-remarks-daca.

4. Julie Zuzamer and Keith McMillan, "Sessions Cites Bible Passage Used to Defend Slavery in Defense of Separating Immigrant Families," *Washington Post*, June 15, 2018, www.washingtonpost.com/news/acts-of-faith/wp/2018/06/14/jeff-sessions-points-to -the-bible-in-defense-of-separating-immigrant-families.

5. Susan Carroll and Lomi Kriel, "Missing Volunteer Pulled from Cypress Creek," *Houston Chronicle*, September 3, 2014.

6. Act of March 26, 1790, ch. 3, I Stat. 103.

7. Peter Schrag, *Not Fit for Our Society: Immigration and Nativism in America* (Berkeley: University of California Press, 2010).

8. Kunal Parker, *Making Foreigners: Immigration and Citizenship Law in America, 1600–2000* (New York: Cambridge University Press, 2011); Gerald Neuman, "The Lost Century of American Immigration Law (1776–1875)," *Columbia Law Review* 93, no. 8 (December 1993): 1833, 1871.

9. Ian Haney López, *White by Law: The Legal Construction of Race* (New York: New York University Press, 2006), 28–29.

10. *Id.*, 29 (citing Dred Scott v. Sanford, 60 US 393 [1857]).

11. Frederick Douglass, *The Dred Scott Decision* (Rochester, 1857).

12. López, *supra*, 29 (citing US Constitution, Fourteenth Amendment).

13. *Id.* (citing United States v. Wong Kim Ark, 169 US 649 [1898]).

14. *Id.* (citing Elk v. Wilkins, 112 US 94 [1884]).

15. *Id.*

16. *Id.*, 30 (citing Nationality Act of 1940, § 201[b], 54 Stat. 1138).

17. John Eastman, "Birthright Citizenship Is Not Actually in the Constitution," *New York Times*, August 24, 2015, www.nytimes.com/roomfordebate/2015/08/24/should-birthright-citizenship-be-abolished/birthright-citizenship-is-not-actually-in-the-constitution.

18. López, *supra*, 33 (citing Act of March 26, 1790, ch. 3, I Stat. 103).

19. *Id.* (citing Act of July 14, 1870, ch. 255, § 7, 16 Stat. 254).

20. In re Camille, 6 F. 256, 257–258 (C.C.D. Or. 1880).

21. See, for example, United States v. Bhagat Singh Thind, 261 US 204, 209 (1923); Lopez, *supra*, 35–77 (discussing the "prerequisite cases" on race and citizenship).

22. López, *supra*, 32–33.

23. Zuzana Cesla, "Fact Sheet: Family Immigration," National Immigration Forum, February 14, 2018, immigrationforum.org/article/fact-sheet-family-based-immigration/; Michael E. Fix and Wendy Zimmerman, "All Under One Roof: Mixed-Status Families in an Era of Reform," Urban Institute, October 6, 1999, webarchive.urban.org/Uploaded PDF/409100.pdf.

24. Nick Miroff, "A Family Was Separated at the Border, and This Distraught Father Took His Own Life," *Washington Post*, June 8, 2018, www.washingtonpost.com/world /national-security/a-family-was-separated-at-the-border-and-this-distraught-father -took-his-own-life/2018/06/08/24e40b70-6b5d-11e8-9e38-24e693b38637_story.html.

25. *Id.*

26. Anne Flaherty, "More Than 260 Migrants Died Trying to Cross the US Southern Border: Report," *ABC News*, December 14, 2018, abcnews.go.com/International /260-migrants-died-cross-us-southern-border-report/story?id=59832675.

27. Joanna Lydgate, "Assembly-Line Justice: A Review of Operation Streamline," policy brief, The Chief Justice Earl Warren Institute on Race, Ethnicity and Diversity, University of California, Berkeley Law School, January 2010, www.law.berkeley.edu/files /Operation_Streamline_Policy_Brief.pdf.

28. Neuman, *supra*, 1833, 1871.

29. Moore v. People of State of Illinois, 55 US (14 How.) 13, 18 (1852).

30. Neuman, *supra*, 1879.

31. Ill. Const. of 1848, art. XIV.

32. Neuman, *supra*, 1869; see also A. Naomi Paik, "Testifying to Rightlessness: Haitian Refugees Speaking from Guantánamo," *Social Text* 104 (2010): 39, 42–43 (detailing the history of US ideas of Haiti and the threat that Haitians posed to the institution of slavery in the United States).

33. Slavery Abolition Act 1833, 3 & 4 Will. IV c. 73 (Eng.) (abolishing slavery in the British Empire).

34. Daniel Kanstroom, *Deportation Nation: Outsiders in American History* (Cambridge, MA: Harvard University Press, 2007), 55–63.

35. *Id.*, 77–83.

36. *Id.*, 63–70.

37. *Id.*, 21–90 (describing the Trail of Tears and Fugitive Slave Laws as the antecedents of American deportation policy); see David Bacon, *Illegal People: How Globalization Creates Migration and Criminalizes Immigrants* (Boston: Beacon Press, 2008), 203–205 (describing how the American system of chattel slavery and Black Codes influenced policies controlling the migration of Chinese and Asian immigrants in the 1800s).

38. Kelly Lytle Hernández, *City of Inmates: Conquest, Rebellion, and the Rise of Human Caging in Los Angeles, 1771–1965* (Chapel Hill: University of North Carolina Press, 2017), 10–13.

39. Martha Menchaca, *Mexican Outsiders: A Community History of Marginalization and Discrimination in California* (Austin: University of Texas Press, 1995); Laura Gómez, *Manifest Destinies: The Making of the Mexican American Race*, 2nd ed. (New York: New York University Press, 2018).

40. Lucy E. Salyer, "*Wong Kim Ark*: The Contest Over Birthright Citizenship," in *Immigration Stories*, ed. David A. Martin and Peter H. Schuck (New York: Foundation Press; Eagan, MN: Thomson/West, 2005), 56–57.

41. People v. Hall, 4 Cal. 399, 403 (1854).

42. *Id.*, 404.

43. Kanstroom, *supra*, 98. Kerry Abrams, "Polygamy, Prostitution, and the Federalization of Immigration Law," *Columbia Law Review* 105, no. 3 (2005): 641, 666–667.

44. Kanstroom, 93–100, 103–107; Bill Ong Hing, *The Making and Remaking of Asian America Through Immigration Policy, 1850–1990* (Stanford: Stanford University Press, 1993), 21–23.

45. New York v. Miln, 36 US (11 Pet.) 102, 142-43 (1837).

46. See Smith v. Turner, 48 US (7 How.) 283, 283-86 (1849).

47. Abrams, 666–667.

48. Hernández, *supra*, 66–67; Jean Pfaelzer, *Driven Out: The Forgotten War Against Chinese Americans* (Berkeley: University of California Press, 2007), 67.

49. Act of Mar. 18, 1870, ch. 230, 1870 Cal. Stat. 330, 330-32.

50. *Id.*, 331.

51. Act of Mar. 18, 1870, ch. 231, 1870 Cal. Stat. 332, 332-33.

52. Abrams, *supra*, 666–667 (construing ch. 231, 1870 Cal. Stat. 332, 332).

53. Act of March 30, 1874, § 70, at 39-40 (amending Cal. Pol. Code §§ 2952, 2953 [1872]) (quoted in Abrams, *supra*, 677).

54. Chy Lung v. Freeman, 92 US 275, 280 (1875).

55. Cong. Globe, 37th Cong., 2d Sess. 2939 (1862) (remarks of Sen. Aaron Sargent). Quoted in Ming M. Zhu, "The Page Act of 1875: In the Name of Morality 9" (unpublished manuscript), March 23, 2010, papers.ssrn.com/sol3/papers.cfm?abstract_id=1577213.

56. 2 Cong. Rec. 4535 (1874) (quoted in Zhu, *supra*, note 64, 10).

57. Abrams, *supra*, 690; see Page Act, ch. 141, 18 Stat. 477, 477-78 (1875).

58. Page Act, §§ 3, 5; see also Abrams, *supra*, 697.

59. Chinese Exclusion Act, ch. 126, § 11, 22 Stat. 58, 61 (1882) (repealed 1943).

60. Chae Chan Ping v. United States, 130 US 581, 595 (1889).

61. Hernández, *supra*, 68.

62. *Id.*, 69.

63. Geary Act of 1892, § 6, 27 Stat. at 25-26.

64. *Id.*, § 4.

65. *Id.*, §§ 2-3.

66. Hernández, *supra*, 72.

67. *Id.*, 73–74.

68. Wong Wing v. United States, 163 US 228, 237-38 (1896); Gerald L. Neuman, "Wong Wing v. United States: The Bill of Rights Protects Illegal Aliens," in *Immigration Stories, supra*, 31, 40.

69. Fong Yue Ting v. United States, 149 US 698 (1893); Gabriel J. Chin, "*Chae Chan Ping* and *Fong Yue Ting*: The Origins of Plenary Power," in *Immigration Stories, supra*, 17.

70. Chae Chan Ping v. United States, 130 US 581 (1889).

71. Brief for Respondents, Fong Yue Ting v. United States, No. 92-1345, 92-1346, 92-1347 (May 10, 1893), 55.

72. Fong Yue Ting, 149 US at 707.

73. *Id.* at 730.

74. *Id.* at 763 (Fuller, C. J., dissenting).

75. *Id.* at 740 (Brewer, J., dissenting).

76. *Id.* at 759 (Field, J., dissenting).

77. *Id.*

78. Alexander, *supra*, 28 (describing the Black Codes).

79. Julia Ann Simon-Kerr, "Moral Turpitude," *Utah Law Review* 2012, no. 2 (2012): 1,001, 1,040.

80. *Id.*

81. Doris Marie Provine, *Unequal Under Law: Race in the War on Drugs* (Chicago: University of Chicago Press, 2007), 65.

82. *Id.*, 65.

83. *Id.*, 67–68.

84. Mikelis Beitiks, "'Devilishly Uncomfortable': In the Matter of Sic—The California Supreme Court Strikes a Balance Between Race, Drugs and Government in 1880s California," *California Legal History* 6 (2011): 229, 238. See also Charles E. Terry and Mildred Pellens, *The Opium Problem* (New York Committee on Drug Addictions, 1928), 807.

85. Provine, *supra*, 71–72.

86. *Id.*, 72 (quoting *Ex parte* Yung Jon, 28 F. 308, 312 [D. Or. 1886]).

87. *Id.*, 70–81.

88. *Id.*, 70–87.

89. Narcotic Drugs Import and Export Act of 1922, ch. 202, 42 Stat. 596, 596-97.

90. Provine, *supra*, 65, 82. See also Carrie Rosenbaum, "What (and Whom) State Marijuana Reformers Forgot: Crimmigration Law and Noncitizens," *DePaul Journal for Social Justice* 9, no. 2 (Summer 2016): 1, 16 (discussing how "racialized and negative views of Mexicans contributed to the criminalization of marijuana"). Rosenbaum cites Jordan Cunnings, "Nonserious Marijuana Offenses and Noncitizens: Uncounseled Pleas and Disproportionate Consequences," *UCLA Law Review* 62, no. 2 (2015): 510, 519, n. 42 (describing how Federal Bureau of Narcotics Commissioner Harry Anslinger "read anti-Mexican statements into the record in a House Ways and Means Committee hearing on marijuana referring to marijuana users as 'degenerate Spanish-speaking residents'").

91. Mae M. Ngai, *Impossible Subjects: Illegal Aliens and the Making of Modern America* (Princeton, NJ: Princeton University Press, 2004), 21–25.

92. *Id.*, 22.

93. *Id.*, 22–27.

94. Hutchinson, *supra*, 484–485 (quoting H.R. Rep. No. 68-350, pt. 1, at 16 [1924]).

95. Ngai, *supra*, 22, 27.

96. *Id.*, 21–25.

97. *Id.*, 49–50

98. *Id.*, 67.

99. See generally *Annual Report of the Commissioner-General of Immigration to the Secretary of Commerce and Labor for the Fiscal Year Ending June 30, 1904*, 138–139.

100. Hernández, *supra*, 134.

101. Ngai, *supra*, 67.

102. *Id.*

103. *Id.*, 137–138.

104. Act of Mar. 4, 1929, Pub. L. No. 70-1018, 45 Stat. 1551.

105. Hernández, *supra*, 139.

106. *Id.*

107. *Id.*, 139–140.

108. Ngai, *supra*, 233.

109. Yolanda Vázquez, "Constructing Crimmigration: Latino Subordination in a 'Post-Racial' World," *Ohio State Law Journal* 7, no. 3 (2015): 600, 621.

110. Ngai, *supra*, 237.

111. *Id.*, 238.

112. *Id.*

113. Gabriel J. Chin, "The Civil Rights Revolution Comes to Immigration Law: A New Look at the Immigration and Nationality Act of 1965," *North Carolina Law Review* 75 (1996): 273–345.

114. Muzaffar Chishti, Faye Hipsman, and Isabel Ball, "Fifty Years On, the 1965 Immigration and Nationality Act Continues to Reshape the United States," Migration Policy Institute, October 15, 2015, www.migrationpolicy.org/article/fifty-years -1965-immigration-and-nationality-act-continues-reshape-united-states.

115. *Congressional Record*, August 25, 1965, 21,812.

116. Lyndon B. Johnson, "President Lyndon B. Johnson's Remarks at the Signing of the Immigration Bill, Liberty Island, New York," October 3, 1965, at LBJ Presidential Library, www.lbjlibrary.org/lyndon-baines-johnson/timeline/lbj-on-immigration.

117. "Table 3: Region and Country or Area of Birth of the Foreign-Born Population: 1960 to 1990," US Census Bureau, updated March 9, 1999, www.census.gov/population /www/documentation/twps0029/tab03.html.

118. Ngai, *supra*, 260–261.

CHAPTER 3: RISE OF THE DEPORTATION MACHINE

1. Robert Pear, "Behind the Prison Riots: Precautions Not Taken," *New York Times*, December 6, 1987, www.nytimes.com/1987/12/06/us/behind-the-prison-riots-precautions -not-taken.html.

2. Douglas S. Massey, "America's Immigration Policy Fiasco: Learning from Past Mistakes," *Daedalus* 5, no. 11 (2013); Rubén G. Rumbaut, "A Legacy of War: Refugees

from Vietnam, Laos and Cambodia," in *Origins and Destinies: Immigration, Race, and Ethnicity in America,* eds. S. Pedraza and R. G. Rumbaut (Cengage, 1996), 315 –20; Mark Tseng-Putterman, "A Century of U.S. Intervention Created the Immigration Crisis," *Medium,* June 20, 2018, medium.com/s/story/timeline-us-intervention -central-america-a9bea9ebc148.

3. Vietnamese Fishermen's Ass'n v. Knights of Ku Klux Klan, 543 F. Supp. 198 (S.D. Tex. 1982); Laura Smith, "The War Between Vietnamese Fishermen and the KKK Signaled a New Type of White Supremacy," *Timeline,* November 6, 2017, timeline.com /kkk-vietnamese-fishermen-beam-43730353df06.

4. Kelly L. Hernández, *Migra!: A History of U.S. Border Patrol* (Berkeley: University of California Press, 2010), 188.

5. Leonard F. Chapman, "Illegal Aliens: Time to Call a Halt!," *Reader's Digest,* October 1976, 188–192; Massey, *supra,* 8; Meagan Flynn, "An 'Invasion of Illegal Aliens': The Oldest Immigration Fear-Mongering Metaphor in America," *Washington Post,* November 2, 2018, www.washingtonpost.com/nation/2018/11/02/an-invasion-illegal-aliens-oldest -immigration-fear-mongering-metaphor-america/?utm_term=.56d20aebfb6a.

6. Leah Nelson, "How Do We Know FAIR Is a Hate Group?" Southern Poverty Law Center, August 10, 2012, www.splcenter.org/hatewatch/2012/08/10/how-do-we-know -fair-hate-group.

7. John Tanton, "'Witan Memo' III," Southern Poverty Law Center, www.splcenter .org/fighting-hate/intelligence-report/2015/witan-memo-iii; Jason DeParle, "The Anti -Immigration Crusader," *New York Times,* April 17, 2011.

8. Carl Lindskoog, *Detain and Punish: Haitian Refugees and the Rise of the World's Largest Immigration Detention System* (Gainesville: University of Florida Press, 2018), 13–35.

9. Alex Stepick III, "The Refugees Nobody Wants: Haitians in Miami," in *Miami Now! Immigration, Ethnicity, and Social Change,* ed. Guillermon J. Granier and Alex Stepick III (Gainesville: University of Florida Press, 1992), 57, 58.

10. *Id.,* 58–60.

11. Peter Heidepriem, "Development in the Executive Branch: Fresh Fears of Deportation for Cubans in the U.S.," *Georgetown Immigration Law Journal* 29 (2015): 305, 308; Associated Press, "Two Decades Later, Mariel Boat Lift Refugees Still Feel Effects of Riot," *Los Angeles Times,* May 5, 2001, articles.latimes.com/2001/may/05/news /mn-59567.

12. Lindskoog, *supra,* 106–107.

13. Marshall Ingwerson, "Pressure Boils in Cuban Camps. Afraid to Return Home but Unwanted in US, Cuban Detainees Are Stuck in a Frustrating Legal Limbo," *Christian Science Monitor,* November 24, 1987, www.csmonitor.com/1987/1124/acuba.html.

14. Leng May Ma v. Barber, 357 US 185, 190 (1958).

15. *Id.*

16. Alexander, *supra,* 190–199.

17. *Id.*

18. *Id.*

19. Khalil Gibran Muhammad, *Condemnation of Blackness: Race, Crime, and the Making of Modern America* (Cambridge, MA: Harvard University Press, 2019) 9, 23–24.

20. Alexander, *supra,* 40–41.

21. *Id.*

22. Elizabeth Hinton, *From the War on Poverty to the War on Crime: The Making of Mass Incarceration in America* (Cambridge, MA: Harvard University Press, 2016), 81.

23. Alexander, *supra*.

24. *Id.*

25. *Id.*, 47.

26. Jonathan Simon, *Governing Through Crime: How the War on Crime Transformed American Democracy and Created a Culture of Fear* (Oxford: Oxford University Press, 2009).

27. Government Accountability Office, *Criminal Aliens: INS's Investigative Efforts in the New York City Area*, July 1985; P. H. Schuck and J. Williams, "Removing Criminal Aliens: The Promise and Pitfalls of Federalism," *Harvard Journal of Law and Public Policy* 22, no. 2 (1999): 367.

28. Immigration Reform and Control Act of 1986 (IRCA), Pub. L. No. 99-603, § 101(a)(1), 100 Stat. 3359, 3360-74.

29. Schuck and Williams, "Removing Criminal Aliens," 370.

30. Anti-Drug Abuse Act of 1986, Pub. L. No. 99-570, § 1751, 100 Stat. 3207, 3207-47 (codified at 8 USC § 1182 [2018]) (allowing deportation of a noncitizen convicted of a violation of "any law . . . of a State, the United States, or a foreign country relating to a controlled substance [as defined in section 102 of the Controlled Substances Act (21 USC 802)]").

31. Alexander, *supra*, 53.

32. *See* Anti-Drug Abuse Act of 1988, Pub. L. No. 100-690, 102 Stat. 4181, 4469-70.

33. 134 Cong. Rec. S17318 (October 21, 1988).

34. Anti-Drug Abuse Act of 1988; Alina Das, "Immigration Detention: Information Gaps and Institutional Barriers to Reform," *University of Chicago Law Review* 80, no. 1 (2013): 137, 147.

35. Anti-Drug Abuse Act of 1988.

36. Ngai, *supra*, 246–48.

37. Immigration Act of 1990, Pub. L. No. 101-649, § 505, 104 Stat. 4978, 5050.

38. *Id.*

39. John Tanton and Wayne Lutton, "Immigration and Crime," *The Social Contract* 3, no. 3 (Spring 1993).

40. *Id.*

41. "U.S. Border Patrol's Implementation of 'Operation Gatekeeper,'" hearing before the Subcommittee on Government Management, Information, and Technology of the Committee on Government Reform and Oversight, 104th Congress, August 9, 1996; Flynn, "An 'Invasion of Illegal Aliens'"; Violent Crime Control and Law Enforcement Act of 1994, Pub. L. No. 103-322, §§ 20301, 130001, 130007, 108 Stat. 1796.

42. Khaled A. Beydoun, *American Islamophobia: Understanding the Roots and Rise of Fear* (Oakland: University of California Press, 2018), 70–74.

43. Nancy Morawetz, "Understanding the Impact of the 1996 Deportation Laws and the Limited Scope of Proposed Reforms," *Harvard Law Review* 113, no. 8 (2000): 1,936.

44. *Id.*

45. Anthony Lewis, "Abroad at Home: 'Cases That Cry Out," *New York Times*, March 18, 2000, www.nytimes.com/2000/03/18/opinion/abroad-at-home-cases-that-cry-out .html.

46. Senator Lamar Smith to Attorney General Janet Reno, November 4, 1999, www .scribd.com/document/236719133/Lamar-Smith-Janet-Reno-letter.

47. US Department of Homeland Security, Bureau of Immigration and Customs Enforcement, *ENDGAME: Office of Detention and Removal Strategic Plan, 2003–2012*, June 27, 2003, www.cryptogon.com/docs/endgame.pdf.

48. Sterling Johnson Jr., "A Reflection on *HCC v. Sale*: A Conversation Between the Honorable Sterling Johnson, Jr. and Professor Brandt Goldstein," *New York Law School Law Review* 61 (2016–17): 69–79, www.nylslawreview.com/wp-content/uploads/sites /16/2017/09/Law-Review-61.1-Johnson.pdf.

49. *Id.*

50. See *supra* Chapter 4; see also Bryan Baker, "Immigration Enforcement Actions: 2016," *Department of Homeland Security Annual Report*, December 2017, 9, www.dhs .gov/sites/default/files/publications/Enforcement_Actions_2016.pdf (finding that about 95 percent of removals in 2016 were immigrants from Mexico, Honduras, Guatemala, or El Salvador); Vázquez, *supra*, 625 (finding that Latinos accounted for only approximately 46 percent of noncitizens living in the United States in 2012).

51. Baker, *supra*, 8.

52. Guillermo Cantor, Mark Noferi, and Daniel E. Martínez, "Enforcement Overdrive: A Comprehensive Study of ICE's Criminal Alien Program," American Immigration Council, November 2015, 3, 17–18, www.americanimmigrationcouncil.org/sites /default/files/research/enforcement_overdrive_a_comprehensive_assessment_of_ices _criminal_alien_program_final.pdf.

53. Juliana Morgan-Trostle and Kexin Zhang, *The State of Black Immigrants*, Black Alliance for Justice Immigration and NYU School of Law Immigrant Rights Clinic, 35, www.stateofblackimmigrants.com/assets/sobi-fullreport-jan22.pdf.

54. *Id.*, 40.

55. *Id.*

56. "Southeast Asian Americans and the School-to-Prison-to-Deportation Pipeline," Southeast Asia Resource Action Center, accessed August 9, 2019, www.searac.org /wp-content/uploads/2018/04/SEAA-School-to-Deportation-Pipeline_0.pdf.

CHAPTER 4: THE PIPELINE

1. "Homeless LGBT Youth in New York City," Ali Forney Center, accessed August 9, 2019, www.aliforneycenter.org/_aliforney/assets/File/Youth%20Crisis%20Stats.pdf.

2. "The Criminal Alien Program (CAP): Immigration Enforcement in Prisons and Jails," American Immigration Council, August 1, 2013, www.americanimmigration council.org/research/criminal-alien-program-cap-immigration-enforcement -prisons-and-jails; Nina Bernstein, "Immigration Officials Often Detain Foreign-Born Rikers Inmates for Deportation," *New York Times*, August 24, 2019, www.nytimes .com/2009/08/25/nyregion/25rikers.html.

3. Khalil A. Cumberbatch, "For Immigrants with Convictions, Punishment Never Ends," *The Hill*, July 4, 2016, thehill.com/blogs/congress-blog/judicial/286309-for -immigrants-with-convictions-punishment-never-ends.

4. *Id.*

5. Bernstein, *supra*.

6. "The Criminal Alien Program," *supra*; Permanent Subcommittee on Investigations of the Committee on Governmental Affairs, *Criminal Aliens in the United States*, Senate Report 104-48, April 7, 1995, www.govinfo.gov/content/pkg/CRPT-104srpt48/html /CRPT-104srpt48.htm.

7. *Criminal Aliens in the United States*.

8. *Id.*

9. US Department of Homeland Security, "ICE Unveils Sweeping New Plan to Target Criminal Aliens in Jails Nationwide," press release, March 28, 2008.

10. Jynnah Radford and Luis Noe-Bustamante, "Facts on U.S. Immigrants, 2017," Pew Research Center, June 3, 2019, www.pewhispanic.org/2019/06/03/facts-on-u-s-immigrants.

11. "ICE Unveils Sweeping New Plan," *supra* (quoting ICE Assistant Secretary Julie Myers).

12. US Department of Homeland Security, *Secure Communities: A Comprehensive Plan to Identify and Remove Criminal Aliens*, July 21, 2009, www.ice.gov/doclib/foia/secure_communities/securecommunitiesstrategicplan09.pdf.

13. Aarti Kohli, Peter L. Markowitz, and Lisa Chavez, "Secure Communities by the Numbers: An Analysis of Demographics and Due Process," The Chief Justice Earl Warren Institute on Law and Social Policy, University of California, Berkeley Law School, October 2011, 3.

14. Gretchen Gavett, "Controversial 'Secure Communities' Immigration Program Will Be Mandatory by 2013," *PBS Frontline*, January 9, 2012.

15. *Id.*

16. *Id.*; Kohli, Markowitz, and Chavez, *supra*.

17. "New York City New Detainer Discretion Law Chart and Practice Advisory," Cardozo Law, Kathryn O. Greenberg Immigration Justice Clinic, updated December 2014, www.immigrantdefenseproject.org/wp-content/uploads/2013/09/Practice-Advisory-2014-Detainer-Discretion-Law-PEP.pdf.

18. Immigrant Defense Project, "This Valentine's Day, Celebrate Best Break Up Ever: ICE out of Rikers," www.immigrantdefenseproject.org/valentines-day-celebrate-best-breakup-ever-ice-rikers/.

19. Liz Robbins, "In a 'Sanctuary City,' Immigrants Are Still at Risk," *New York Times*, February 27, 2018.

20. US Immigration and Customs Enforcement, "ICE Arrests over 450 on Federal Immigration Charges During Operation 'Safe City,'" press release, September 28, 2017, www.ice.gov/news/releases/ice-arrests-over-450-federal-immigration-charges-during-operation-safe-city.

21. Huyen Pham, "287(g) Agreements in the Trump Era," *Washington and Lee Law Review* 75, no. 3 (Summer 2018): 1,253–1,286, scholarlycommons.law.wlu.edu/cgi/viewcontent.cgi?article=4609&context=wlulr.

22. Heather Lynn Wood, "Juana Villegas Now Has Legal Standing to Live in the U.S.: Other New Mothers May Not Be So Lucky," *Nashville Scene*, October 30, 2014, www.nashvillescene.com/news/article/13056653/juana-villegas-now-has-legal-standing-to-live-in-the-us-other-new-mothers-may-not-be-so-lucky; Julia Preston, "Immigrant, Pregnant, Is Jailed Under Pact," *New York Times*, July 20, 2008, www.nytimes.com/2008/07/20/us/20immig.html.

23. Jonathan Meador, "Sheriff Daron Hall Announces the End of Davidson County's Controversial Deportation Program, But Questions Remain," *Nashville Scene*, August 23, 2012, www.nashvillescene.com/news/article/13044557/sheriff-daron-hall-announces-the-end-of-davidson-countys-controversial-deportation-program-but-questions-remain.

24. Randy Capps et al., "Delegation and Divergence: 287(g) State and Local Immigration Enforcement," Migration Policy Institute, January 2011, www.migrationpolicy.org/research/delegation-and-divergence-287g-state-and-local-immigration-enforcement.

25. Marc R. Rosenblum and William A. Kandel, "Interior Immigration Enforcement: Programs Targeting Criminal Aliens," Congressional Research Service, December 20, 2012, fas.org/sgp/crs/homesec/R42057.pdf.

26. Capps et al., *supra*.

27. Aarti Shahani and Judith Greene, "Local Democracy on ICE: Why State and Local Governments Have No Business in Federal Immigration Law Enforcement," Justice Strategies, February 2009, www.justicestrategies.org/sites/default/files/JS-Democracy-On-Ice.pdf.

28. *Id.*

29. Rebekah Barber, "Voices of Resistance: How to Unseat an ICE-Collaborating Sheriff," *Facing South*, November 16, 2018, www.facingsouth.org/2018/11/voices-resistance-how-unseat-ice-collaborating-sheriff.

30. "National Map of 287(g) Agreements," Immigrant Legal Resource Center, May 22, 2019, www.ilrc.org/national-map-287g-agreements.

31. Kohli, Markowitz, and Chavez, *supra*.

32. *Id.*

33. Arizona v. United States, 567 US 387 (2012).

34. Nigel Duara, "Arizona's Once-Feared Immigration Law, SB 1070, Loses Most of Its Power in Settlement," *Los Angeles Times*, September 15, 2016, www.latimes.com/nation/la-na-arizona-law-20160915-snap-story.html; Elvia Diaz, "'Show Me Your Papers' Still Is the Law, but Now Everyone Is Happy?" *AZ Central*, September 19, 2016, www.azcentral.com/story/opinion/op-ed/elviadiaz/2016/09/19/show-me-your-papers-sb-1070/90435066.

35. Ian Gordon and Tasneem Raja, "164 Anti-Immigration Laws Passed Since 2010? A MoJo Analysis," *Mother Jones*, March/April 2012, www.motherjones.com/politics/2012/03/anti-immigration-law-database.

36. Julie Turkewitz, "In New York, a 20-Year-Old Policy Suddenly Prompts a Lawsuit," *The Atlantic*, May 1, 2012.

37. Padilla v. Kentucky 559 US 356, 364 (2010).

38. *Id.*

39. Erica Goode, "Stronger Hand for Judges in the 'Bazaar' of Plea Deals," *New York Times*, March 22, 2012, www.nytimes.com/2012/03/23/us/stronger-hand-for-judges-after-rulings-on-plea-deals.html.

40. Alina Das, "Problem Solving Courts," *Criminal Justice Review* 33 (2018): 308.

41. Joanna Jacobbi Lydgate, "Assembly-Line Justice: A Review of Operation Streamline," *California Law Review* 98, no. 2 (2010): 481–482; Maya Srikrishnan, "Operation Streamline Is Here," Voice of San Diego, July 16, 2018, www.voiceofsandiego.org/topics/news/border-report-operation-streamline-is-here/.

42. Lydgate, *supra*, 481–482.

43. *Id.*

44. *Id.*, 491–495; Judith L. Greene, Beth Carson, and Andrea Black, "Indefensible: A Decade of Mass Incarceration of Migrants Prosecuted for Crossing the Border," Justice Strategies and Grassroots Leadership, July 2016, 30–32.

45. Lydgate, *supra*, 488–491.

46. *Id.*

47. *Id.*, 493–494.

48. *Id.*

49. *Id.*, 494–495.

50. Brad Heath, "DOJ: Trump's Immigration Crackdown 'Diverting' Resources from Drug Cases," *USA Today*, June 22, 2018, www.usatoday.com/story/news/2018/06/22/zero-tolerance-immigration-crackdown-diverting-resources-drug-cases/727532002/.

51. Lydgate, *supra*, 487.

52. *Padilla*, 559 US at 373.

CHAPTER 5: THE CAGE

1. Dominique Mosbergen, "ICE Has a Record-Breaking 52,000 Immigrants in Detention, Report Says," *Huffpost*, May 21, 2019, www.huffpost.com/entry/ice-detainees-record_n_5ce39a0fe4b0877009939c17; Sharita Gruberg, "How For-Profit Companies Are Driving Immigration Detention Policies," Center for American Progress, December 18, 2015, www.americanprogress.org/issues/immigration/reports/2015/12/18/127769/how-for-profit-companies-are-driving-immigration-detention-policies.

2. Demore v. Kim, 538 US 510 (2003).

3. "Three-fold Difference in Immigration Bond Amounts by Court Location," TRAC Reports, July 2, 2018, trac.syr.edu/immigration/reports/519/.

4. American Civil Liberties Union, "Alternatives to Immigration Detention: Less Costly and More Humane Than Federal Lock-Up," fact sheet, accessed August 9, 2019, www.aclu.org/other/aclu-fact-sheet-alternatives-immigration-detention-atd.

5. Mazin Sidahmed, "Assembly Members Slam Orange County Jail over Immigrant Detention Conditions," *Documented*, November 29, 2018, documentedny.com/2018/11/29/assembly-members-slam-orange-county-jail-over-immigrant-detention-conditions.

6. Salvado Rizzo, "The Facts About Trump's Policy of Separating Families at the Border," *Washington Post*, June 19, 2018, www.washingtonpost.com/news/fact-checker/wp/2018/06/19/the-facts-about-trumps-policy-of-separating-families-at-the-border/?utm_term=.6bff58c59bd8.

7. See *supra* Chapter 3.

8. Leng May Ma v. Barber, 357 US 185, 190 (1958).

9. Jonathan Simon, "Refugees in a Carceral Age: The Rebirth of Immigration Prisons in the United States," *Public Culture* 10, no. 3 (1998): 577, 579–580, 599.

10. Anti-Drug Abuse Act of 1988, Pub. L. No. 100-690, 102 Stat. 4181, 4469-70.

11. Antiterrorism and Effective Death Penalty Act of 1996 (AEDPA), Pub. L. No. 104-132, § 440(c), 110 Stat. 1214 (April 24, 1996); Illegal Immigration Reform and Immigrant Responsibility Act of 1996 (IIRIRA), Pub. L. No. 104-208, Div. C, § 303(b), 110 Stat. 3009 (September 30, 1996).

12. *IIRIRA*, §302(a).

13. *Id.*

14. Adam Snitzer, "The Nation's Largest Private Prisons Operator Is Based in Florida. And Profits Are Up," *Miami Herald*, April 22, 2019, www.miamiherald.com/news/business/biz-monday/article227477119.html.

15. American Civil Liberties Union, "Warehoused and Forgotten: Immigrants Trapped in Our Shadow Private Prison System," June 2014, www.aclu.org/sites/default/files/assets/060614-aclu-car-reportonline.pdf.

16. Bethany Carson and Eleana Diaz, "Payoff: How Congress Ensures Private Prison Profit with an Immigrant Detention Quota," Grassroots Leadership, April 2015, grassrootsleadership.org/reports/payoff-how-congress-ensures-private-prison-profit

-immigrant-detention-quota#2; Eric Pianin, "A Senator's Shame," *Washington Post*, June 19, 2005, www.washingtonpost.com/wp-dyn/content/article/2005/06/18/AR2005 061801105.html?noredirect=on.

17. Carson and Diaz, *supra*.

18. J. Rachel Reyes, "Immigration Detention: Recent Trends and Scholarship," Center for Migration Studies, March 26, 2018, cmsny.org/publications/virtualbrief-detention.

19. US Immigration and Customs Enforcement, *Fiscal Year 2018 ICE Enforcement and Removal Operations Report*, 2018, www.ice.gov/doclib/about/offices/ero/pdf/eroFY 2018Report.pdf.

20. "Untangling the Immigration Enforcement Web," National Immigration Law Center, September 2017, www.nilc.org/issues/immigration-enforcement/untangling -immigration-enforcement-web.

21. Ryan Devereaux, "A Mother's Appeal to the Supreme Court: 'I Had to Fight to Stay in the Country for My Children,'" *The Intercept*, November 30, 2016, theintercept .com/2016/11/30/i-had-to-fight-to-stay-in-the-country-for-my-children-a-mothers -deportation-appeal-before-the-supreme-court/; "Why We Must Abolish the 1886 Laws," National Immigrant Justice Center, www.immigrantjustice.org/staff/blog/why-we -must-abolish-1996-law-has-destroyed-thousands-families-video.

22. N.J. Advocates for Immigrant Detainees et al., "Isolated in Essex: Punishing Immigrants Through Solitary Confinement," American Friends Service Committee re-port, 2016, 5–6, www.afsc.org/resource/isolated-essex-punishing-immigrants-through -solitary-confinement.

23. *Id.*, 6.

24. Scott Bixby and Betsy Woodruff, "Trans Woman Was Beaten in ICE Custody Before Death, Autopsy Finds," *Daily Beast*, November 26, 2018.

25. Human Rights Watch et al., *Code Red: The Fatal Consequences of Dangerously Substandard Medical Care in Immigration Detention*, 2018, www.aclu.org/sites/default /files/field_document/coderedreportdeathsicedetention.pdf; Meera Senthilingam, "Half of Recent Immigrant Detainee Deaths Due to Inadequate Medical Care, Report Finds," CNN, June 20, 2018, www.cnn.com/2018/06/20/health/immigrant-detainee-deaths -medical-care-bn/index.html.

26. Sandra E. Garcia, "Independent Autopsy of Transgender Asylum Seeker Who Died in ICE Custody Shows Signs of Abuse," *New York Times*, November 27, 2018, www.nytimes.com/2018/11/27/us/trans-woman-roxsana-hernandez-ice-autopsy.html.

27. See, for example, Southern Poverty Law Center et al., *Shadow Prisons: Immigrant Detention in the South*, November 21, 2016, 14–16, www.splcenter.org/sites/default /files/ijp_shadow_prisons_immigrant_detention_report.pdf; National Prison Rape Elimination Commission Report, June 2009, 21–23, www.ncjrs.gov/pdffiles1/226680 .pdf; Human Rights Watch, *Detained and At Risk: Sexual Abuse and Harassment in United States Immigration Detention*, August 25, 2010, 8–14, www.hrw.org/sites/default /files/reports/us0810webwcover.pdf.

28. Nina Bernstein, "Immigrant Jail Tests U.S. View of Legal Access," *New York Times*, November 2, 2009, www.nytimes.com/2009/11/02/nyregion/02detain.html.

29. Nina Bernstein, "Immigrants in Detention to Be Sent Out of State," *New York Times*, January 15, 2010, www.nytimes.com/2010/01/15/nyregion/15ice.html.

30. Nina Bernstein, "Illness Hinders Plans to Close Immigration Jail," *New York Times*, February 23, 2010, www.nytimes.com/2010/02/24/nyregion/24varick.html.

31. New York University School of Law Immigrant Rights Clinic and New Jersey Advocates for Immigration Detainees, *Immigration Incarceration: The Expansion and Failed Reform of Immigration Detention in Essex County, NJ*, March 2012, www.law.nyu .edu/sites/default/files/upload_documents/Immigration%20Incarceration.pdf.

32. *Id.*

33. Adam Cox and Ryan Goodman, "Detention of Migrant Families as 'Deterrence': Ethical Flaws and Empirical Doubts," *Just Security*, June 22, 2018, www.justsecurity .org/58354/detention-migrant-families-deterrence-ethical-flaws-empirical-doubts.

34. *Id.*

35. Arnold Giammarco, "After 50 Years as a Legal Immigrant, I Spent 18 Months in Immigration Detention Without a Bail Hearing," *The World*, Public Radio International, November 30, 2016, www.pri.org/stories/2016-11-30/after-50-years-legal-immigrant -i-spent-18-months-immigration-detention-without.

36. R.I.L-R v. Johnson, 80 F. Supp. 3d 164, 189 (D.D.C. 2015).

37. Center for Human Rights and International Justice at Boston College, *Returning to the United States After Deportation: A Guide to Assess Your Eligibility*, August 2011, www.bc.edu/content/dam/files/centers/humanrights/pdf/Returning%20to%20the%20 US%20AfterDeportation%20-%20A%20Self-Assessment%20FINAL.pdf.

38. Complaint, Giammarco v. Beers, No. 3:13-cv-01670-VLB (D. Conn. November 12, 2013), www.law.yale.edu/system/files/documents/pdf/Clinics/vlsc_giammarco _complaint.pdf/. See also Decl. of Sharon Giammarco (on file with counsel); "U.S. Army Veteran Returns Home After YLS Clinics Secure Settlement," *YLS Today*, Yale Law School, July 27, 2017, law.yale.edu/yls-today/news/us-army-veteran-returns-home -after-yls-clinics-secure-settlement.

39. Homeland Security Advisory Council, *Report of the Subcommittee on Privatized Immigration Detention Facilities*, December 1, 2016, www.dhs.gov/sites/default/files /publications/DHS%20HSAC%20PIDF%20Final%20Report.pdf; Matthew Nanci, "Protest Denounces Orange County Jail Agreement with ICE," *Record Online*, July 8, 2019, www.recordonline.com/news/20190708/protest-denounces-orange-county-jail -agreement-with-ice.

40. Livia Luan, "Profiting from Enforcement: The Role of Private Prisons in U.S. Immigration Detention," Migration Policy Institute, May 2, 2018, www.migrationpolicy .org/article/profiting-enforcement-role-private-prisons-us-immigration-detention.

41. Homeland Security Advisory Council, *supra*.

42. Ian Urbina, "Using Immigrants as a Pool for Cheap Labor," *New York Times*, May 24, 2004, www.nytimes.com/2014/05/25/us/using-jailed-migrants-as-a-pool-of-cheap -labor.html; Elise Foley, "Immigrant Freed from 19-Month Detention: 'I Treat My Dogs Much Better Than the Detainees Are Treated,'" *Huffington Post*, May 18, 2011, www .huffingtonpost.com/2011/05/18/immigrant-freed-from-detention_n_863893.html; Richard Fausset, "Could He Be a Good American?" *Los Angeles Times*, June 4, 2011, www .latimes.com/nation/la-na-deportation-story-htmlstory.html; Yana Kunichoff, "'Voluntary' Work Program Run in Private Detention Centers Pays Detained Immigrants $1 a Day," *Truthout*, July 27, 2012, www.truth-out.org/news/item/10548-voluntary -work-program-run-in-private-detention-centers-pays-detained-immigrants-1-a-day; Kelsey Sheehy, "Saga Highlights Kinks in Immigrant Detention System," *San Diego Tribune*, April 23, 2011, www.sandiegouniontribune.com/sdut-saga-highlights-kinks-in -immigrant-detention-2011apr23-story.html.

43. Madison Paul, "How a Private Prison Company Used Detained Immigrants for Free Labor," *Mother Jones*, April 3, 2017; Alexandra Levy, "Who Has Most to Gain from Trump's Immigration Policies? Private Prisons," *Washington Post*, June 29, 2018; Jacqueline Stevens, "One Dollar Per Day: The Slaving Wages of Immigration Jail, from 1943 to Present," *Georgetown Immigration Law Journal* 29, no. 3 (Spring 2015).

44. Paul, *supra*.

45. Bixby and Woodruff, *supra*.

46. Matt Zapotosky, "The Justice Department Closed This Troubled Private Prison. Immigration Authorities Are Reopening It," *Washington Post*, October 27, 2016; Seth Freed Wexler, "Federal Officials Ignored Years of Internal Warnings About Deaths at Private Prisons," *The Nation*, June 15, 2016, www.thenation.com/article/federal-officials-ignored-years-of-internal-warnings-about-deaths-at-private-prisons.

47. US Department of Justice, Office of the Inspector General, *Review of the Federal Bureau of Prisons' Monitoring of Contract Prisons*, August 2016; Wexler, *supra*.

48. Deputy Attorney General Sally Q. Yates, memorandum to acting director, Federal Bureau of Prisons, on "Reducing Our Use of Private Prisons," August 18, 2016.

49. Homeland Security Advisory Council, *supra*.

50. Laura Sullivan, "Prison Economics Help Drive Ariz. Immigration Law," *Morning Edition*, NPR, October 28, 2010, www.npr.org/2010/10/28/130833741/prison-economics-help-drive-ariz-immigration-law.

51. Mirren Gidda, "Private Prison Company GEO Group Gave Generously to Trump and Now Has Lucrative Contract," *Newsweek*, May 11, 2017, www.newsweek.com/geo-group-private-prisons-immigration-detention-trump-596505.

52. Fredreka Schouten, "Private Prisons Back Trump and Could See Big Payoffs with New Policies," *USA Today*, February 23, 2017, www.usatoday.com/story/news/politics/2017/02/23/private-prisons-back-trump-and-could-see-big-payoffs-new-policies/98300394; Alice Speri, "Private Prisons Were Thriving Even Before Trump Was Elected," *The Intercept*, November 28, 2016, theintercept.com/2016/11/28/private-prisons-were-thriving-even-before-trump-was-elected.

53. Schouten, *supra*.

54. "GEO Group," Open Secrets, accessed August 9, 2019, www.opensecrets.org/lobby/clientsum.php?id=D000022003&year=2017; "CoreCivic, Inc.," *Open Secrets*, accessed August 9, 2019, www.opensecrets.org/lobby/clientsum.php?id=D000021940&year=2017.

55. Meredith Hoffman, "Prison Company Struggles to Get License to Hold Children," Associated Press, April 20, 2017, apnews.com/adbd71efcfaf4b9a96c379face79fbe9.

56. Peter Wagner and Alexi Jones, "State of Phone Justice: Local Jails, State Prisons, and Private Phone Providers," Prison Policy Initiative, February 2019, www.prisonpolicy.org/phones/state_of_phone_justice.html.

57. Sara Wakefield and Christopher Wildeman, "How Parental Incarceration Harms Children and What to Do About It," National Council on Family Relations policy brief, January 2018, www.ncfr.org/sites/default/files/2018-01/How%20Parental%20Incarceration%20Harms%20Children%20NCFR%20Policy_Full%20Brief_Jan.%202018_0.pdf.

58. Wendy Sawyer and Peter Wagner, "Mass Incarceration: The Whole Pie 2019," Prison Policy Initiative, March 19, 2019, www.prisonpolicy.org/reports/pie2019.html.

59. US Government Accountability Office, *Criminal Alien Statistics: Information on Incarcerations, Arrests, Convictions, Costs, and Removals*, July 17, 2018, www.gao.gov/products/GAO-18-433.

CHAPTER 6: THE "LOSS OF ALL
THAT MAKES LIFE WORTH LIVING"

1. Ng Fung Ho v. White, 259 US 276, 284 (1922); Bridges v. Wixon, 326 US 135, 147 (1945).

2. Tim Padgett-Kingston, "The Most Homophobic Place on Earth?" *Time*, April 12, 2006, content.time.com/time/world/article/0,8599,1182991,00.html.

3. Beth C. Caldwell, *Deported Americans: Life After Deportation to Mexico* (Durham, NC: Duke University Press, 2019).

4. David Brotherton and Luis Barrios, *Banished to the Homeland: Dominican Deportees and Their Stories of Exile* (New York: Columbia University Press, 2011).

5. Howard Dean Bailey, "I Served My Country. Then It Kicked Me Out," *Politico*, April 10, 2014, www.politico.com/magazine/story/2014/04/howard-dean-bailey-deported-i-served-my-country-and-then-it-kicked-me-out-105606?o=3; American Civil Liberties Union of California, *Discharged, Then Discarded: How U.S. Veterans Are Banished by the Country They Swore to Protect*, July 2016, www.aclusandiego.org/wp-content/uploads/2017/07/DischargedThenDiscarded-ACLUofCA.pdf.

6. Sarah Stillman, "When Deportation Is a Death Sentence," *The New Yorker*, January 8, 2018, www.newyorker.com/magazine/2018/01/15/when-deportation-is-a-death-sentence.

7. Ryan Autullo and Taylor Goldenstein, "Immigrant Taken by ICE from Austin Courthouse Was Killed in Mexico," *Statesman*, updated September 25, 2018, www.statesman.com/NEWS/20170920/Immigrant-taken-by-ICE-from-Austin-courthouse-was-killed-in-Mexico.

8. "Criminalizing Survival Curricula," Survived and Punished, accessed August 9, 2019, survivedandpunished.org/criminalizing-survival-curricula; Mexican National Institute of Public Health, "Migrants Suffering Violence While in Transit Through Mexico: Factors Associated with the Decision to Continue or Turn Back," *Journal of Immigrant and Minority Health* 16, no. 1 (June 2014); Doctors Without Borders, *Forced to Flee Central America's Northern Triangle: A Neglected Humanitarian Crisis*, May 2017, www.doctorswithoutborders.org/sites/default/files/2018-06/msf_forced-to-flee-central-americas-northern-triangle.pdf#page=10.

9. Dara Lind, "The US Has Made Migrants at the Border Wait Months to Apply for Asylum. Now the Dam Is Breaking," *Vox*, November 28, 2018, www.vox.com/2018/11/28/18089048/border-asylum-trump-metering-legally-ports.

10. Max Rivlin-Nadler, "The 'Streamline' Program to Prosecute Immigrants Is Ensnaring Kids by Mistake," *The Appeal*, August 10, 2018, theappeal.org/the-streamline-program-to-prosecute-immigrants-is-ensnaring-kids-by-mistake.

11. Brent S. Wible, "The Strange Afterlife of Section 212(c) Relief: Collateral Attacks on Deportation Orders in Prosecutions for Illegal Reentry After St. Cyr," *Georgetown Immigration Law Journal* 19, no. 4 (2005): 455, 462; Immigration Act of 1990, Pub. L. 101-649, § 511, 104 Stat. 4978; Illegal Immigration Reform and Immigrant Responsibility Act of 1996, Pub. L. No. 104-208, § 304(a)(3), (b); 110 Stat. 3009-594 to -597.

12. INS v. St. Cyr, 533 US 289, 326 (2001).

13. Nancy Morawetz, "Understanding the Impact of the 1996 Deportation Laws and the Limited Scope of Proposed Reforms," *Harvard Law Review* 113, no. 8 (2000).

14. Human Rights Watch, *Forced Apart (by the Numbers): Non-Citizens Deported Mostly for Nonviolent Offenses*, April 2009, www.hrw.org/sites/default/files/reports/us0409web.pdf.

15. Seth Freed Wessler and Julianne Hing, "Torn Apart," in *Beyond Walls and Cages: Prisons, Borders, and Global Crisis,* eds. Jenna M. Loyd, Matt Mitchelson, and Andre Burridge (Atlanta: University of Georgia Press, 2012), 152–162; Race Forward, *Shattered Families: The Perilous Intersection of Immigration Enforcement and the Child Welfare System,* November 2, 2011, www.raceforward.org/research/reports/shattered-families.

16. Alina Das, "The Immigration Penalties of Criminal Convictions: Resurrecting Categorical Analysis in Immigration Law," *New York University Law Review* 86, no. 6 (December 2011): 1,669–1,760, www.nyulawreview.org/wp-content/uploads/2018/08/NYULawReview-86-6-Das.pdf.

17. *Id.*

18. Stephen H. Legomsky, "Deportation and the War on Independence," *Cornell Law Review* 91, no. 2 (2006): 369, 375–376.

19. "In re A-B-: Attorney General Holds that Salvadoran Woman Fleeing Domestic Violence Failed to Establish a Cognizable Particular Social Group," *Harvard Law Review Recent Adjudication,* December 10, 2018, harvardlawreview.org/2018/12/in-re-a-b.

20. Das, "Immigration Penalties," 1686.

CHAPTER 7: POLITICS OF FEAR

1. Julia Prodis Sulek, "S.F. Shooting Victim Kate Steinle: 'She Was About Loving People,' Friends Say," *Mercury News,* July 8, 2015, www.mercurynews.com/2015/07/08/s-f-shooting-victim-kate-steinle-she-was-about-loving-people-friends-say; John Diaz, "Exclusive: Kate Steinle's Family Talks About the Anguish and Frustration," *San Francisco Chronicle,* November 30, 2017, www.sfchronicle.com/opinion/article/Exclusive-Kate-Steinle-s-family-speaks-12396710.php; Joe Mozingo and Brittany Mejia, "The Kathryn Steinle Murder Trial: Why the Jury and Trump Saw Two Different Cases," *Los Angeles Times,* December 2, 2017, www.latimes.com/local/lanow/la-me-kate-steinle-analysis-20171202-story.html.

2. Katy Steinmetz, "Kate Steinle: Victim of Deadly 'Russian Roulette' or a Tragic Accident?" *Time,* November 21, 2017, time.com/5032771/kate-steinle-immigration-closing-arguments.

3. Steinle v. San Francisco, 230 F. Supp. 3d 994, 1004 (N.D. Cal. 2017).

4. Mozingo and Mejia, *supra.*

5. *Id.*

6. Dara Lind, "'Immigrants Are Coming Over the Border to Kill You' Is the Only Speech Trump Knows How to Give," *Vox,* January 9, 2019, www.vox.com/2019/1/8/18174782/trump-speech-immigration-border.

7. Julián Aguilar and Alexa Ura, "Border Communities Have Lower Crime Rates," *Texas Tribune,* February 23, 2016, www.texastribune.org/2016/02/23/border-communities-have-lower-crime-rates.

8. Human Rights Watch, *Forced Apart (By the Numbers)*; David Bier, "60% of Deported 'Criminal Aliens' Committed Only Victimless Crimes," *Cato Institute,* June 6, 2018, www.cato.org/blog/60-deported-criminal-aliens-committed-only-victimless-crimes-few-violent-crimes.

9. Sam Wolfson, "Are Donald Trump's Claims About the Caravan of 7,000 Migrants Accurate?" *The Guardian,* October 24, 2018, www.theguardian.com/us-news/2018/oct/22/fact-check-trumps-claims-migrant-caravan; Jordan Fabian, "Trump:

Migrant Caravan 'Is an Invasion,'" *The Hill*, October 29, 2018, thehill.com/homenews /administration/413624-trump-calls-migrant-caravan-an-invasion.

10. Adam Serwer, "Trump's Caravan Hysteria Led to This," *The Atlantic*, October 28, 2018, www.theatlantic.com/ideas/archive/2018/10/caravan-lie-sparked-massacre-american -jews/574213.

11. Mark Hetfeld, "Because We Are Jewish," *Jewish Philanthropy*, June 20, 2017, ejewishphilanthropy.com/because-we-are-jewish.

12. Jeremy Diamond, "Donald Trump: Ban All Muslim Travel to U.S.," CNN, December 8, 2015, www.cnn.com/2015/12/07/politics/donald-trump-muslim-ban -immigration/index.html.

13. Theodore Schleifer, "Donald Trump: 'I Think Islam Hates Us,'" CNN, March 10, 2016, www.cnn.com/2016/03/09/politics/donald-trump-islam-hates-us/index.html.

14. Hebrew Immigrant Aid Society, "HIAS Statement on Muslim Ban Supreme Court Ruling," June 26, 2018, www.hias.org/hias-statement-muslim-ban-supreme -court-ruling.

15. Hebrew Immigrant Aid Society, "National Refugee Shabbat," accessed August 9, 2019, www.hias.org/national-refugee-shabbat.

16. Masha Gessen, "Why the Tree of Life Shooter Was Fixated on the Hebrew Immigrant Aid Society," *The New Yorker*, October 27, 2018, www.newyorker.com/news /our-columnists/why-the-tree-of-life-shooter-was-fixated-on-the-hebrew-immigrant -aid-society.

17. Deepa Iyer, "3 Years After the Sikh Temple Massacre, Hate-Violence Prevention Is Key," *Colorlines*, August 5, 2015, www.colorlines.com/articles/3-years-after -sikh-temple-massacre-hate-violence-prevention-key; Faith Karimi, "Kansas Man Who Killed an Indian Engineer at a Bar Gets Life in Prison," CNN, May 5, 2018, www.cnn.com/2018/05/05/us/kansas-bar-shooting-killer-sentenced/index.html; Amanda Jackson, Emanuella Grinberg, and Nicole Chavez, "Police Believe the El Paso Shooter Targeted Latinos. These Are the Victims' Stories," CNN, August 7, 2019, www.cnn.com/2019/08/04/us/el-paso-shooting-victims/index.html.

18. Alex Nowrasteh, "Terrorism and Immigration: A Risk Analysis," *Cato Institute Policy Analysis* no. 798, September 13, 2016, www.cato.org/publications/policy-analysis /terrorism-immigration-risk-analysis#full; New America, "In Depth: Terrorism in America After 9/11," accessed August 9, 2019, www.newamerica.org/in-depth/terrorism -in-america/who-are-terrorists; Brian Michael Jenkins, "The Origins of America's Jihadists," Rand Corporation, updated December 5, 2017, www.rand.org/pubs/perspectives /PE251.html; George Washington University Program on Extremism, *ISIS in America: From Retweets to Raqqa*, December 2015, extremism.gwu.edu/isis-america.

19. Alex Nowrasteh, "New Government Terrorism Report Provides Little Useful Information," *Cato at Liberty* blog, Cato Institute, January 16, 2018, www.cato.org/blog /new-government-terrorism-report-nearly-worthless.

20. Luiz Romero, "US Terror Attacks Are Increasingly Motivated by Right-Wing Views," *Quartz*, October 24, 2018, qz.com/1435885/data-shows-more-us-terror-attacks -by-right-wing-and-religious-extremists.

21. New America, *supra*.

22. Jenkins, *supra*.

23. "NYC Terror Attack: Sayfullo Saipov Was Here on Diversity Visa, Trump Says. What Is That?" *USA Today*, November 1, 2017, www.usatoday.com/story/news/nation -now/2017/11/01/nyc-terror-attack-sayfullo-saipov-here-diversity-visa-trump-says -what-that/820352001.

24. Holly Yan and Dakin Andone, "Who Is New York Terror Suspect Sayfullo Saipov?" CNN, updated November 2, 2017, www.cnn.com/2017/11/01/us/sayfullo-saipov-new -york-attack/index.html; Kim Barker, Joseph Goldstein, and Michael Schwirtz, "Finding a Rootless Life in U.S., Sayfullo Saipov Turned to Radicalism," *New York Times*, November 1, 2017, www.nytimes.com/2017/11/01/nyregion/sayfullo-saipov-truck -attack-manhattan.html.

25. New America, *supra*; "Domestic Radicalization Research Yields Possible Keys to Identifying Extremists on the Path to Terrorism," National Institute of Justice, June 26, 2018, www.nij.gov/topics/crime/terrorism/Pages/domestic -radicalization-yields-possible-keys-to-identifying-extremists.aspx.

26. Dina Sayedahmed, "Long Before Halloween Attack, NYPD Spying on Sayfullo Saipov's Mosque Broke Down Community Bonds," *The Intercept*, November 10, 2017, theintercept.com/2017/11/10/sayfullo-saipov-new-york-attack-nypd-spying-mosque; Adam Goldman and Matt Apuzzo, "NYPD: Muslim Spying Led to No Leads, Terror Cases," Associated Press, August 21, 2012, www.ap.org/ap-in-the-news/2012/nypd -muslim-spying-led-to-no-leads-terror-cases.

27. Registration and Monitoring of Certain Nonimmigrants from Designated Countries, AG Order No. 2612-2002, 67 Fed. Reg. 57032 (September 3, 2002); Khaled A. Beydoun, *American Islamophobia: Understanding the Roots and Rise of Fear* (Oakland: University of California Press, 2018), 101.

28. Beydoun, *supra*, 101.

29. See Shoba Sivaprasad Wadhia, "Business as Usual: Immigration and the National Security Exception," *Dickinson Law Review* 114, no. 4 (2010): 1,485, 1,500, 1,502.

30. Beydoun, *supra*, 101.

31. Wadhia, *supra*, 1,507–508.

32. *Id.*

33. Center for Constitutional Rights, "National Security Entry-Exit Registration System (NSEERS) Freedom of Information Act (FOIA) Request," January 3, 2017, ccrjustice.org/home/what-we-do/our-cases/national-security-entry-exit-registration -system-nseers-freedom.

34. Wadhia, *supra*, 1,499.

35. *Id.*

36. *Id.* (quoting Muzaffar Chishti et al., "Migration Policy, America's Challenge: Domestic Security, Civil Liberties, and National Unity After September 11," Migration Policy Institute, March 2003, 154, www.migrationpolicy.org/research/americas -challenge-domestic-security-civil-liberties-and-national-unity-after-september-11).

37. *Id.*, 1,520.

38. Janet Reitman, "U.S. Law Enforcement Failed to See the Threat of White Nationalism. Now They Don't Know How to Stop It," *The New York Times Magazine*, November 3, 2018, www.nytimes.com/2018/11/03/magazine/FBI-charlottesville-white-nationalism -far-right.html.

39. Philip Bump, "Trump Again Smears a Large Immigrant Community with the Violent Actions of a Few People," *Washington Post*, May 23, 2018, www.washingtonpost .com/news/politics/wp/2018/05/23/trump-again-smears-a-large-immigrant-community -with-the-violent-actions-of-a-few-people.

40. Eileen Guo, "ICE and the Banality of Spin," *Topic*, March 2019, www.topic.com/ ice-and-the-banality-of-spin.

41. Dara Lind, "Trump's 'Animals' Remark and the Ensuing Controversy, Explained," *Vox*, updated May 21, 2018, www.vox.com/2018/5/18/17368716/trump -animals-immigrants-illegal-ms-13.

42. "What You Need to Know About the Violent Animals of MS-13," White House update, May 21, 2018, www.whitehouse.gov/articles/need-know-violent-animals-ms-13.

43. Jennifer M. Chacon, "Whose Community Shield? Examining the Removal of the 'Criminal Street Gang Member,'" *The University of Chicago Legal Forum* 2007, no. 1 (2007): 317, 327–329.

44. *Id.*, 329.

45. US Department of the Treasury, "Treasury Sanctions Latin American Criminal Organization," press release, October 11, 2012, www.treasury.gov/press-center/press -releases/pages/tg1733.aspx.

46. Bump, *supra.*

47. Hannah Dreier, "I've Been Reporting on MS-13 for a Year. Here Are the 5 Things Trump Gets Most Wrong," *ProPublica*, June 25, 2018, www.propublica.org/article /ms-13-immigration-facts-what-trump-administration-gets-wrong.

48. *Id.*

49. *Id.*

50. Timothy D. Sini to Senate Committee on Homeland Security and Governmental Affairs, "Testimony Regarding MS-13," May 22, 2017, www.hsgac.senate.gov/imo/media /doc/Testimony-Sini-2017-05-241.pdf.

51. Dreier, *supra.*

52. *Id.*

53. Benjamin Mueller, "New York Compels 20 School Districts to Lower Barriers to Immigrants," *New York Times*, February 19, 2015, www.nytimes.com/2015/02/19 /nyregion/new-york-compels-20-school-districts-to-lower-barriers-to-immigrants.html.

54. See US Immigration and Customs Enforcement, "Operation Raging Bull," www.ice.gov/features/raging-bull (accessed September 30, 2019).

55. US Immigration and Customs Enforcement, "ICE's Operation Raging Bull Nets 267 Arrests," November 16, 2017, www.ice.gov/news/releases/ices-operation-raging -bull-nets-267-ms-13-arrests.

56. *Id.*; US Department of Justice, "22 MS-13 Members and Associates Charged Federally in ICE's MS-13 Targeted 'Operation Raging Bull' Which Netted a Total of 267 Arrests," press release, November 16, 2017, www.justice.gov/opa/pr/22-ms-13-members -and-associates-charged-federally-ice-s-ms-13-targeted-operation-raging-bull.

57. Hannah Dreier, "How a Crackdown on MS-13 Caught Up Innocent High School Students," *The New York Times Magazine*, December 27, 2018, www.nytimes .com/2018/12/27/magazine/ms13-deportation-ice.html.

58. *Id.*

59. Alice Speri, "NYPD Gang Database Can Turn Unsuspecting New Yorkers into Instant Felons," *The Intercept*, December 5, 2018, theintercept.com/2018/12/05 /nypd-gang-database; REALSEARCH Action Research Center, *Tracked and Trapped: Youth of Color, Gang Databases and Gang Injunctions*, Youth Justice Coalition, December 2012, www.youth4justice.org/wp-content/uploads/2012/12/TrackedandTrapped.pdf.

60. Sara Libby, "Scathing Audit Bolsters Critics' Fears About Secretive State Gang Database," *Voice of San Diego*, August 11, 2016, www.voiceofsandiego.org/topics/public -safety/scathing-audit-bolsters-critics-fears-secretive-state-gang-database.

61. Annie Sweeney, "Lawsuit Alleges Chicago Police Department's Massive Gang Database Discriminatory, Inaccurate," *Chicago Tribune*, June 20, 2018, www.chicago tribune.com/news/local/breaking/ct-met-chicago-police-gang-database-lawsuit -20180619-story.html; Mick Dumke, "Like Chicago Police, Cook County and Illinois Officials Track Thousands of People in Gang Databases," *ProPublica*, July 19, 2018, www.propublica.org/article/politic-il-insider-additional-gang-databases-illinois -cook-county.

62. Maryam Saleh, "Chicago's Promise," *The Intercept*, January 28, 2018, theintercept .com/2018/01/28/chicago-gangs-immigration-ice.

63. Sini, *supra*.

64. US Immigration and Customs Enforcement, "Fugitive Operations," updated June 7, 2017, www.ice.gov/fugitive-operations.

65. Michael Wishnie, Margot Mendelson, and Shayna Strom, "Collateral Damage: An Examination of ICE's Fugitive Operations Program," Migration Policy Institute, February 2009, www.migrationpolicy.org/research/ice-fugitive-operations-program.

66. Ramirez v. Reddish, No. 18-cv-00176-JNP (D. Utah 2017); Jessica Miller, "Utah Family Sues Immigration Officers, Says Agents Intimidated Them and Frightened Their Children During Two Warrantless Searches," *Salt Lake Tribune*, February 27, 2018, www.sltrib.com/news/2018/02/27/alcu-utah-sues-ice-us-marshals-service-over -alleged-warrantless-swat-style-searches-of-heber-familys-home.

67. Sarah Holder, "The Real Intention Behind the Recent ICE Raids Is Intimida- tion," *Pacific Standard*, July 30, 2019, psmag.com/social-justice/the-real-intention -behind-the-recent-ice-raids-is-intimidation; Mijente, *Blueprint for Terror: How ICE Planned Its Largest Immigration Raid in History*, mijente.net/icepapers/#15621673398 96-6a452e08-a607.

68. See *supra*, Chapter 5.

69. Doe v. Robertson, 751 F.3d 383 (5th Cir. 2014); Doe v. United States, 831 F.3d 309, 319 (5th Cir. 2016).

70. Office of Inspector General, "About Us," www.oig.dhs.gov/about.

71. Office of Inspector General, *Concerns About ICE Detainee Treatment and Care at Detention Facilities*, December 11, 2017, 4, www.oig.dhs.gov/sites/default/files/assets /2017-12/OIG-18-32-Dec17.pdf.

72. Office of Inspector General, *DHS Open Unresolved Recommendations Over Six Months Old, as of September 30, 2018*, November 30, 2018, 2, www.oig.dhs.gov/sites /default/files/DHS-Open-Recommendations-As-Of-093018_113018.pdf.

73. *Id.*

74. Compare, for example, Office of Inspector General, *ICE Field Offices Need to Improve Compliance with Oversight Requirements for Segregation of Detainees with Mental Health Conditions*, September 29, 2017, www.oig.dhs.gov/sites/default/files /assets/2017-11/OIG-17-119-Sep17.pdf (noting misuse of solitary confinement of de- tainees with mental health needs) with Office of Inspector General, *Concerns About ICE Detainee Treatment*, 6–7 (reporting continued misuse of solitary confinement); see also Department of Homeland Security, *Office for Civil Rights and Civil Liberties, Fiscal Year 2017 Annual Report to Congress*, November 27, 2018, 36 (noting that the majority of complaints opened in fiscal year 2017 concerned mental health care), www.dhs.gov /sites/default/files/publications/crcl-fy-2017-annual-report_0.pdf.

75. Office of Inspector General, *ICE's Inspections and Monitoring of Detention Facil- ities Do Not Lead to Sustained Compliance or Systemic Improvements*, June 26, 2018, 2, www.oig.dhs.gov/sites/default/files/assets/2018-06/OIG-18-67-Jun18.pdf.

76. Tara Tidwell Cullen, "ICE Released Its Most Comprehensive Immigration Detention Data Yet. It's Alarming," National Immigrant Justice Center, March 13, 2018, immigrantjustice.org/staff/blog/ice-released-its-most-comprehensive-immigration-detention-data-yet.

CHAPTER 8: JUSTICE FOR ALL

1. Jennifer Stave et al., "Evaluation of the New York Immigrant Family Unity Project: Assessing the Impact of Legal Representation on Family and Community Unity," Vera Institute of Justice, November 2017, storage.googleapis.com/vera-web-assets/downloads/Publications/new-york-immigrant-family-unity-project-evaluation/legacy_downloads/new-york-immigrant-family-unity-project-evaluation.pdf.

2. Robert Farley, "Obama's Actions 'Same' as Past Presidents?" FactCheck.org, updated November 24, 2014, www.factcheck.org/2014/11/obamas-actions-same-as-past-presidents.

3. American Immigration Council, "Reagan-Bush Family Fairness: A Chronological History," fact sheet, December 9, 2014, www.americanimmigrationcouncil.org/research/reagan-bush-family-fairness-chronological-history.

4. US Immigration and Customs Enforcement, memorandum from John Morton, "Exercising Prosecutorial Discretion Consistent with the Civil Immigration Enforcement Priorities of the Agency for the Apprehension, Detention, and Removal of Aliens," June 17, 2011, www.ice.gov/doclib/secure-communities/pdf/prosecutorial-discretion-memo.pdf; US Department of Homeland Security, memorandum from Jeh Johnson, "Policies for the Apprehension, Detention and Removal of Undocumented Immigrants," November 20, 2014, www.dhs.gov/sites/default/files/publications/14_1120_memo_prosecutorial_discretion.pdf.

5. US Department of Homeland Security memorandum from Jeh Johnson, *supra*.

6. *Id.*

7. Ingrid V. Eagly, "Immigration Protective Policies in Criminal Justice," *Texas Law Review* 95, no. 245 (2016): 300–302.

8. *Id.*

9. "Why Can't Undocumented Immigrants Just 'Get Legal'? And Other Immigration Reform FAQ," *America's Voice*, americasvoice.org/why-dont-immigrants-come-here-legally-and-other-frequent-questions-about-immigration-reform/#hottopics (accessed September 30, 2019).

10. Christian Penichet-Paul, "Border Security Along the Southwest Border," National Immigration Forum, March 11, 2019, immigrationforum.org/article/border-security-along-the-southwest-border-fact-sheet.

11. Rebecca Sharpless, "'Immigrants Are Not Criminals': Respectability, Immigration Reform, and Hyperincarceration," *Houston Law Review* 53, no. 3 (2016).

12. National Immigration Forum, *Community and Courtroom Responses to Immigration Detainers*, January 2012, https://immigrationforum.org/article/community-courtroom-responses-immigration-detainers/.

13. Antonio Olivo, "Cook County Bucks Immigration Officials," *Chicago Tribune*, September 8, 2011, www.chicagotribune.com/news/ct-xpm-2011-09-08-ct-met-county-immigration-policy-2-20110908-story.html; Toni Preckwinkle et al., Policy for Responding to ICE Detainers, Ordinance 11-O-73, September 7, 2011, immigrantjustice.org/sites/default/files/Cook%20County%20Detainer%20Ordinance%20(enacted).pdf.

14. Sam Dolnick, "In Change, Bloomberg Backs Obstacle to Deportation," *New York Times*, September 30, 2011, www.nytimes.com/2011/10/01/nyregion/law-expected-in-new-york-city-would-hamper-inmate-deportations.html.

15. "The History of the #Not1More Campaign," Not One More Deportation, January 1, 2013, www.notonemoredeportation.com/the-history-of-the-not1more-campaign.

16. Immigrant Legal Resource Center, "Immigration Detainers Legal Update: Key Court Decisions on ICE Detainers as of July 2018," July 2018, www.ilrc.org/sites/default/files/resources/immig_detainer_legal_update-20180724.pdf.

17. Make the Road New York, "City Council Passes Historic Legislation Limiting Involvement with Federal Immigration Authorities at NYC Department of Corrections," press release, November 3, 2011, maketheroadny.org/city-council-passes-historic-legislation-limiting-involvement-with-federal-immigration-authorities-at-nyc-department-of-corrections; Matt Flegenheimer, "New York City Proposal Would Limit Detention of Migrants," *New York Times*, October 2, 2014, www.nytimes.com/2014/10/03/nyregion/city-would-stop-honoring-many-immigrant-detainment-orders.html; National Immigration Forum, *supra*; American Civil Liberties Union of New York, testimony before the New York City Council in support of legislation limiting the detention and deportation of immigrants, January 25, 2013, www.nyclu.org/en/publications/testimony-new-york-city-council-support-legislation-limiting-detention-and-deportation.

18. Make the Road New York, *supra*; Flegenheimer, *supra*; National Immigration Forum, *supra*; American Civil Liberties Union of New York, *supra*.

19. Vera Institute of Justice, "Launch of New York Immigrant Family Unity Project (NYIFUP)," press release, November 7, 2013, www.vera.org/newsroom/launch-of-new-york-immigrant-family-unity-project-nyifup.

20. Vera Institute of Justice, "New York City Becomes First Jurisdiction in Nation to Provide Universal Representation to Detained Immigrants Facing Deportation," press release, June 26, 2014, www.vera.org/newsroom/press-releases/new-york-city-becomes-first-jurisdiction-in-nation-to-provide-universal-representation-to-detained-immigrants-facing-deportation.

21. Peter L. Markowitz et al., *Accessing Justice: The Availability and Adequacy of Counsel in Immigration Proceedings*, Yeshiva University Cardozo School of Law, 2011, cardozo.yu.edu/sites/default/files/New%20York%20Immigrant%20Representation%20Study%20I%20-%20NYIRS%20Steering%20Committee%20%281%29.pdf.

22. Vera Institute of Justice, *Evaluation of the New York Immigrant Family Unity Project*, November 2017, www.vera.org/publications/new-york-immigrant-family-unity-project-evaluation.

23. Gloria Pazmino, "Mark-Viverito Breaks with de Blasio Over Legal Funding for City's Undocumented Immigrants," *Politico*, May 2, 2017, www.politico.com/states/new-york/city-hall/story/2017/05/02/mark-viverito-breaks-with-de-blasio-over-legal-funding-for-citys-undocumented-immigrants-111723.

24. *Id.*; Roshan Abraham, "Major Impact Seen from Mayor's Carve-Out of Deportation Defense Program," *City Limits*, July 10, 2017, citylimits.org/2017/07/10/major-impact-seen-from-mayors-carve-out-of-deportation-defense-program; Gloria Pazmino, "Anonymous Donation Settles City Hall Dispute over Immigrant Legal Services," *Politico*, July 31, 2017, www.politico.com/states/new-york/city-hall/story/2017/07/31/anonymous-donation-settles-city-hall-dispute-over-immigrant-legal-services-113701.

25. Abraham, *supra*.

26. *Id.*

27. Chicago Police Department, "Responding to Incidents Involving Citizenship Status," Special Order S06-14-03, December 31, 2015, directives.chicagopolice.org /directives/data/a7a57b42-12ab41ab-48212-ab41-c1f5b5ad5c097076.html.

28. Erase the Database, "Targeted: Early Findings on Chicago's Gang Database," press release, February 6, 2017, erasethedatabase.com/2018/02/09/new-report-on-gang -database-details-harms-to-chicago-residents.

29. Barber, *supra*.

30. Ingrid Eagly and Steven Shafer, "Access to Counsel in Immigration Court," American Immigration Council special report, September 28, 2016, www.american immigrationcouncil.org/research/access-counsel-immigration-court.

31. US Immigration and Customs Enforcement, "ICE Opens Its First-Ever Designed-and-Built Civil Detention Center," press release, March 13, 2012, www.ice.gov /news/releases/ice-opens-its-first-ever-designed-and-built-civil-detention-center.

32. Felipe De La Hoz, "Hudson County Wants to Stop Holding ICE Detainees. Where Will They Go?" *WNYC News*, New York Public Radio, October 2, 2018, www.wnyc.org /story/hudson-county-wants-stop-holding-ice-detainees-where-will-they-go.

33. California Bill SB-29, 2017–18, leginfo.legislature.ca.gov/faces/billTextClient .xhtml?bill_id=201720180SB29; Freedom for Immigrants, *Guide to Dignity Not Detention*, static1.squarespace.com/static/5a33042eb078691c386e7bce/t/5a8c74b9e2c483 c4083fa156/1519154364279/Dignity_Not_Detention_Guide+.pdf.

34. Illinois General Assembly, Public Act 101-0020, 2019, www.ilga.gov/legislation /publicacts/fulltext.asp?Name=101-0020; Washington Bill 5497, 2019-20, establishing a statewide policy supporting Washington state's economy and immigrants' role in the workplace, http://lawfilesext.leg.wa.gov/biennium/2019-20/Pdf/Bills/Senate%20Passed %20Legislature/5497-S2.PL.pdf; California Bill AB-32, 2019–20, leginfo.legislature.ca .gov/faces/billTextClient.xhtml?bill_id=201920200AB32.

35. Deputy Attorney General Sally Q. Yates, memorandum to acting director, Federal Bureau of Prisons, on "Reducing Our Use of Private Prisons," August 18, 2016; Homeland Security Advisory Council, *Report of the Subcommittee on the Privatized Immigration Detention Facilities*, December 1, 2016, www.dhs.gov/sites/default/files /publications/DHS%20HSAC%20PIDF%20Final%20Report.pdf.

36. Detention Watch Network and Center for Constitutional Rights, "New Information from ICE ERO's July Facility List," www.detentionwatchnetwork.org/sites/default /files/DWN%20Spreadsheet%20Memo.pdf.

37. Mijente, "Free Our Future: An Immigration Policy Platform for Beyond the Trump Era," June 2018, https://mijente.net/wp-content/uploads/2018/06/Mijente -Immigration-Policy-Platform_0628.pdf.

38. Ryan Devereaux, "Bodies in the Borderlands," *The Intercept*, May 4, 2019, theintercept.com/2019/05/04/no-more-deaths-scott-warren-migrants-border-arizona.

EPILOGUE

1. Mike DeBonis, "House GOP Passes Measure Lauding ICE; Democrats Withhold Votes in Protest," *Washington Post*, July 19, 2018, www.washingtonpost.com /powerpost/house-gop-passes-measure-lauding-ice-democrats-withhold-votes-in -protest/2018/07/18/a9d8fd78-8a97-11e8-a345-a1bf7847b375_story.html.

2. Jonathan Easley, "Democrats Warn Push for Border Crossing Decriminalization Will Prove Costly in 2020," *The Hill*, July 11, 2019, thehill.com/homenews

/campaign/452531-democrats-warn-push-for-border-crossing-decriminalization
-will-prove-costly.

3. John Burnett, "See the 20+ Immigration Activists Arrested Under Trump," NPR,
March 16, 2018, www.npr.org/2018/03/16/591879718/see-the-20-immigration-activists
-arrested-under-trump.

4. Asher Stockler, "As Trump's DOJ Prosecutes Aid Worker, Humanitarian Groups
Promise Continued Support for Migrants," *Newsweek*, May 29, 2019, www.newsweek
.com/work-continues-humanitarian-groups-vow-support-migrants-doj-prosecutes
-aid-1438793.

5. Ryan Devereaux, "Journalists, Lawyers, and Activists Working on the Border Face
Coordinated Harassment from U.S. and Mexican Authorities," *The Intercept*, Febru-
ary 8, 2019, theintercept.com/2019/02/08/us-mexico-border-journalists-harassment;
John Bowden, "Pastor Put on Watchlist After Work with Migrants at Border Sues US
Government," *The Hill*, July 10, 2019, thehill.com/homenews/administration/452385
-pastor-put-on-watchlist-after-work-with-migrants-at-border-sues-us.

INDEX

JULIANA THOMAS

ALINA DAS is an immigrant rights activist, lawyer, and professor at New York University (NYU) School of Law. Das is the codirector of the NYU Immigrant Rights Clinic, a leading institution in national and local struggles for immigrant rights. She defends the rights of immigrants facing deportation and partners with community groups on immigrant rights campaigns. Her legal scholarship has been published by prominent law journals and cited by the US Supreme Court. Das is the recipient of numerous awards for advocacy and teaching, including the Immigrant Defense Project Champion of Justice Award, the Daniel Levy Memorial Award for Outstanding Achievement in Immigration Law, the New York State Youth Leadership Council Outstanding Attorney Award, the NYU Dr. Martin Luther King Jr. Faculty Award, and the NYU Law School Podell Distinguished Teaching Award. Das is a frequent commentator on immigration law and policy for national and local media outlets. She lives in Brooklyn, New York.